Life Defined
by Jesus Christ

What Jesus Did and Did Not Say

about Life, Death, the Soul, and Eternity

Su Z Kane

Life Defined
by Jesus Christ

What Jesus Did and Did Not Say

about Life, Death, the Soul and Eternity

www.LifeDefined.Life

Su Z Kane

© 2017

© 2018 Second Edition

Contents

Copyrights - Permissions

Greek-English Interlinear New Testament verses are from:
http://www.scripture4all.org

Sublinear texts in the Greek-English Interlinear can include:

Disclaimer

The statements made in this book regarding correct translation and interpretation of the Bible are my opinion (the author) and not a declaration of fact.

Strong differences of opinion as to how the original Greek or Hebrew should be interpreted have been debated for millennia. My opinion on the correctness of the interpretation or translation are focused on particular words or phrases at any given time and merely reflect my viewpoints.

From time to time throughout this book, I will disagree with certain words used in many English Bible translations. These disagreements or criticisms reflect my opinion and are not statements of fact.

I am actually very thankful for the English translations that exist, for they have been the basis of my faith and growth as Christian and a means of spreading the light of the gospel of Jesus to millions of people throughout the world for centuries.

It is my hope that some future translations will transliterate the 5 words that I focus on in this book, and let the educated reader decide for themselves what God's Word is saying.

Display of Words

In many Bible verses throughout this book, I will display the original Greek word (or its root) next to the translated English word in parentheses.

These Greek words do not appear in any English translation that I am currently familiar with. Rather, I have displayed the Greek word as a teaching aid. I also incorporate some screenshots from a Greek-English Interlinear New Testament, where the original Greek words can be seen and read.

Resources and References

At the end of this book, I provide a list of resources and references

Preface

I believe the views that I have expressed in this book regarding the interpretation of the Greek words *psuche* and *zoe* are true.

However, I don't believe that my salvation (nor anyone else's) is dependent upon having a totally accurate understanding of how Jesus used *psuche* and *zoe* in his teaching. We are saved by belief in who Jesus is and what he has done for us. Holding to that truth is essential.

Even when Jesus taught small groups of people, they usually did not understand everything he said. But those who laid hold to who he was and held onto their belief, even in spite of their questions, became children of God.

If we make "absolute correctness" a gauge of our walk with God and our spiritual maturity, then we have missed the point about the gift of salvation that comes only through Jesus, not through any works of our own.

Having said that, I do believe an accurate understanding of Jesus' teaching will clarify his message and purpose. The importance of this clarity cannot be overstated. Without clarity, our doctrine, our emphasis, and our lives will be out of step with Jesus' message.

But make no mistake about it. My salvation is based on wholeheartedly believing that Jesus is who he claimed to be—the Messiah, the Son of God—and counting on the fact of his death and resurrection.

> *John 1:12-13 But as many as received him—to those who believe in his name—he gave to them authority to become children of God, who were born not of blood, nor of the will of the flesh, nor of the will of a husband, but of God (LEB)*

Note: This book is intended to be a catalyst for dialogue.

I truly welcome comments, critique, and open discussion.

Comments can be made at www.LifeDefined.life

Part One

Clarifying Psuche

1

Choose Your Words Carefully

My Journey

My journey began over twenty years ago, when I started doing a word search on the English word "life." In some instances, the way the word "life" was used in the New Testament just didn't make sense to me. I began my study using *The NIV Exhaustive Concordance*. It quickly became evident that the single English word "life" had been translated from two different Greek words. These two Greek words account for almost all the instances where "life" appears in English translations of the New Testament.

It also became obvious to me that there was a clear pattern in the way Jesus used the Greek words *psuche* and *zoe*. As I progressed in the study it became apparent that *psuche* and *zoe* were in fact, very different in their meaning, especially in the manner that Jesus and the New Testament authors used these words.

The fact that these two original Greek words are not visible to English readers of the New Testament generates several critical problems. The first problem is that using a single word "life" for both *psuche* and *zoe* actually **conceals** what Jesus, Paul, and others in the New Testament originally said. Secondly, the English words that have been inserted in lieu of *psuche* and *zoe* have literally **changed** what Jesus and Paul said. There are other even more serious problems that are intertwined with this, which we will examine in detail at as we progress through the book.

> The English words **life** and **soul**, which have been inserted in lieu of **psuche** and **zoe**, have actually changed the original message of Jesus

In addition, I found that approximately half of the occurrences of the Greek word *psuche* had also been translated into the English word "soul!" This was confusing and appeared to be a somewhat arbitrary choice of words. Especially in light of my understanding of the word "soul" at that time in my life, the insertion of these significantly different English words "life" and "soul" for the single Greek word *"psuche"* seemed to introduce ambiguity into what was originally a singular concept.

In order to truly know what Jesus emphasized in his teachings, we have to know how he defined these two highly divergent words: *psuche* and *zoe*.

History of Translations

English translations are a fairly recent occurrence in the history of the New Testament. Since I speak English, I can only comment on what I see in the English translations. However, this is significant because, over the last five centuries, English translations have had a major shaping effect on church doctrines worldwide.

In my opinion, the misunderstanding of these words in the last millennium (not just in English) have detrimentally influenced the Christian message and the global perceptions of immortality, death, and Hell.

2

My Purpose for Writing This Book

It is my hope that, as you read this book, you will clearly see how Jesus defined "life" and its incredible significance.

I believe you will see how we have missed the **core message of Jesus' teachings** by not understanding his use of several key words. Were it not for the fact that these words form the very foundation of his teaching, possibly this book would not need to be written. Again, it is my hope that when you see how Jesus clearly used these key words, it will remove the obscurity that has distorted Jesus' primary message for centuries.

Unfortunately, this misunderstanding has generated its own offspring of doctrinal errors (beliefs that are not true). These errors have permeated traditional Christian beliefs for over a thousand years.

Cutting to the Chase

This book unwraps **a lot**. I will take you through understanding what Jesus said versus what he did not say. As it turns out, what he did *not* say has become a significant portion of mainstream Christianity's doctrine. To be frank, part of what we have believed is simply false.

At the risk of oversimplifying the situation, just let me say this: immortality as most Christians understand it is just not reality. There are two main prevailing views on this topic: the traditional view and the conditional view. I happen to hold to the conditional view. I believe in **conditional immortality**.

I held to the traditional view for most of my life. It was not until I began a long study on Jesus' use of the words "life," "death," "soul," and "eternity" that I began to question my beliefs and eventually came to see that Jesus was talking about something entirely different than what I had believed most of my life.

Please look at the definitions below. These definitions are a bit simplified at this point.

Traditional Viewpoint

The "**Traditional**" view is associated to the belief that Hell is a place of everlasting torment, burning, darkness, and separation from God, where unbelievers will spend eternity. The traditional view believes the **second death** does not mean actual death but rather is symbolic, signifying eternal spiritual separation from God. This separation would also include the everlasting torment and excruciating suffering associated with Hell.

Conditional Immortality

The "**Conditional**" view holds to the belief that man is mortal. The Conditional view believes the Bible clearly teaches that man does not "have an **immortal soul**," but rather that man "is a **soul**" and that the soul is mortal. Immortality is not an innate aspect of mankind's nature. Conditionalists have the understanding that a person receives **immortality** via the gift of **Eternal Life** when that person wholeheartedly believes the truth about Jesus' identity.

Conditionalists believe a person's immortality is "**conditional**" upon this gift of salvation. Immortality comes only from the impartation of the Holy Spirit into the believer. This deposit of the Holy Spirit imparts eternal life unto the believer.

Conditionalists believe that the unbeliever is destroyed (or perishes) in the lake of fire. This means that the unbeliever ceases to exist at some point after being thrown into the lake of fire, which is aptly and repeatedly called the **second death** in the book of Revelation. (see Revelation 2:11, 20:6, 20:14, 21:8).

Thus, Conditionalists hold to the belief that when any person dies (passes away from their earthly life), that is their first death. They believe that unbelievers are cast into the lake of fire (the **second**

death) and at some point thereafter will be destroyed. (The Greek word Jesus uses for perish or destroy is "appolumi").

I would like to say that I did not initially arrive at my conclusions on conditionalism from a focused study on *Hades* and *Gehenna*. Rather, I came to my conclusions primarily from studying Jesus' teachings on *zoe*, *psuche*, death, and perishing.

My purpose is to help you to see what Jesus actually said two thousand years ago, uncluttered by tradition, dogma, and the powerful paradigms that have so wrongly shaped Jesus' words for over a millennium.

After you see what Jesus and the New Testament authors really said, I believe you will clearly understand the gift of immortality that Jesus gives to those who believe in him. The goal of this book is to bring clarity in lieu of the obscurity that has for so long choked out the truth of Jesus' primary message.

Life

Defined

3

Five Unseen Words

There are 5 Greek words that permeate the New Testament, (particularly Jesus' teaching), that are basically unrecognizable in the English translations. These 5 words form the very foundation of Jesus' message of salvation, yet they remain essentially unseen by the English reading Christian.

The first two words that we will tackle in Parts 1 & 2 are *psuche* and *zoe*. These words are interpreted interchangeably in current English translations, when in actuality, Jesus used these words in stark contrast to each other. Jesus would never have used these two key words interchangeably.

Furthermore, one of these words (*psuche*) is translated into 2 significantly different English words (life and soul), without any Biblical reason to do so. This dissection of the word *psuche* has injected significant ambiguity into Jesus teachings, which we will uncover in the chapters ahead.

Psuche and *zoe* form the very foundation of Jesus' teaching, but Jesus' intent with these words is totally invisible in English Bibles. Even worse, these two words have been inconsistently replaced by two English words that end up actually changing Jesus' original message.

In addition, the Greek words *Hades* and *Gehenna* are not clearly differentiated in English translations, nor in main stream Christian teachings. These 2 words are directly tied and contrasted to psuche and zoe, but this impossible to see in English Bibles.

Furthermore, Gehenna is always translated as "Hell" when in reality the concept of "Hell" that most Christians believe is not at all what Jesus was teaching about when he referred to Gehenna, which was actually a physical location just outside of Jerusalem.

Hades and Gehenna are two completely different events (or venues) that people may face after their earthly death, but their differences are impossible to see in many English Bibles, as they are both translated as "Hell". The way Jesus and the New Testament writers used these words show that these two words are significantly different. Both words are indeed tied to the existence of mankind after their earthly death, yet their important differences are rarely clarified in main stream Christianity.

The other word is "appolumi" which means "utterly destroy" or "perish". The frequent use of this word throughout the New Testament is also directly connected to all 4 of these other words. However, the widespread misunderstanding of the other 4 words results in the inevitable twisting of the word "appolumi" to fit the paradigm of the traditional view. Thus although the English word "perish" does indeed appear in the English Bibles, the vast majority of Christian teaching twists this word to make it mean "ruin" as opposed to the original meaning of "destroy". We will cover these last 3 words in detail in Part 3.

Having a clear definition of these 5 words *as Jesus used them* is vitally essential to understanding Jesus message of salvation. Without this clarity, our understanding will be vague and misinformed.

In Parts 1 & 2, we focus on *psuche* and *zoe*. If you understand Jesus teaching on these 2 highly important words, the other words will naturally be interpreted correctly. They will fall into place, so to speak. For this reason, it is very important to understand Parts 1 & 2, prior to digging into Part 3.

I believe the tail has wagged the dog metaphorically speaking, with regard to *psuche* and *zoe*. Our Christian doctrine has been so heavily focused on perpetuating the false doctrine of "Hell", that this paradigm has shaped our interpretation (ignoring the vitally distinct differences) of *psuche* and *zoe*. This paradigm has also injected other ideas into Jesus teaching that were not originally there.

Important Note: *Jesus used words and phrases frequently that were directly tied to Old Testament words and phrases. Without understanding these connections that Jesus is making (when he refers back to scriptures and prophecies in the Old Testament), you will indeed mis-interpret many of the scriptures that we discuss in this book.*

Jesus was 100% tied in to the Old Testament in his teaching. His teachings on psuche, zoe, death, destruction, eternity, Hades and Gehenna can only be correctly understood by seeing the direct connections that Jesus makes to Old Testament scripture and imagery.

There are 5 Greek words that permeate the New
Testament, (particularly in Jesus' teaching),
that are basically unrecognizable
in current English Bibles

Life

Defined

4

Why Is This a Big Deal?

I have heard some people say, "What difference does it really make what you believe about this?" or "Why is this a big deal?"

I would partially agree with these questions. Let me explain. It is not a big deal, in the sense that I don't believe it is necessary to have an accurate understanding of the afterlife in order to be saved.

Clarity Is Vitally Important

Having said that, here is why I think having a clear understanding of **Eternal Life** (*oe*) is important.

Jesus' teachings on **Eternal *Zoe*** are part of the big picture of the entire Bible from Genesis to Revelation. If we don't understand this concept, we will miss the details of this big picture as it reveals itself from Genesis through Revelation. If we do not understand these concepts, we will be propagating untruths that are actually detrimental to the gospel's message.

Using the metaphor of a rudder on a ship, if we do not have clarity in our understanding of Jesus' message, we will be like a ship without a rudder. We will continue sailing while wavering in obscurity and ambiguity. We will be unable to give straight, clear answers to those who depend on us for truth, like our children, family, and friends. Without clarity, we will also portray lies about the character of God and his plan for saving man to the unsaved.

Without clarity, we will never have a grip on Jesus' true message and purpose, which Jesus dedicated his three-year ministry to explaining and demonstrating to the world. We will never be completely in step with God, Jesus, or the Holy Spirit. We will always be out of sync with God's ultimate purpose.

If you believed in Jesus as Lord, Savior, and the Son of God, then you are saved. Perhaps you have shared that message with others who have believed and are saved. So, as far as your salvation is concerned, you are good to go. But, wouldn't you like to be able to accurately understand what you are saved from, and also be able to convey that clearly to those you share the gospel with?

Isn't the message that Jesus strove to convey during his three years of ministry important enough to clearly understand it, instead of projecting a false and confusing message?

> Wouldn't you like to be able to accurately understand what you are saved from, and also be able to convey that clearly to others?

Can We Accurately Know What Words Jesus Used?

The era in which Jesus lived was one of great transition in language, culture and politics. Since the time of Alexander the Great's conquests, Hellenism (Greek culture and language) had spread throughout much of the Middle East and Europe.

Being a Jew himself, and speaking primarily to Jews during the beginning of his ministry, Jesus likely spoke Aramaic when teaching Jews.

However, as the Jews found themselves in this sea of "Greek language & culture", they adapted to speak and write the Greek language, in order to be able to function and do commerce in society at large. So it is likely that Jesus could communicate in Greek, as well as Aramaic, and probably Hebrew.

We know that Jesus quoted from the Septuagint, (The Septuagint is the Old Testament written in Greek), as it was the predominant Old Testament text that was available in his day. The Septuagint was written approximately 200-300 years before the time of Jesus.

Therefore it can be assumed that Jesus read Greek and could communicate in Greek. But let's get back to our question. Can we accurately know what Jesus actually said, if he originally spoke in Aramaic or even in Hebrew? How can we be sure what words Jesus actually used when he spoke of life, death, the soul, and eternity?

Jesus did not actually write any of the New Testament, but rather others wrote about him. The authors of the gospels, wrote their gospel narratives in Greek because it was the "common" language of that part of the world and era.

Therefore we are totally dependent upon these Greek texts for an accurate understanding of Jesus teachings. If Jesus spoke in Aramaic, then the gospel writers took it upon themselves to express Jesus teachings in Greek to the greatest accuracy they were capable of.

In other words, the gospel writers made it a point to choose Greek words that would accurately convey what Jesus said. There are 4 gospels that record Jesus teachings. Two of these authors were with Jesus throughout his ministry and were extremely familiar with both his teachings and his intent. (Matthew and John).

Mark likely had been with Jesus during the latter part of Jesus' ministry hearing Jesus teaching in-person and also learning from the apostles that had been with Jesus all along. Luke was a dedicated historian, and did painstaking research in order to write his gospel.

As you progress through reading this book, you will see quotes of Jesus from each of the gospels, particularly the gospel of John. I believe John carefully chose how he crafted his gospel, as well as his three letters (1,2 and 3 John), and the book of Revelation. I believe that John chose his words with precision in order to reflect the precise message that Jesus taught. John chose Greek words that accurately showed Jesus purpose, intent, and the primary message that Jesus sought to convey.

So regardless of whether Jesus taught in Aramaic, Hebrew or Greek, I believe the words used by the authors accurately reproduce what Jesus said, and the intent of his message. I believe the gospel writers saw this as their ultimate God-given responsibility.

In the end, we are totally dependent on the words carefully chosen by the gospel authors. If they did not choose their words carefully to accurately reflect what Jesus said (even if Jesus spoke in a different language), then at best we only have an approximation of what he said.

It is incumbent for me to believe that what John said in all of his writing accurately conveys what Jesus said and the message Jesus intended to convey. John was one of Jesus' closest confidants and apostles.

Of all writers, John's writing is trustworthy, or else, nothing is trustworthy.

If we cannot rely on what John said, believing that he was inspired by the Holy Spirit, thus accurately reproducing Jesus what said and intented to convey, then we are woefully relegated to be left with wishfully interpreting the New Testament as we see fit.

I choose to believe John's account of what Jesus said (in the original Greek text of John's gospel) can be depended on, to precisely and accurately reflect Jesus word's and intent. I believe that is the case for the other three gospels as well.

Throughout this book, I frequently refer to the words that Jesus "precisely" chose in his teachings. I also refer to the significance Jesus imparted to these words by the way he used them in his teachings. I just want to go on record, that I know it is likely that Jesus spoke in Aramaic during most of his teaching, thus he would have used equivalent words in that language.

Emotional Effect

Very often those who hold to the traditional view use the idea of "emotion" to discredit those who hold to the "conditional" view. This is not only unfair, but very inaccurate. The totality of verses that support the conditional view dwarf those used by the traditional view. In fact all of the verses that the traditional view uses for support, upon closer inspection fully support the conditional view.

The traditional view infers that conditionalists don't have the "stomach" to hold onto the view of eternal suffering of the unbeliever. Again, not only is this untrue, it is totally irrelevant to this entire dicussion. To insult conditionalists by saying they are primarily driven by emotion is being dismissive of their earnest and biblical approach.

It is indeed truth that the conditionalists seek to bring to light.

Life

Defined

5

Jesus' Concept of Life

Throughout Jesus' ministry, Jesus taught a great deal about life. You might think that sounds a bit non-specific. After all, everyone has something to say about life, right? Ask anyone over eighteen years of age about the "meaning of life," and you will likely get as many different answers as the number of people you ask. Most of these answers would probably center on a few specifics about leaving a legacy for your loved ones, seizing the day, leaving no regrets, and many other bits of good advice or humor. Some of these meanings can be a bit warm and fuzzy without any real specifics—the kind of saying you might see on a greeting card.

But, this in no way represents what Jesus is talking about when he spoke about life. The things that Jesus said about life got people's attention.

Some people thought he was crazy. Others were convinced he was the Messiah. Still others wanted to kill him. Jesus never offered warm and fuzzy greeting card material.

When someone left after hearing Jesus, they didn't leave that encounter thinking they had just heard an interesting philosopher or sage. They left convinced he was both the Messiah and someone they were willing to follow and even die for, or that he was insane, or that he was politically dangerous.

To understand what Jesus said about life, we have to know how he defined it, and that is where a big problem comes in. English versions of the Bible commonly translate two very different Greek words that Jesus used throughout his teaching into a single word: "life." It is important to understand that in the Greek language common to the Roman Empire at that time, either of the words Jesus used could easily be translated today as "life" in today's English.

You might be thinking, "Okay, so what is the big deal?" Well, as you will shortly see, it is the way that Jesus used these words that inspired thousands and thousands of believers to lovingly, fearlessly, and willingly sacrifice their lives as they shared Jesus' teachings with others in the first two to three centuries after Jesus' resurrection.

> English versions of the Bible translate two
> very different Greek words that Jesus used
> throughout his teaching into a single word - **Life**

Do today's English versions of the Bible accurately deliver his original message? My answer would be, yes . . . mostly yes. Maybe even ninety-nine percent accurate.

However, in my opinion, this one percent has garbled key concepts of Jesus' message, leading to significant ambiguity and obscuring his core message. The English translations deliver the gist of Jesus' teaching, but I believe they fail to accurately define the most vital core teachings that drove Jesus in his preaching.

Follow with me as we methodically unravel misconceptions that have existed for centuries due to the lack of Jesus' intended meaning being accurately conveyed.

As you move ahead, let me assure you that I am not using smoke and mirrors to try to manipulate you into seeing something that is not there. I am sharing what I have learned over twenty years of searching God's direction and clarity in his word.

Indeed, it was my lack of clarity with respect to several verses in the Bible that drove my search. The standard answers of my day that I was familiar with just did not seem sufficient.

It is that search, and the answers that followed it, that I would like to share with you.

In Him Was Life

To introduce Jesus and his concept of life, I would like to follow the course set by the apostle John. John was one of Jesus' companions throughout his ministry and was known as one of his apostles. John wrote one of the gospels. (There are four gospels in the New Testament. Each gospel records the life and teachings of Christ.) Of all the authors in the New Testament, John records more of Jesus' teachings on life than any other author.

As we go through this study, we are going to zero in on specific verses that contain the word "life." Each of these verses is located within a larger context, which I would encourage you to read outside of this book. But, for the purpose of this study (and to keep the book from running too long), we are going to focus on the words associated with life.

Now, before you are tempted to think that this is going to be some sort of boring philosophical analysis, let me assure you; it is anything but boring.

You are likely to see some core teachings of Jesus that you never knew existed.

In the first chapter of John's gospel, John begins with an introduction of Jesus. John does not refer to Jesus by name here but instead refers to Jesus as "the Word." There are several important concepts that John introduces about Jesus, but, again, for the sake of this study we are focusing on **life**.

Life
Defined

6

John's Introduction of Jesus

John 1:1-4 In the beginning was the Word, and the Word was with God, and the Word was God. This one was in the beginning with God. All things came into being through him, and apart from him not one thing came into being that has come into being. In him was life, and the life was the light of humanity. (LEB)

Let's Look at One Facet of This Introduction

In 1:5, John introduces Jesus by saying, "In him was **life**."

Obviously, the term "life" as coined here by John has very special significance. Notice that John did not say that Jesus was lively or had a charismatic personality, nor did he say he was an invigorating or energizing person. Now, suppose one of your friends was going to introduce you to someone new, and your friend told you ahead of time that this person is going to be full of life. You might conclude that this person would be joyful, exuberant, or full of electrifying, contagious energy. That would certainly be the kind of person one might want for a politician, someone to head up a fund-raiser, a proponent of a good cause, or to invite to a party.

But, in John's introduction of Jesus, John sets us up for a concept that is going to be the most vital underlying theme in all of Jesus' teachings. John will develop this in detail throughout his gospel and, in fact, expounds upon it in two of his other books (1 John and the Book of Revelation). The other gospel writers also support this critical concept by recording many of Jesus' teachings regarding life.

This concept of life being in Jesus is so critical in John's gospel that John summarizes his purpose for writing this gospel as follows:

*John 20:30-31 Now Jesus also performed many other signs in the presence of the disciples which are not recorded in this book, but these things are recorded in order that you may believe that Jesus is the Christ, the Son of God, and that by believing you may have **life** in his name. (LEB)*

John also concludes the end of his letter in 1 John with the same emphasis.

*1 John 5:11-13 And this is the testimony: that God has given us eternal **life**, and this **life** is in his Son. The one who has the Son has the **life**; the one who does not have the Son of God does not have the **life**. These things I have written to you who believe in the name of the Son of God, in order that you may know that you have eternal **life**. (LEB)*

> John sets us up for a concept that is going to become the most vital underlying theme in Jesus' teachings

I Am Writing This Book from My Perspective

I grew up in a Christian home and church. I had a solid Christian education and upbringing. However, as a young man, I became somewhat comfortable with the fact that certain verses in the Bible seemed obscure to me. I was okay with that for the most part, because I felt I knew and understood the concepts that were important for me to be saved. I knew God's plan for saving me from my sins included me having a genuine faith in Jesus as the son of God, born of a virgin, and that Jesus led a sinless life, was crucified on the cross, and was raised from the dead on the third day.

I believed his death on the cross was necessary to pay for my sins so that I might be forgiven, become a child of God, and live forever in heaven when my life on this earth was done. I believed that

Jesus was the promised Messiah—that he indeed was the Christ. I had no doubt about it. I was a baptized believer, and I was open about my faith. This summary of my understanding is a little simplistic but covers the main points of my belief at the time.

My Early Understanding

When I was in my thirties, I began to question certain verses and concepts. My understanding up to that time was:

- Since I had been given Eternal Life, when I died, I would go to heaven.
- I could not actually enter heaven until after my life on earth was over.

Entering this heavenly type of environment obviously could not come to pass until after I died. I was okay with that. In fact, I was great with that. I was saved from my sins! I was a child of God. I was very thankful and mindful of my state and the grace I constantly lived under. I felt assured knowing that in spite of my sins, Jesus had a place prepared for me in his home, in his kingdom.

On the Other Hand

Although I was very comfortable with my confidence in Eternal Life/heaven being a wonderful existence that I would experience **after** I died, I would occasionally run into Bible verses that would still give me **"Uhhhh . . . just exactly what is that saying?"** moments.

Some verses in the Bible still confused me enough to ponder about them. For many years, I brushed these verses under the rug, saying, "Well, after all, God has this all under control, so I don't need to fret over these verses because:

- The confusion may just be due to the language difference of the time

- Or . . . the customs of that time

- Obviously, someone smarter than me has figured this out, because nobody at church besides me seems to have a hang-up with these verses.

- Plus, I'm having a hard enough time living by the verses that I do understand, so why concern myself over these less significant verses.

- Last of all, I assumed these verses were not going to change any of my overall belief, so I just decided to move on and pretend that I didn't see them or that they weren't a big deal.

- Hmmmmm . . .

For Example

Every time I ran into the following verses (Matthew 18:8-9), I could never quite make sense of what Jesus was saying.

> *Matt. 18:8-9 And if your hand or your foot causes you to sin, cut it off and throw it from you! It is better for you to enter into life crippled or lame than, having two hands or two feet, to be thrown into the eternal fire! And if your eye causes you to sin, tear it out and throw it from you! It is better for you to enter into life one-eyed than, having two eyes, to be thrown into fiery hell! (LEB)*

Let me explain where I got stuck on this verse. My understanding (at that time) of being raised from the dead to eternal life included an important stipulation: I would have a new body of some sort. It would obviously be a heavenly body in essence, with some sort of physical aspect to it. Again, I wasn't clear on this, but I was comfortable leaving these details up to God.

But, this is where my hang-up with these verses began. According to my understanding at that time, I was sure that if I had some sort of physical deformity or disability in this present world, my old body would be replaced with a new heavenly body, a better one. In fact, it would be a perfect body with no disease, disabilities, or missing parts!

In my mind, if eternal life with Christ didn't include a new body, then I had to be missing something.

So, my hang-up with the verses above had to do with the "missing parts!" These verses were throwing me into confusion. In 18:8, Jesus says that if your hand or foot is causing you to sin, cut it off and throw it from you, because it is better for you to enter into life crippled or lame than to be thrown into the eternal fire with two hands or two feet.

The only other option here was to assume there was a gap in my current understanding. Losing a hand, foot, or eye didn't leave too much open to interpretation, so I felt like I understood that part of his statement. And, while I may not have totally understood the part about being thrown into the eternal fire, there was no doubt in my mind that I didn't want to end up there. My desire was to enter life, but this was the part that confused me and was at odds with my beliefs and understanding at the time.

If there was a gap in my understanding at that time of what Jesus said, the gap had to do with what Jesus meant by the term "life." My understanding of life was that it implied heaven or eternal life in some way.

In fact, my understanding at that time was that eternal life and heaven were equivalent, although the connection was a bit blurry to me. In addition, I believed I could not enter heaven or eternal life until my temporal life on earth was over. That is, until after I died.

But, how could that possibly be heaven if I could enter it retaining some sort of disability or deficiency in my earthly body?

I finally began to see that I must be missing an important part of the picture. There had to be more to entering life than just dying and going to heaven. Otherwise, how could an individual be assured of a new body without blemish? This just didn't make sense to me.

Obviously, there was something wrong with my understanding of the concept of "entering life." My assumption that entering life was synonymous with going to heaven had to be flawed.

I concluded that my current definition of life was incorrect. There had to be another explanation. I needed a clear definition of the term "life" in the context that Jesus used it.

> I needed a clear definition of the word "Life"
>
> in the context that Jesus used it

7

Lack of Clarity Obscures Vital Details

When I was a kid about five years old, my family spent a summer in Colorado. My dad was finishing up some course work on a college degree at a Colorado university. On weekends, we would occasionally drive to see some of the beautiful country that was within driving distance. I don't remember much about the weekend excursions, but I do remember seeing the photos that my dad took. They were black and white and clearly showed our family as well as the beautiful mountains.

My dad had an old camera that looked like a small box. It was a typical family camera of that time and only had a single fixed lens. At that time, the photos looked great. But, as decades went by and camera technology improved, it became clear that the old black and white photos were actually not clear. That is, you could make out pretty much everything in the photo, but nothing was really crisp. None of the leaves on trees in the photo could be individually seen, and there were no distinct edges on anyone or anything in the photo. The old photos were . . . somewhat blurry.

Now, if I had really needed to see some fine detail in the photos, I would have been out of luck. With today's technology, no one would think a blurry photo is acceptable. Blurry photos lack important details that are vital to having a clear picture.

Remember how I discussed my lack of understanding of some of Jesus' teachings when I was a much younger man? My understanding was blurry, just like my old black and white photos. I was missing key details of what Jesus intended in some of the things he taught.

In a similar manner, I believe that most Christians lack a clear understanding of the most vital concept of Jesus' teachings. Why do I say vital? Because, as I believe you will see by the time you are through reading this book, Jesus' message about life and death is foundational to all of his teachings. Not having this understanding will prevent you from having the clarity that Jesus intended. You will indeed go through your journey with a blurry interpretation of scripture.

In my opinion, Jesus' use of the Greek words that have been translated into English as "life" transcended the normal definition of his day. If you were to use the standard *Koine* Greek dictionary of Jesus' day (if such a thing existed) to look up the words that Jesus used when he spoke of "life" or "soul," for instance, you would not find definitions that adequately define the way Jesus used these words. In fact, it is indeed the way that Jesus uses these words that so heavily defines them and makes them vitally important.

The two Greek words I am speaking of are *psuche* and *zoe*. Jesus used both of these words frequently throughout his teachings. Both Greek words are translated into English as "life" throughout the New Testament.

In my opinion, each word has powerful but completely different meanings. To further complicate things, the English word "life" does not adequately define either of these Greek words.

In fact, Jesus uses these two words in such a way that they almost appear to be polar opposites. As you go through this book, each chapter will bring you closer to understanding why these two words were so different in Jesus' teachings.

Remember, the difference between these two influential and highly divergent words is totally hidden in the English versions of the Bible. But, by the time you are done reading this book, I hope the difference will be laser sharp in your mind, and you will clearly see the life-changing implications of his teaching.

On occasion, Jesus will use these significantly different words, *psuche* and *zoe*, in the same conversation. However, English versions of the Bible will use the same English word "life" as the translation for both original Greek words. This results in significant loss of meaning and lack of clarity as to what Jesus said. **I cannot overstate this!**

These mistranslated (in my opinion) words have heavily obscured vital points of Jesus' teachings! We are in essence missing key points of Jesus' teachings as they are either altogether missing or have been misconstrued in our English Bibles.

> There is a great deal of meaning that is lost when you take two different words used with significantly different meaning and translate both of them into a single word that does not adequately define *either* of the original words

For instance, there are other Greek words in the New Testament where this translation issue is commonly seen as well. The Greek words *agape* and *philos* are often both translated into a single English word "love." Each original word has a unique intent and definition as the author or speaker used them. *Agape* describes unconditional love, like a parent would have for their child. *Philos* describes a love that is loyal and committed, like a friendship. Yet in the English translations, we usually just find the English word "love." As you can see, some of the original intent is lost.

The loss of intent in the words translated as "life" is much more significant because they are such **key words** in Jesus' teachings. Not having a clear understanding of these **original key words** will lead to obscurity and ambiguity, as we will soon see.

If we don't clearly see how he used them, the rest of our doctrine will be an improvisation, held together by a disarray of assumptions.

> Not having a clear understanding of **key words**
> will lead to obscurity and ambiguity

What Created This Lack of Clarity?

To summarize thus far, there are three primary reasons for the lack of clarity today as to what Jesus said about life:

1. Jesus created unique definitions for the words *psuche* and *zoe* by the way he used them.

2. Most English Bible translations do not distinguish between these two words when translating them as "life" (both words are translated into the singular word "life").

3. The English word "life" is inadequate to define either of these Greek words in the way that Jesus used them.

Important! Your Personal Definition

Before you move on to the next chapter, on a piece of paper write your own definition of the words "life" and "soul." Writing down your definitions will help clarify what your understanding is at this time.

This will give you a baseline so that you can come back and compare your present understanding to any changes that may occur as you move ahead. Keep your current definitions handy (maybe in a journal or notebook) so that you can refer to them later.

8

The Ramifications of *Psuche*

Perplexity of *Psuche* in the New Testament

The common language of the Roman Empire during the first century AD was called *Koine'* Greek (*Koine* means "common"). The New Testament (written during the first century) was originally written in *Koine'* Greek. In order to best understand what Jesus and the New Testament authors were saying, translators have sought to go back to the oldest Greek manuscripts of the New Testament books that are available. (Koine' Greek is considered an ancient language, and is different from modern Greek).

We are going to look at two Greek words in these New Testament manuscripts that are often translated into the English word "life." For the moment, we are going to focus on the use of the Greek word *psuche* (pronounced "psoo-kay").

We will look at *zoe* (pronounced "dzo-ay'") later in this book.

The Greek word *psuche* is used throughout the New Testament. It is often used by Jesus in his teachings and is thus recorded frequently throughout the four gospels. Jesus did not actually write any of the New Testament books with his own pen. Instead, others wrote about Jesus.

The four gospels were written about Jesus' life, ministry, and teachings. Jesus' ministry and teachings took place over a period of three years, when Jesus was in his early thirties. At the end of those three years, Jesus was crucified. On the third day, he resurrected from the dead.

The book of Acts is about the early years of the church immediately after Jesus' resurrection and ascension into heaven. The rest of the New Testament is written as exhortation and instruction to believers in the churches during the first century after his resurrection. Much of this writing focused on Jesus' teachings, the truth about who he was, and the salvation that comes only through him.

Now, back to our focus on the Greek word *psuche*. *Psuche* appears 104 times in the New Testament. It is overwhelmingly (over ninety-five percent of the time) translated into the English words "life" or "soul." On a few occasions, it is translated as "heart," "mind," "person," or "self."

Strong's Definition of *Psuche*

Let's take a look at the definition for *psuche* in *Strong's Exhaustive Concordance*. *Strong's* is a widely accepted concordance and dictionary of the Bible. Strong's definition of *psuche* is given as:

> **Short Definition: the soul, life, self**
>
> **Definition:** *(a) the vital breath, breath of life, (b) the human soul, (c) the soul as the seat of affections and will, (d) the self, (e) a human person, an individual.*

We will look at this definition in more detail later. But, we can assume the translators used these commonly held definitions of *Psuche* as their basis for translating *psuche* into English. However, as we will shortly see, there appear to be several huge problems **in the way that** *psuche* was translated.

On the following pages, I list several verses in which the word *psuche* has been used by New Testament authors. The English words translated as "life" or "soul" are shown in bold next to the original Greek word, *psuche*.

Splitting up Psuche

As you read these verses, keep in mind that each time you see the word "life" or "soul," these two words have been translated from the single Greek word *psuche*. The English translator **chose** to translate *psuche* into "life" or "soul" as they deemed best in each of these verses.

I am not saying their choice was arbitrary. On the contrary, the translators made a careful choice based upon their understanding.

However, in my opinion translating *psuche* into these two significantly different words has created obscurity of the original word used by the speaker (most often Jesus himself).

The resulting ambiguity has perpetuated significant false beliefs throughout the Christian world, distorting key doctrines within the faith.

Translating **psuche** into these two significantly different words has created an enormous obscurity of the original intent of the speaker (most often Jesus himself)

The resulting ambiguity has perpetuated significant false beliefs throughout Christianity, distorting key doctrines within the faith

Life
Defined

9

Ambiguity of *Psuche* in English

In the verse below, an angel tells Joseph (Jesus' earthly father) in a dream to leave Egypt and return to Israel.

> *Matt. 2:19-20 Now after Herod had died, behold, an angel of the Lord appeared in a dream to Joseph in Egypt, saying, "Get up, take the child and his mother and go to the land of Israel, for those who were seeking the **life (psuche)** of the child are dead. (LEB)*

Herod's soldiers had orders to kill all male babies two years old and younger. With this understanding, would you say the soldiers were seeking to take Jesus' life or his soul? Would you suppose the soldiers would be capable of killing the soul of a child?

The next verse comes from Jesus' Sermon on the Mount.

> *Matt. 6:25 For this reason I say to you, do not be anxious for your **life (psuche),** what you will eat, and not for your body, what you will wear. Is your **life (psuche)** not more than food and your body more than clothing? (LEB)*

It makes sense that the English word "life" was chosen here. As an English-speaking person, my life would seem to be closely associated with such things as food and clothing, certainly more so than my soul.

But, this strictly due to the fact that, as an English-speaking person, my definition of the word "soul" is much different than my definition of the word "life," while, in reality, there was no distinction in Jesus' mind between these two concepts. Jesus used the single word *psuche*.

Matt. 10:28 And do not be afraid of those who kill the body but are not able to kill the soul (psuche), but instead be afraid of the one who is able to destroy both soul (psuche) and body in hell (Gehenna). (LEB)

If the word "life" were to be used here (instead of "soul"), would this verse make any sense to you?

In the English translation, we get the distinct impression that the word "soul" is a unique word when in fact, it does not exist in the Greek New Testament as a unique word.

So, the question arises: Is Jesus talking about a person's soul being destroyed in Hell (*Gehenna*), or their life being destroyed, or something else?

This next verse comes from a session of Jesus' teachings.

Luke 14:26 "If anyone comes to me and does not hate his own father and mother and wife and children and brothers and sisters, and furthermore, even his own life (psuche), he cannot be my disciple. (LEB)

It's hard to wrap your brain around the idea of hating your own *soul.* Maybe hating your own *life* would make sense to a Christian, in the hopes of saving your *soul,* but hating your own *soul?*

Splitting up *psuche* into the **divergent** concepts of "life" and "soul" has injected ambiguity and confusion.

In the English translation, we get the distinct impression that the word "Soul" is a unique word when in fact, it does not exist in the Greek New Testament as a unique word.

The Critical Question of Intent

As mentioned before, we really need to ask ourselves what Jesus' **intent** was in his message when he used the word *psuche*. As we progress through this book, you will see how **critical** this word was in Jesus' primary message.

Yet, in the English translations, his intent is not only hidden (in my opinion), it has been twisted into concepts that Jesus never projected.

In other words, because of the way *psuche* has been divided up during translation, **Jesus' original intent** has not only been garbled and obscured, it has also been replaced by **someone else's intent.**

> In most current English translations, Jesus intent is not only hidden, it has been twisted into concepts that Jesus never projected

The paradigm of the translator has been subtly inserted into the verse, obscuring what Jesus said and replacing it with what the translator thought the verse should say.

> *Matt. 10:39 The one who finds his **life (psuche)** will lose it, and the one who loses his **life (psuche)** because of me will find it. (LEB)*

How would this context change if the English word "soul" had been used here instead of "life?"

If inserting the word "soul" here does not make sense, then perhaps we should not be carving up *psuche* as we see fit. Perhaps this quote is an indicator that we are not using the word correctly.

Perhaps exchanging "soul" for "life" in this quote does not make sense because the definitions of *life* and *soul* are so firmly etched in our minds as separate concepts. It is abnormal for us to think of them as essentially the same thing.

But, in Jesus' mind, they were exactly the same . . . they were *psuche*.

We need to clearly understand the message that Jesus conveyed during his three years of teaching and ultimately gave his life for. We cannot settle for a twisted, confusing assumption that is not true.

Here is another teaching of Jesus from the gospel according to Mark.

> **Mark 10:45** *For even the Son of Man did not come to be served, but to serve, and to give his **life (psuche)** as a ransom for many. (LEB)*

I have a big question for you: What did Jesus come to give?

His life? His soul? Or his *psuche*?

You may be asking yourself, "Why do I have to choose?" I would in turn ask you, "Would you prefer someone else to choose for you?"

Because, in effect, someone else already has.

Someone else has chosen the word you have come to know and understand, and it does *not* accurately reflect what Jesus said.

> **Matt. 16:26** *For what will a person be benefited if he gains the whole world but forfeits his **life (psuche)**? Or what will a person give in exchange for his **life (psuche)**? (LEB)*

Is there a difference in forfeiting one's life versus forfeiting their soul? If so, what is the difference? Most English Bible versions actually translate both instances of the word psuche as "soul" in in the verse above.

In reality, *psuche* does not distinguish between life and soul in any way! Your *psuche* is simply who you are.

In other words, **your *psuche* is you.**

Let's Clarify *Psuche*

In Jesus' mind, *psuche* was the **total** essence of that person. *Psuche* comprised a person's life, their heartfelt emotions, their will, their inner self . . . their consciousness. Jesus did not break *psuche* down into components.

Psuche is not some aspect or component of a person. Nor is *psuche* something that a person possesses.

A person's *psuche* **is** that person.

This use of *psuche* is consistent for all instances of the word throughout the New Testament, regardless of the speaker or author.

Where Did the Ambiguity Come From?

The ambiguity crept in when a single, clearly defined word was later arbitrarily interpreted into two highly divergent concepts that fit the belief system of the prevailing Roman culture.

This ambiguity was initiated and perpetuated by the prevailing Greek paradigm that the *soul was immortal*, when in fact, the Bible **never** associates immortality with the word *psuche*.

The cultural paradigm of the "immortality of the soul" was a firm belief of the Hellenistic culture that the Jews found themselves in. This paradigm of the "immortality of the soul" began to permeate into Christian circles during the period from around AD 180 to AD 500. This incorrect but powerful paradigm drove the divergence of *psuche* into the separate concepts of *life* and *soul*. This paradigm of the "immortal soul" became a firmly entrenched foundational belief about AD 500, supplanting Jesus' original teaching. The idea of the immortal soul has remained as a highly infuential doctrine in Christianity ever since.

Jesus' original teaching has become heavily corrupted by the divergence of *psuche*.

This next verse comes from a conversation between Jesus and Peter.

> *John 13:37-38* *Peter said to him, "Lord, why am I not able to follow you now? I will lay down my **life (psuche)** for you!" Jesus replied, "Will you lay down your **life (psuche)** for me? Truly, truly I say to you, the rooster will not crow until you have denied me three times (LEB)*

The translator thought "life" made more sense than "soul" here. Based upon the common understanding of the word "soul" in our culture, laying down one's *soul* would not even be conceivable.

> *Heb. 10:39* *But we are not among those who shrink back to destruction, but among those who have faith to the preservation of our **souls (psuche)**! (LEB)*

What is it that those who have faith are preserving? What happens to those who shrink back? If they are destroyed, then just exactly what is destroyed? What is preserved for those who have faith? Their lives or their souls?

And just exactly how does this preserving take place?

As you will see later, this is one of scores of verses that clearly demonstrate conditionalism. But you miss this entirely, unless you understand how the New Testament writers defined *psuche* and *zoe.*

The next verse comes from 1 John.

> *1 John 3:16* *We have come to know love by this: that he laid down his **life (psuche)** on behalf of us, and we ought to lay down our **lives (psuche)** on behalf of the brothers. (LEB)*

Did Jesus lay down his life for us? Or his soul? Jesus laid down his *psuche* for us. This theme of Jesus giving his *psuche* for mankind is repleat throughout the New Testament. But this theme is basically hidden in current versions of the English Bible. As a result we fail to see the true purpose of Jesus death.

42

Maybe just using the original word *psuche* would help the reader have a clearer understanding of what Jesus said.

> **James 1:21** *Therefore, putting aside all moral uncleanness and wicked excess, welcome with humility the implanted message which is able to save your **souls (psuche)**.* *(LEB)*

What is going to be saved: our souls or our lives?

Again, if you don't understand the significance of how *psuche* was seen by the New Testament authors, you will miss the emphasis of this verse.

Jesus is speaking (in the verse below) to his disciples shortly before he is betrayed and crucified. He is referring to his own death that will take place during his crucifixion.

> **John 15:13** *No one has greater love than this: that someone lay down his **life (psuche)** for his friends* *(LEB)*

Jesus' **intent** is complete in the single word *psuche*.

Yet we have taken the liberty to dissect *psuche* into our perceived English components, which has resulted in us injecting new, **unintended** concepts into what he said.

Life
Defined

10

Focusing on Jesus' Use of *Psuche*

We are now going to look at three different sections in the gospels where Jesus uses the word *psuche* multiple times during a single conversation. This will help to clarify how this word was defined in Jesus' mind. This will also build a foundation for later sections where we will look at how Jesus **contrasts** this word with another, much more powerful word . . . *Zoe*.

As you will see in this chapter, *something very alarming occurs* in each instance of the English translations.

In each case, *psuche* is translated into two different words ("life" and "soul") within a few sentences of each other.

> When Jesus used the word **psuche**, he never intended to convey two different meanings!

The Parable of the Rich Fool

These verses contain one of Jesus' parables. In this parable, Jesus uses the word *psuche* five times. Yet, it is translated as "soul" twice and "life" three times. Most English versions actually translate the first three as "soul" and the last two as "life". In addition some English translations translate the first two occurrences as "self".

> *Luke 12:16-23 And he told a parable to them, saying, "The land of a certain rich man yielded an abundant harvest. And he reasoned to himself, saying, 'What should I do? For I do not have anywhere I can gather in my crops.' And he said, 'I will do this: I will tear down my barns and build larger ones, and I will gather in there all my grain and possessions. And I will say to my* **soul (psuche),** *"Soul (psuche),* *you have many possessions stored up for many years. Relax, eat, drink, celebrate!"' But God said to him, 'Fool! This night your* **life (psuche)** *is demanded from you, and the things which you have prepared—whose will they be?' So is the one who stores up treasure for himself, and who is not rich toward God!" And he said to his disciples, "For this reason I tell you, do not be anxious for your* **life (psuche),** *what you will eat, or for your body, what you will wear. For* **life (psuche)** *is more than food, and the body more than clothing. (LEB)*

Why were the first two occurrences translated as "soul" but the last three as "life?" Most likely, the translator felt like this made the most sense based upon his or her paradigm.

Jesus certainly did not intend two different concepts here. To Jesus, the word *psuche* contained only a single concept; a person's *psuche* was that person.

The use of the word "soul" injects and propagates the false notion of the innate immortality of "man's soul". Jesus never implied this, nor taught this, nor is the "immortal soul" taught anywhere in the Bible.

> To Jesus, the word **psuche** was a single concept,
> a person's **psuche** was that person

Destruction of and Losing One's *Psuche*

In Matthew 10, Jesus sends out his apostles to proclaim that the kingdom of heaven has come near. He encourages them not to be afraid of those who might kill them for their message.

In fact, in the decades to follow, ten of these twelve men would indeed be killed for sharing their message about Jesus.

> *Matt. 10:28 And do not be afraid of those who kill the body but are not able to kill the **soul (psuche)**, but instead be afraid of the one who is able to destroy both **soul (psuche)** and body in hell (Gehenna). (LEB)*

A few verses later (a few seconds later in the conversation), Jesus revisits this statement with his apostles, with an emphasis on the willingness to follow him.

> *Matt. 10:38-39 And whoever does not take up his cross and follow me is not worthy of me. The one who finds his **life (psuche)** will lose it, and the one who loses his **life (psuche)** because of me will find it. (LEB)*

Let's take a close look at these verses. In 10:28, *psuche* has been translated twice as "soul." A few seconds later in the conversation (10:39), *psuche* has been translated twice as "life." Why?

Jesus did not use two different words here nor did he mean to imply two different concepts. But, that is what exactly what we have ended up with in the English translation: two significantly divergent words that portray two powerfully different concepts.

Read these verses a second time and ask yourself: "If I exchange the English word "soul" for "life" and visa-versa, how would that affect my understanding of these verses?"

Based on your own current paradigm, if you had been forced to choose between using one of these two words, would you have done anything differently? Perhaps you can see how powerful a paradigm can be.

But, was it the best choice? More importantly, do the words chosen accurately portray what Jesus was trying to say? Or do the words chosen actually obscure his original message?

Or, even worse, could the words *chosen* actually *change* his message?

Holding on to the belief that a person has an "immortal soul", makes it impossible to see Jesus true teaching.

Saving Your *Psuche*

In Matthew 16, Jesus explains to his disciples that he is going to Jerusalem and will be betrayed, killed, and raised from the dead. It is in the context of this conversation where Jesus again emphasizes the importance of being willing to lose your *psuche* in order to gain your *psuche*.

Psuche is used four times in these verses and is translated into both "life" and "soul" in the English translation.

Let's play a bit of a game. This time, I am repalcing the words "life" and "soul" with the Greek word *psuche* in the following verses. Which instances do you think would read as "soul" or "life" in the typical English translation?

> **Matt. 16:24-26** *Then Jesus said to his disciples, "If anyone wants to come after me, let him deny himself and take up his cross and follow me. For whoever wants to save his **psuche** will lose it, but whoever loses his **psuche** on account of me will find it. For what will a person be benefited if he gains the whole world but forfeits his **psuche**? Or what will a person give in exchange for his **psuche**? (LEB)*

Well, how did you do?

The Lexham English Bible actually translates all four instances as "life". But most English translations insert each of the words "soul" and "life" twice.

Previously, we discussed the paradigm of the "immortal soul." Notice how natural it would be (if you were influenced by that paradigm) to insert the word "life" into the first two sentences where *psuche* was used, and "soul" into the last two sentences of these verses.

But was that what Jesus had in mind? No! It was absolutely not his intention! This will become increasingly clear as we progress through the upcoming chapters.

Life

Defined

11

Three Huge Problems with *Psuche*

At first glance, we might think that in each of the examples above, translating *psuche* into the English word "life" or "soul" seems fairly innocent. These words might initially seem suitable for use in the context in which they are used.

On the other hand, there are three huge problems with this.

Psuche Problem 1: Ambiguity

First, the words "life" and "soul" have very different meanings to the typical English-speaking person.

Typical English understanding of the word "life": A person's life consists of who they are, what they are doing with their time on earth, their attitudes, their personality, their relationships, the period from their birth to their death, the process of living, and so on. Your definition might vary from mine a bit, but it is probably similar.

Typical English understanding of the word "soul": The word "soul" connotes some spirit-like, ethereal component of the person that has an **immortal** nature to it. The soul is thought of as transcending a person's life on earth. The soul is commonly thought of as the "inner person" that lives on after that person dies an earthly death. Again, your definition might vary from mine a bit, but it is probably similar.

We have ended up with two distinctly different (divergent) words when, in fact, there was originally only one word (*psuche*). Splitting up *psuche* into two divergent words has garbled what Jesus originally said, injecting **ambiguity** that did not exist in the original Greek texts.

Psuche Problem 2: Immortality

The second problem occurs specifically with the word "soul." Most English-speaking people believe that the Bible teaches that the soul is **immortal**.

In reality, the Bible *never, never* teaches this, nor implies this, either directly or indirectly.

The idea that man has a soul is not biblical. Furthermore, there is not a unique word in the Greek New Testament that specifically means *soul*. Yet, in the English translation that is exactly what we have ended up with.

To reiterate, there is no unique word in the Bible that means "soul" that parallels the commonly held belief of the "immortal soul" held by most English speaking people.

The idea of *psuche* being immortal originated with Socrates and Plato, centuries before Jesus' time. But, Jesus and the New Testament authors never used the word with this understanding.

This falsely held notion of the "immortal soul" has significantly distorted the context of Jesus' teachings. However, it is this very notion of the "immortal soul" that drives much of traditional Christian doctrine and belief. This incorrect understanding has itself generated additional incorrect doctrines.

Due to the far-reaching consequences of this incorrect notion of the "immortal soul," we need to be sure we understand how Jesus and the New Testament authors understood and used this word. Only after we clearly understand how they defined *psuche* can we move on to a much more important word: *zoe*.

What I can say at this point is that *psuche* refers to a person. It is that simple.

A person is a *psuche*. They don't **have a *psuche***, they **are a *psuche***.

Is a Soulish Perspective Okay?

Psuche can refer to the inner person in their thoughts, emotions, and will. In that sense it could be considered to be the *soul* of that person. However, this is an English innovation.

Inserting "soul" for *psuche* could be seen as a fairly innocent translation if done with this understanding.

But, due to the fact that the prevailing belief that the soul is immortal, this ends up being anything but innocent. Instead, it has tragically undermined Jesus' clear message of salvation.

How many times have you heard the phrase "immortal soul?" This phrase does not appear anywhere in the Bible . . . period. This notion is strictly an innovation of man and is not in the scriptures.

Replacing *psuche* with the word "soul" has inserted a corrupting element of influential doctrine that never existed in Jesus' teaching nor in the original Greek—nor was it ever intended to.

In my opinion, it would be best to do away with the word "soul," since it is so misleading. But if it is necessary to use the word, then just think of it this way: you do not have a **soul**, but, rather you are a **soul**. And most importantly you are merely a **mortal**, unless and until you have been saved and given the gift of Eternal Life *(Zoe)*.

> Due to the the prevailing belief that the **soul** is immortal, inserting the English word **"soul"** in the Bible ends up being anything but innocent. Instead, it has tragically undermined Jesus' clear message of salvation.

The concept of the "immortal soul" was not taught by Jesus nor was it taught by any New Testament authors. Rather, the New

Testament authors taught that God alone is immortal. In fact, historically, this idea of the "immortal soul" was unheard of from the early church leaders for almost 150 years after the resurrection of Jesus.

This idea of the "immortal soul" (from the prevailing Greek culture) eventually began to creep into the Christian Church by the end of the second century AD and, by the sixth century, had taken over as the predominant Christian belief regarding the soul.

Psuche Problem 3: Obscuring *Zoe*

In the next couple of chapters, we will see where inserting the word "life" for *psuche* has created its own set of issues.

The problem that occurs with inserting the word "life" for *psuche* is that it ends up obscuring Jesus' use of a much more powerful word, which he used extensively throughout his ministry.

Let me briefly explain. The word *zoe* is one of the most powerful and influential words in the New Testament, especially and explicitly because of the way Jesus uses *zoe*.

Here is where the problem begins. Zoe is always translated as "life" in English bibles. *Psuche* is also translated as "life" about half of the time. *The obscurity occurs because the English reader never has any idea that Jesus used two very different words in his teaching,* often in contrast to one another, because both words have been translated as "life."

As a result, we end up being totally unaware of the major differences in how Jesus used these two words and their profound impact on the *truth* of his message.

This third problem has resulted in **severe consequences** that extend throughout Christian doctrine, heavily obscuring and distorting the profound truth that Jesus taught.

This is the biggest of the three *psuche* problems, but each problem has enormous implications and is entangled with the other two.

The problem that occurs with inserting the word **life** for **Psuche**, is that it ends up masking Jesus' use of a much more important word… **"Zoe"** (also translated as **Life**), which Jesus used extensively throughout his ministry

12

Let's Try to Clear This Up

Remember when we defined *psuche* at the beginning of the book? To recap, Strong defines *psuche* as:

*Short Definition: **the soul, life, self***

Definition: (a) the vital breath, breath of life, (b) the human soul, (c) the soul as the seat of affections and will, (d) the self, (e) a human person, an individual.

As we have seen from Strong's definition, the idea of life, soul, or self each convey some singular aspect of *psuche*. But, it's only when they are combined as an integral part of *psuche*'s definition that one begins to understand the original intent. None of those words adequately defines *psuche* when used singularly.

As we have already mentioned, one aspect of *psuche* is "the soul as the seat of affections and will." This idea in and of itself is innocent enough. It is not until one ascribes immortality to the soul that this becomes a real problem.

Now, think back to the definition you wrote down earlier for the words life and soul. Were your definitions for these two words essentially the same?

More than likely there was a clear difference in your definitions.

As we move ahead with this study, just hold on to the fact that the New Testament authors used the word *psuche* to define the entirety of a person (excluding their body). They never contemplated that someone would break up psuche into components that support a particular paradigm, as has obviously taken place (in my opinion) in the English translations.

But, *psuche* is not the main focus of our study. While it is very important to remove the confusion that the dissection of *psuche* has created, it is not as important as zeroing in on what Jesus did say.

Jesus' focus was not on *psuche*. His focus was heavily on *zoe*, but we would never know that by reading a current English Bible.

> Jesus' focus was not on **psuche.**
>
> His focus was heavily on **zoe!**
>
> But we would never know that by
>
> reading a current English Bible

13

The Influence of Key Words

As it turns out, the words "life" and "soul" have become key words in the New Testament.

A key word is a word that strongly influences how the New Testament is understood as a whole, as well as how subsequent doctrine is interpreted and developed. A key word has far-reaching effects, permeating every corner of the gospel message.

"Life" and "soul" have been key words for millenia when, in fact, these two highly divergent words never existed in the Greek New Testament! Thus, we have ended up with two heavily influential key words that are not in the original Bible.

Even worse, these faux key words, "life" and "soul," have supplanted the real key words that Jesus used, *psuche* and *zoe*. The loss of meaning that has taken place as a result has radically altered the message of Jesus, distorting major components of his original teaching.

> **Life** and **Soul** became (and unfortunately have remained) critically influential key words for centuries when in fact, these two highly divergent words never existed in the Greek New Testament!

Psuche Issues Are Not Our Biggest Problem

I wish I could say the misunderstanding stopped with *psuche*.

But, in fact, further ambiguity is introduced when the word *zoe* is translated as "life," and no effort is made to distinguish it from the instances where *psuche* is translated as "life."

These two words (*psuche* and *zoe*) were clearly different in the minds of Jesus and the New Testament authors, yet this distinction is completely ignored and obscured in the English translations. We do not get even a subtle hint that there might be a difference in their intended meanings.

But, the difference is very significant indeed.

In fact, you could say that your "life" depends on the critical nature of their difference. However, since we have not yet clearly defined the word "life," this concept is likely still nebulous to you. Please hang in there with me, as we see Jesus message clearly and powerfully unfold.

"Life" as Jesus defines it, is the main key word throughout the New Testament. However, it has been obscured by millenia of translation due to very powerful paradigms.

Further ambiguity is introduced when the word **Zoe** is translated as **Life,** and no effort is made to distinguish it from the instances where **Psuche** is translated as **Life**

These two words (*Psuche* and **Zoe**) were very different in the minds of Jesus and the New Testament authors, yet this distinction is completely ignored, and is in fact totally obscured in the English translations!

Reminder: As noted in the front disclaimer: Statements made in this book regarding correct translation and interpretation of the Bible are my opinion (the author) and not a declaration of fact.

As you have seen, I disagree with certain words used in many English Bible translations. These disagreements and criticisms reflect my opinion and are not statements of fact.

Life
Defined

14

Analyzing a More Powerful Word

So far, we have limited our word study to the use of the word *psuche* and have sought to clarify how it was used by the New Testament authors as well as by Jesus.

Now, we are going to delve into a new word: *Zoe*. This word is actually infused with much more meaning than the word *psuche* **in the way that Jesus uses it**. This is actually one of the most powerful words in the Bible, which will become clear as we progress.

Earlier, we looked at Matthew, Mark, and Luke's accounts of a dialogue that Jesus had with his followers when he was teaching them about "saving their *psuche*." In the gospel according to John, we see a similar conversation. However, in John's gospel, Jesus adds a second word to this teaching that has huge significance.

To read the whole dialogue, refer to John 12. But, for this example, we are only looking at one verse, which will sound very familiar with one major exception.

> **John 12:25** *The one who loves his **life** loses it, and the one who hates his **life** in this world preserves it for eternal **life**. (LEB)*

There are three words translated into English as "life" in this verse. Now, let's take a closer look by examining the original Greek words.

See below:

> **John 12:25** *The one who loves his **life (psuche)** loses it, and the one who hates his **life (psuche)** in this world preserves it for eternal **life (zoe)**. (LEB)*

We can see that the first part of this verse matches what we have already seen in the other three gospels. But, at the end of this verse, Jesus uses the word *zoe*.

Why would Jesus do this?

The English translator obviously didn't think it was substantially different from *psuche*, as both words are both translated as "life." The English reader would never know that Jesus used a different word or that he might have intended some other meaning than what the translator has given us.

But, do Psuche and Zoe both mean "Life"?

Was there an intentional difference in how Jesus was using these two words? If so, what is the difference? Even if the difference is only subtle, shouldn't we know what it is and be able to make that discernment for ourselves?

When you examine the obvious pattern of how Jesus and the New Testament authors *intentionally* used these words, it becomes clear that these two words *do not* mean the same thing.

The concept of "life" that is typically understood by the English speaking person, actually does a very poor job of defining either of these original Greek words. Translating both of them as "life" does an injustice to the original teaching, and in fact *masks* what Jesus actually said.

You don't have to be a Greek scholar to see this. You can easily see this obvious pattern of use in the reference materials that I refer to in this book.

One More Example

One other verse I'd like to look at is in 1 John. Notice that the English translation inserts the word "life" or "lives" in four instances. However, the Greek word *zoe* is used in the first two instances, and *psuche* is used in the last two. Is this difference significant?

> *1 John 3:14-16* We know that we have passed over from death to **life (zoe)** because we love the brothers. The one who does not love remains in death. Everyone who hates his brother is a murderer, and you know that every murderer does not have eternal **life (zoe)** residing in him. We have come to know love by this: that he laid down his **life (psuche)** on behalf of us, and we ought to lay down our **lives (psuche)** on behalf of the brothers *(LEB)*

There is a difference, and it is *huge*.

In fact, if you don't clearly understand how John is using these two words, you not only miss the powerful point he is making here, but you will also leave thinking you truly understand what was said when, in fact, *you do not even have a clue*.

Before we move on, let me make a point.

Every time Jesus uses the word *zoe*, it is **always** translated into English as "life." Yet, English versions of the Bible do not provide you with any way to discern which Greek word is being translated as "life." It could be either *psuche* or *zoe*, but you wouldn't know which one without referring to the original Greek text.

Jesus picked his words **precisely**. Yet, in our English translations, there is no way to discern between these two very powerful and distinct words. For example, in the verse we just read (John 12:25), Jesus talks about a person losing their *psuche*. He then says you can keep it for *eternal zoe*.

As you will see, the word *zoe* would not make sense at all in place of *psuche*, and there is absolutely no way *psuche* would work in the place of *zoe*. John 12:25 happens to be a very powerful and insightful verse into Jesus' teachings. But, we miss ninety-nine percent of it by not knowing exactly what Jesus was saying.

By the time you are done reading this book, you should be able to accurately determine (95% of the time) which word Jesus is using as you read the New Testament without even referring to a Greek text. You will learn to identify the word by the context of how it is being used. Jesus and the authors of the New Testament were very consistent in their use of *psuche* and *zoe* and how they defined these words by their use.

Every time Jesus uses the word **Zoe**, it is always translated into English as **Life**. Yet, English versions of the Bible do not provide you with any way to know which Greek word is being translated as **Life**. It could be either **Psuche** or **Zoe**, but you wouldn't know which one without referring to the original Greek text.

Jesus and the writers of the gospels deliberately chose their words, but we totally miss this in the current English translations.

Sneak Preview of *Zoe*

I have hesitated to give you the definition of *zoe* before Jesus reveals it in John's gospel. John writes his gospel in such a way that *zoe* becomes the most powerful underlying theme in the whole book. The most efficient way to get a full understanding of *zoe* is to see how Jesus unwraps it in John's gospel and how Jesus contrasts this word with several other words, including *psuche*.

Unlike *psuche*, Strong's definition of *zoe* doesn't give us a clear understanding of this key word in the context of how Jesus used *zoe* in his teachings.

For now, let it suffice to say that the simplified definition of *zoe* is "life as God has it." Whereas, in contrast, you could say that p*suche* is "life as man has it." (Again, this is a bit oversimplified).

For a full understanding, it is crucial that we see how Jesus, Paul, and others define and contrast these two words.

> For now, let it suffice to say that the simplified definition of **Zoe** is "Life as God has it"
>
> Whereas, in contrast, you could say that **Psuche** is "Life as man has it"

An Avalanche of Misunderstanding

The lack of understanding of how these words are connected prevents us from comprehending the primary message of Jesus' teachings, what he died for, and the huge implications of his resurrection.

In addition, the lack of understanding of how Jesus precisely used these two words has resulted in other words also not being accurately understood. It's as if *psuche*'s divergent translation started an avalanche of ambiguity that spread to other highly influential words of Jesus, resulting in the devastation of Jesus' original message.

However, by the time we finish reviewing the gospel according to John, you will likely have a totally new understanding of Jesus' teaching that will free your mind from this ambiguity, confusion, and deception. Even the Old Testament will come alive for you in ways you may have never seen before.

This is a Matter of Life and Death

Understanding the original intent of Jesus' words
is truly a matter of life and death.

I cannot overemphasize the importance of this.
But at this point we are just beginning to unveil
how Jesus defines both Life and Death.

Please continue with me as we unwrap this
vital teaching that was Jesus' primary focus.

Using a Metaphor of Theater

Here is where we stand at this point. There are two key words that are highly visible in the English New Testament, which *never* existed in the original Greek New Testament!

These "key words" are *Life* and *Soul*.

Using a metaphor of theater, we could call these two key words "impostors." Imagine a play in which impostors have taken center stage over the two real (original intended) key words that Jesus used.

Life and *Soul* are counterfeits, mimicking *Psuche* and *Zoe* but delivering a completely different message.

As we have already seen, the original single Greek word *Psuche* has been translated into two very different English words, which has culminated in these two key words *Life* and *Soul* becoming the focal point of the whole show. Thus, the audience focuses on these phony actors *Life* and *Soul,* even though they never existed in the original script.

Jesus' intended main character *Zoe*, is never recognized by the audience, because *Zoe* has been hidden backstage. The original script has been revised so that *Life* and *Soul* have been given all of the speaking roles. The pinnacle of the show was originally intended to occur with the introduction and demonstration of *Zoe*. But *Zoe* is never heard from in the English version of the show, even though *Zoe* was originally the leading character throughout Jesus' teachings!

Instead, *Zoe* has been dressed in the same clothes and makeup as *Life but is not allowed to speak*. As a result, the most important character in the script has been relegated to the status of an unrecognizable extra in the crowd!

Are you tracking with me?

Zoe is always translated as *Life*, just as *Psuche* has been translated as *Life* about half of the time. Since the theater audience cannot tell the difference between the impersonator (*Life-Psuche*) and the real main character (*Zoe*) because the actors look the same to the them, they totally miss the real intended message of the show!

Psuche and *Zoe* were supposed to be the main characters in the show, but we have ended up with a show that has substituted two impostors: *Soul* and *Life*. No one is quite sure where these counterfeit actors came from, and the voices of the original intended characters are muted in the background, where they cannot be heard.

This is all taking place while the impostors have stolen the show! The audience has missed the real plot, as the importance of the true characters has been totally obscured by the impostors.

The audience is satisfied thinking they have seen the real show when tragically, the original life-saving, empowering message is relegated to obscurity without the audience having a clue as to what they missed.

> **Psuche** and **Zoe** were supposed to be the main characters in the show, but we have ended up with a show that has substituted two impostors: **Soul** and **Life**.

We Have Ended up with Wrong Key Words!

Jesus' intended key words were *zoe* and *psuche*. Yet, these two words are totally obscured in the English translations.

We have instead ended up with the key words **life** and **soul** (horrible substitutes), which have tragically garbled and hijacked Jesus' message.

15

Jesus Defines Life in His Own Terms

Introducing Jesus' Use of the Word *Zoe*

Earlier in the book, I discussed one of the verses that prompted me to undertake this study. Each time I read Matthew 18:8-9, I could never quite make sense of what Jesus was saying.

> *Matt. 18:8-9 And if your hand or your foot causes you to sin, cut it off and throw it from you! It is better for you to enter into **life** crippled or lame than, having two hands or two feet, to be thrown into the eternal fire! And if your eye causes you to sin, tear it out and throw it from you! It is better for you to enter into **life** one-eyed than, having two eyes, to be thrown into fiery hell! (LEB)*

These verses contained some connotation that was hidden from me; I couldn't decipher its true meaning. For many years, I was forced to just let it pass by because I did not understand the meaning of a key word in the verse.

What was the word "life" supposed to mean to me? As we have already seen, "life" has been translated into English from two different Greek words without any effort to discriminate their meanings. In many cases, one of those words has been translated as "soul."

With the loss of the word's original intent, how could I possibly know what Jesus was saying here? My own preconceptions left me totally unable to bring this verse into practical application for me.

So, let's take a look at this verse with its Greek root listed next to "life".

> **Matt. 18:8-9** *And if your hand or your foot causes you to sin, cut it off and throw it from you! It is better for you to enter into **life (zoe)** crippled or lame than, having two hands or two feet, to be thrown into the eternal fire! And if your eye causes you to sin, tear it out and throw it from you! It is better for you to enter into **life (zoe)** one-eyed than, having two eyes, to be thrown into fiery hell! (LEB)*

That does makes a difference. Now, I can see that Jesus is not using *psuche* here but *zoe*. So, I can likely deduce that Jesus is not talking about a person's "life" or "soul" (which a living person would already possess). So, Jesus has to be talking about something different. The concept of "life" or "soul" wouldn't make sense here anyway.

Zoe has to have some other meaning that would illuminate this and help this verse make sense. But, how do I know what that meaning is?

As previously mentioned, if I could get a copy of a Greek dictionary from the time Jesus was preaching and looked up the word *zoe*, would it give me the understanding I need? Even if no such dictionary exists, I could look at Greek literature from that time period and get a general idea of how the word *zoe* was used.

But . . . did Jesus use *zoe* in a unique way?

A Patent Illustration

Let me illustrate using a law that is very much in effect today in almost all nations worldwide: patent law. Almost all countries respect other countries' patent laws to some degree. If you apply for a utility patent in the United States, your patent application will be closely evaluated by a patent examiner from the United States Patent and Trademark Office.

During the evaluation of the patent application, the patent examiner closely reviews every detail of your patent application.

The examiner will compare the claims you are making in your application by examining key concepts and equivalent words from patents all over the world. If the examiner can find any "prior art" (previously patented inventions or descriptions of the device) then the examiner will be obligated to deny any correlated claims in your patent.

The success of any patent hinges upon whether its claims can be defended against a lawsuit. The claims are the most important part of the patent. It is the patent examiner's job to find reasons to deny the claims within any patent application. If the examiner can deny all of the claims, then the patent will not be granted. A person or company can enter as many claims as they want in their application, but the examiner will put forth their best effort to deny every claim. However, if the applicant is successful in even getting only one of their claims through the process, then they are granted a patent.

This part of the examiner's job is very important. The US Patent and Trademark office does not want to grant patents with weak claims. If they did, the courts would be tied up with an overwhelming number of lawsuits. However, if a claim is very strong, then it is less likely to be litigated by someone seeking to challenge the patent.

As you can see, the strength of a patent is only as good as its **claims**. Now, here is the catch: the **key words** contained in the claims are dependent upon how those key words are defined by their use in the **body of the patent**. The claims are the last part of a patent application. Before an applicant itemizes their claims, they must first describe the need for the invention and how this device solves that need.

Any **wording** contained in the **claims** that is not defined by its use in the **body of the patent** will be considered as a basis for the examiner to deny that claim. The importance of this is paramount. If the examiner denies a claim based on the fact that the body of the patent does not define a key word used in the claim, then there is no opportunity for the applicant to go back and revise the supporting wording in the body of the patent!

For instance, let's say I have applied for a patent for a device that contains a "carriage" somewhere in the device, and the "carriage" performs an important function in the use of my device. Then, I used the word "carriage" in one of the claims of my patent application. If I have not defined the word "carriage" by my use of the word in the body of my application and I do not have a "carriage" depicted and explained in my engineering drawing, then the examiner will likely deny my claim on the basis there is no "carriage" defined in my application. In other words, there is not enough supporting information to clarify my definition of "carriage."

It is quite possible that the "carriage" in my patent barely resembles a "carriage" in the minds of most people, but I chose to use the word "carriage" because it was the best word I could think of. Thus, the word "carriage" has been defined by the way I used it in my application. The examiner doesn't really care how a key word is used or defined by the general public. The merits of the claims are totally dependent on the how the **key word** was defined in the body of the patent.

If clarifying a word can cost millions of dollars to defend in a ptent lawsuit, then is it not possible to say that Jesus' use of a word can indeed define it in a way that is unique and different than the normal basis for the word in Jesus' culture?

Ask yourself, if God came down and explained himself in a very spiritual sense that was foreign to mortals, what language or words would he use to do this? Out of necessity, he would be restricted to the people's common language, using words they were already familiar with. Then, he might use metaphors to describe spiritual truths that are beyond the human experience. This is exactly what Jesus does throughout his ministry.

For instance, when Jesus spoke with Nicodemus in John 3, he chided Nicodemus for his failure to already recognize the spiritual truth about being born again. He told Nicodemus, "If you don't understand when I speak to you of earthly things, then how will you understand when I speak to you of heavenly things?"

It is indeed this aspect that describes Jesus' use of the word *zoe*. *Zoe* was the closest earthly word available to define a spiritual truth that surpassed the common use of the word. Being born again was the metaphor he used in combination with the word *zoe* while describing the process to Nicodemus.

So, the question ultimately comes down to this: Does the word *zoe* convey a unique definition that is generated by Jesus' unique use of the word? My answer is absolutely **yes**! In fact, it is his very use of the word that is so profound and should clarify every believer's understanding of the core of Jesus' message.

In fact, failing to see this core concept of *zoe* as Jesus defines it will prevent any believer from fully understanding Jesus' teachings.

Failing to see this core concept of **Zoe** as Jesus defines it will prevent any believer from fully understanding Jesus' teachings!

Life
Defined

16

Understanding Zoe

Over the years, I have taken my kids and their friends to several waterparks. One of my favorites has a lazy river that meanders in a loop through the park. There are four or five entrances with steps where one can get in or out of the lazy river. Now, the largest entrance is near the front of the park, and most people get in there, but you can get in or out at any of the entrances.

Once you understand the concept of *zoe* as Jesus defines it, the scriptures will make more sense to you anywhere you open them up. The hard part for me is deciding where to begin this study with you. We could get into the water anywhere along the river and do just fine. But, what makes the most sense?

I certainly did not begin my study at the beginning. My study began with questions I had over a twenty-year period regarding several scattered scriptures that just didn't seem to make sense. It was only after a long struggle with comparing and studying that it came together like a puzzle for me. That's not an optimal way to teach or train, so I have decided to use the gospel according to John as map for this journey.

As we embark on a journey through the gospel according to John, I would like to point out something that I believe is particularly unique to John's gospel. I think of the four gospels as narratives that describe Jesus' life, teachings, miracles, etc. in a timeline, so to speak. Each author seemed to record the events that they thought would be of importance to their particular audience as they occurred, beginning with Jesus' birth, selecting his apostles, his teachings, betrayal, death, resurrection, etc.

But, in John's gospel, something significantly different occurs: John masterfully reveals the concept of *Zoe*.

If you will forgive me for using the vernacular of my day, John was all over *zoe*! He introduces the concept during his introduction of Jesus, then gradually reveals more and more about *zoe* as he progresses through his gospel. It is comparable to an artist gradually revealing a magnificent sculpture as he chisels away the stone chip by chip. The sculptor already knows what the final image is, but it is unveiled in stages for the observer. John records Jesus' own teachings about *zoe* progressively, defining it in steps.

It is probable that Jesus spoke of *zoe* many times and in many different venues. But, John selectively and methodically reveals Jesus' teachings to us about *zoe* so that we can grasp it in small bites. As we see Jesus reveal this truth, we begin to understand that *zoe* is the most powerful underlying theme in the gospel according to John.

> **Zoe** is the most powerful underlying
> theme in the Gospel of John

You may be asking, "If this concept does exist, why hasn't it already been explained and taught?"

My answer is that there is significant evidence that this concept is exactly what the church taught for approximately the first two to three centuries of its existence.

So, your next question might be, "Why is this so difficult to understand?"

My reply: it is not difficult at all. Let me repeat that. The concept of *zoe* as Jesus taught it is not complicated at all. It is in fact less complicated than most Christians' current understanding of Eternal Life. But, educating ourselves on what Jesus actually taught requires us to unlearn some things that are not true.

Untangling Knots, One at a Time

Having inaccurate words in the English translation has created tangled misconceptions that have lasted for centuries. The concept of *zoe* is not complicated at all, but it has been **obscured** by inaccurate and ambiguous wording. Thus, the complication comes with untangling knots of obscurity and replacing those with **clarity**.

Have you ever had to untangle a fishing line, an extension cord, necklace, or maybe the wires to your earbuds? It's a pain, isn't it? Imagine having to untangle a long string that had scores of tangles that have been tightly pulled together. You have to figure out which one you want to untangle first and then gradually untangle each one, until you have a string free of tangles.

We are going on a journey through the New Testament, untangling knots one a time. After we untie a few knots, it will gradually become clear where Jesus is leading us with *zoe*.

Note: As we progress through "untangling" these knots, there will be sections where you may wish that I would just give you a definition or explanation right then and there. I honestly don't know of a way to just cut to the final explanation without building definitions one step at a time and, in some cases, intentionally creating questions that I do not answer until I can lay out the facts.

I regret that this may leave you temporarily confused in some sections, but as we progress, my hope is that this confusion will be replaced by absolute clarity.

As you progress throught this study, you may feel defensive or that you need to make arguments against what I am saying in your mind. That's ok, please just keep an open mind as you proceed.

Seeing Things in Full Color

When I was a kid, our family had an old, black-and-white television. My friends and I would spend hours watching our favorite TV shows. We thought B&W TV was the coolest thing ever! I can't remember how long we had our B&W TV, but I do remember the excitement that all the kids in our neighborhood shared when we heard about the new color TVs that were soon to be available at the department store. We couldn't even imagine what that would be like!

Eventually one of the neighboring kids' parents purchased one of these new, amazing TV sets. All of the kids couldn't wait to hang out at the friend's house and watch a TV show in full color. I can clearly recall the amazement that we all felt at being able to see our favorite western TV show in vibrant color.

We had no idea how much vibrancy we had been missing! These colors obviously existed when the show was originally filmed, but they were muted in the background in the B&W display.

But, with the new color TV, the shows seemed so much more exciting to watch. Seeing the shows in full color changed the whole experience. Things just popped off the screen that were previously monotone in appearance.

As you begin to understand what Jesus actually said in the original Greek, this may be how you start to feel. Important details that you never noticed before will become vibrant and powerful. Old familiar phrases from the Bible (both Old and New Testaments) will take on new meaning as you see the original intent that was there all along but has subsequently been obscured.

Part Two

Jesus Defines Zoe

Life
Defined

17

Following the Gospel of John

John 1

Let's start by stepping into the first few verses of the gospel according to John, chapter one. John introduces Jesus by saying several things about him, but the key concept we are focusing on for this study is what John says about *zoe*.

> John 1:4 In him was **life (zoe)**, and the **life (zoe)** was the light of humanity. *(LEB)*

John points out that "**In Him was Life**"

There is something here to take note of. John only interjects his personal comments about *zoe* **twice** in his gospel. John inserts his comment here as an introduction to *zoe*, and then, toward the end of the gospel, he concludes with a summary of *zoe* (John 20:30-31). The rest of the *zoe* scriptures in John are taken directly from Jesus' teachings and conversations (and one from John the Baptist).

> John introduces Jesus, emphasizing,
>
> "**In Jesus was Life (Zoe)**"

What is John trying to say here? Isn't his statement a little unusual? If so, what are the possible implications of this statement? Is this how you would introduce someone?

As you go through the possibilities of what John intends here, let's make a multiple-choice list. You decide which one makes the most sense at this point. You might even want to add an option of your own for now.

- Jesus is alive (not a zombie).

- Jesus is a living human being, not just a spirit.

- Jesus is a very lively person with a lot of charisma.

- Jesus has extra wisdom that gives him insight from God, which is enlightening to others.

- Other?

Reflection

Please take a minute and write down what you think John meant by this statement:

"In Jesus was life . . ."

Now, let's ask ourselves a few questions:

- Why did John emphasize that Jesus had life in himself?

- How is it possible that this life could be the light of mankind?

- Maybe the biggest question we should be asking ourselves is this - **Is the fact that Jesus had life (*zoe*) in himself different from you and me?**

If you are a Christian, how influential has this part of John's introduction of Jesus been in your understanding of who Jesus is? I'm guessing you probably haven't given it too much thought.

As a young man, I used to work for a company selling concrete brick. Most people wouldn't know the difference between a concrete brick and a clay brick.

However, if you know what to look for, you can easily tell the difference between clay and concrete brick. Occasionally, when I am driving around with my wife in the car, I'll see a house with concrete brick. I'll point it out to my wife, and she will look at me like, "Really, ok, I am pretending to be interested".

But, we are all like this in one way or another. We go through life not noticing certain things around us until, one day, we learn about something new through school or work. We then begin to notice that new thing we learned about is all around us. We never noticed it before because we didn't know enough about it to appreciate it.

That is exactly what's happening in John 1:4.

You may have not paid much attention to John's statement—"In Jesus was life."—because you didn't know its **implications.**

Dear reader, I pray with all my heart, that is about to change.

Milestones

Key Concepts Defined

What we have learned about life (*Zoe*) thus far:

> ➤ In Jesus was *Zoe*.

> ➤ *Zoe* was the light of mankind.

What we don't know:

> ➤ What exactly is *Zoe*?

> ➤ Why is this so important that John felt he needed to introduce Jesus in this way?

> ➤ Do I have *Zoe*?

Life

Defined

18

John 3

Next Up . . . Nicodemus

In John 3:1-22, Jesus is approached by a man named Nicodemus. I encourage you to read this narrative in its entirety, as it is a very powerful dialogue. But, for now, let's zero in on just the verses that contain *zoe*.

About halfway through this narrative, Jesus tells Nicodemus the following:

> **John 3:16** *For in this way God loved the world, so that he gave his one and only Son, in order that everyone who believes in him will not perish, but will have **eternal life (zoe)** (LEB)*

Interesting! By believing in Jesus, a person can have **eternal *zoe***. Notice that Jesus did **not** use the word *psuche*. Trust me, this is no insignificant detail. The term "eternal *psuche*" **never** occurs in the Bible. Every time the term "eternal life" appears, it occurs as a combination of the Greek word *zoe* and another Greek word *aionion*, which means "unto the ages," "everlasting," or "eternal."

> Every time the term "Eternal Life" appears, it occurs as a combination of the Greek word **Zoe** and another Greek word **aionion**, which means "unto the ages," "everlasting," or "eternal"

Let's pause for a second and ask ourselves a few questions. As you read each question, take time to reflect on each one.

Your answer to these questions could be life changing.

➤ Why did Jesus use *zoe* instead of *psuche* for this term? Would it have made any difference?

➤ Referring back to John 1:4, how is the fact that Jesus had life (*zoe*) in himself different from you and me?

➤ Or are we any different? Is life (*zoe*) in us as typical human beings?

➤ Or is this something unique about Jesus that is different than you and me?

> ➤ If we indeed have the same life (*zoe*) as Jesus, then why did John feel it was important to point this out in John 1:4?

Furthermore

If the statement that John made in his introduction—"In Jesus was Life"—is true, and this can't be said about you and me . . . then the statement that Jesus made to Nicodemus becomes that much more interesting.

Because Jesus just told Nicodemus he can have *zoe* . . . and he can have it for *eternity*!

> If the statement John made in his introduction
> **"In Jesus was Life"**—is true, and this can't be
> said about you and me, then the statement
> that Jesus made to Nicodemus
> becomes much more interesting!!
>
> Because Jesus just told Nicodemus that he could
> have **Life (Zoe)** and have it for **Eternity**

John the Baptist Understood the Concept of *Zoe*

In John 3:22-36, John (the apostle and author of the gospel according to John) records an interaction between John the Baptist (a different John, not the author) and some of John the Baptist's disciples. During this conversation, John the Baptist explains several important things to his disciples about Jesus. He proclaims that Jesus is the Son of God. Then, in the very last verse of this conversation, John the Baptist states the following:

> *John 3:36 The one who believes in the Son has **eternal life (zoe),** but the one who disobeys the Son will not see **life (zoe)** —but the wrath of God remains on him (LEB)*

In the first half of this verse, John the Baptist essentially says the same thing that Jesus told Nicodemus.

*The one who believes in the Son has **eternal life (zoe)***

But, it's the second part of the verse that answers one of the questions we were pondering.

*but the one who disobeys the Son will not see **life (zoe)** —but the wrath of God remains on him.*

John the Baptist points out that anyone who disobeys or rejects the Son (Jesus) will not see life (*zoe*).

From what John the Baptist just said, it sounds like *zoe* is something that I don't already have. According to what John the Baptist just said, if I don't believe in Jesus, I will not see *zoe*.

This clearly indicates that we (as humans) don't initially have *Zoe*.

Summary of John 3

- If I believe in Jesus, I will receive eternal life (*zoe*).

- On the flip side, if I reject Jesus, I will not see life (*zoe*).

- If I reject Jesus, I remain under God's wrath.

- I can conclude that I do not have *zoe* as an inherent part of my nature.

Would you agree it safe to say that we don't have *zoe* intrinsically as a part of us before we believe in Jesus?

If this statement is indeed true, then what is it about *zoe* that makes it so different than *psuche*?

A few peskier questions are now in order. Remember, we are trying to untangle a very tight knot, and this one has **a lot** of wraps in it.

What does John the Baptist mean when he says that some will not see Life (*Zoe*)?

This seems very definitive and terribly restrictive. He indicates there is no way for an unbeliever to have *zoe* in any form or percentage. It is not a matter of not having more of *zoe*, it is not having *zoe* at all.

Also, the last section of this verse indicates that in order for me to receive *zoe*, I must get out from under God's wrath. How does God's wrath figure into all this? It sounds as though I am already under God's wrath, and I need to remove it by believing in Jesus.

Somehow removing his wrath is a prerequisite for me getting *zoe*.

This leads to a few more very important questions:

- If I start out being under God's wrath and I don't have *zoe* (life), then just what do I have?
- What is my life status?
- What would be the opposite of not having eternal *zoe*?

There are so many tangles in this knot! The gospel according to John definitely has our attention. Let's see what John has in store for us next.

Life

Defined

19

John 4

The Woman at the Well Needs Life (*Zoe*)

In John 4:1-26, Jesus encounters a Samaritan woman who comes to draw water at a well outside of the town she lives in. Jesus uses a conversation about getting water from the well as a segue into his purpose for meeting this woman.

Jesus wants to give her *zoe*, just like he wants to give *zoe* to you and me.

> *John 4:13-14 Jesus answered and said to her, "Everyone who drinks of this water will be thirsty again. But whoever drinks of this water which I will give to him will never be thirsty for eternity, but the water which I will give to him will become in him a well of water springing up to **eternal life (zoe)**." (LEB)*

Reminder: Every time the phrase "eternal life" occurs, it always uses the word *zoe* and not *psuche*. In fact, this phrase occurs again in this chapter in verse 36.

> *John 4:36 The one who reaps receives wages and gathers fruit for **eternal life (zoe)**, in order that the one who sows and the one who reaps can rejoice together (LEB)*

This presents another important question: What is the connection of the word ***zoe*** to "**eternity**" (*aionion*)? This is just one more tangle in our strand of knots. We will untangle all of these knots, one precept at a time, as we follow John's unveiling of *zoe* in his gospel.

Milestones

Key Concepts Defined

What we have learned about Zoe thus far:

- ➤ In Jesus was *Zoe*.

- ➤ *Zoe* was the light of mankind.

- ➤ If I believe in Jesus, I will receive eternal *Zoe*.

- ➤ On the flip side, if I reject Jesus, I will not see life (*Zoe*).

- ➤ If I reject Jesus, I remain under God's wrath.

- ➤ I do not have *Zoe* as an inherent part of my nature.

What we don't know:

- ➤ What exactly is *Zoe*?

- ➤ Why is this so important that John felt he needed to introduce Jesus in this way?

- ➤ How does God's wrath fit into this?

- ➤ What exactly is the difference between *psuche* and *zoe*?

- ➤ What is the connection of the word *Zoe* to "eternity?"

Now for a very important question ...
If I do not initially have *Zoe*,
then just exactly what do I have?

20

John 5

Jesus Defines Life (*Zoe*)

As we move into John 5, John provides further details to his introduction of Jesus—"In Him was life (*zoe*)." He records Jesus' conversation with a group of Jewish leaders, in which Jesus himself defines *zoe*.

> *John 5:21-29 For just as the Father raises the dead and **makes them alive (root word is zoe)**, thus also the Son **makes alive (root word is zoe)** whomever he wishes. For the Father does not judge anyone, but he has given all judgment to the Son, in order that all people will honor the Son, just as they honor the Father. The one who does not honor the Son does not honor the Father who sent him. Truly, truly I say to you that the one who hears my word and who believes the one who sent me has **eternal life (zoe)**, and does not come into judgment, but has passed from death into **life (zoe)**.*

> *"Truly, truly I say to you, that an hour is coming—and now is here—when the dead will hear the voice of the Son of God, and the ones who hear will live. For just as the Father has **life (zoe)** in himself, thus also he has granted to the Son to have **life (zoe)** in himself. And he has granted him authority to carry out judgment, because he is the Son of Man. "Do not be astonished at this, because an hour is coming in which all those in the tombs will hear his voice and they will come out—those who have done good things to a resurrection of **life (zoe)**, but those who have practiced evil things to a resurrection of judgment. (LEB)*

This section is very revealing. Jesus begins by talking about God his Father raising the dead and giving them life (the root of *zoe* is used here). Jesus then explains that he is capable of giving life (*zoe*) as well, because God his Father has sent him and enabled him to do so. The crux of this whole discourse comes down to 5:26, shown below:

> **John 5:26** *For just as the Father has **life (zoe)** in himself, thus also he has granted to the Son to have **life (zoe)** in himself. (LEB)*

Did you just catch this? Jesus explains that *zoe* is an intrinsic aspect of who God is. God the Father has this life (*zoe*) in himself! *Zoe* is part of his nature as God.

Pause and make sure you recognize this point! This mysterious word *zoe* has just been defined by Jesus, going beyond the definitions of his day with a divine significance.

Zoe is the Type of Life That God Has!

The Father has life (*zoe*) in himself, and he has granted Jesus to have life (*zoe*) in himself.

This is the definition that we have been looking for!

Jesus has just used a common word in the Greek language for "life." But, he has clearly given it huge significance that far exceeds the current definition of his day.

This *zoe* as Jesus has just defined it is life of a **divine** nature.

> **Zoe** is the type of Life that God has.
> The Father has Life (**Zoe**) in himself,
> and he has granted that Jesus
> also has Life (**Zoe**) in himself

What did Jesus say about those that he gives this *zoe* (life) to?

Believers cross over from death to life (*zoe*). From this, we can unravel another knot.

First, we now know that God the Father and Jesus the Son have *zoe* intrinsically. We can further deduce that no one else has *zoe* intrinsically. Any other creature that has *zoe* has it because it has been bestowed upon them by the Father or Jesus.

This mysterious word *zoe* has just been defined by Jesus with a very special significance. This *zoe* is the type of life that God has. The Father has life (*zoe*) in himself, and he has granted that Jesus have life (*zoe*) in himself.

So, What Is Our Initial Status?

Next, Jesus defines us (humans) as not having life (*zoe*) intrinsically but rather existing in a state of death.

> *John 5:24 Truly, truly I say to you that the one who hears my word and who believes the one who sent me has **eternal life (zoe)**, and does not come into judgment, but has passed from death into **life (zoe)**. (LEB)*

Not until we believe in Jesus is this *zoe* (life) bestowed upon us. We then cross over from death to life (zoe). At that point, our status changes from "dead" to "alive." We initially start out in a state of being dead. Pretty sobering, isn't it?

Those who believe in Jesus cross over from a status of **Death** to to a status of **Life (Zoe)**

Milestones

What we have learned about *Zoe* thus far:

➢ In Jesus was *Zoe*.

➢ If I believe in Jesus, I will receive Eternal *Zoe*.

➢ On the flip side, if I reject Jesus, I will not see life (*Zoe*).

➢ If I reject Jesus, I remain under God's wrath.

➢ I do not have *Zoe* as an inherent part of my nature.

➢ *Zoe* is defined by Jesus as "the life that God the Father has in himself."

➢ The Father has granted that Jesus has *Zoe* in himself.

➢ *Zoe* is an innate part of the divine nature of the Father and the Son (Jesus).

➢ No humans have *Zoe* as an innate part of themselves.

➢ Humans are initially in a state of death.

➢ Humans that believe cross over from death to life (*Zoe*).

We will unwrap just exactly what this state of death entails in a later chapter, but we have just bitten off some pretty huge definitions.

As Jesus continues this difficult conversation with the Jewish leaders, he reiterates that they must come to him to receive this life (*zoe*). Jesus is very direct with them, confronting them about their stubbornness of heart.

> **John 5:36-40** *But I have a testimony greater than John's, for the works which the Father has given to me that I should complete them—the very works which I am doing—these testify about me, that the Father has sent me. And the Father who sent me, that one has testified about me. You have neither heard his voice at any time nor seen his form. And you do not have his word residing in yourselves, because the one whom that one sent, in this one you do not believe. You search[p] the scriptures because you think that you have* **eternal life (zoe)** *in them, and it is these that testify about me. And you are not willing to come to me so that you may have* **life (zoe)**. *(LEB)*

Jesus chastises the Jewish leaders because they searched the scriptures, supposing that the scriptures would somehow lead them to Eternal Life, yet they failed to recognize that the scriptures were pointing to Jesus. As a result, they refused to come to Jesus for life.

This is unfortunate, for Jesus is the only source for life (*zoe*).

It is interesting that Jesus acknowledges that the Jewish leaders knew what the real issue was (death), and that they searched the scriptures to understand God's solution to death. Yet their hard hearts prevented them from recognizing that the scriptures indeed pointed to God's solution – Jesus himself.

Definitions

Let's summarize some definitions that we understand up to this point. Further defining is still to come, but let's review what we learned thus far.

Psuche: (life, soul, self) Basically the human life, consisting of a person's consciousness. It is the heart of who that person is—their existence. A person's *psuche* is that person. English translators have used either "life" or "soul," as they deemed best, to translate *psuche*.

> **Note:** There is never any indication in the Bible that *psuche* has any eternal or immortal properties. As you may remember, Eternal Life is only associated with *Zoe*.

Zoe: Life as God has it. This is the inherent state that God is in. Immortality is one of the primary defining aspects of *Zoe*.

Dead: The state that man is in until and unless he/she believes in Jesus. This death will be explained by Jesus in greater detail in the upcoming chapters.

You and Me: We do not have *Zoe* in and of ourselves. We intrinsically exist in a state of death unless we believe in Jesus. Until we believe in Jesus, our life consists of mortal *psuche*, nothing more.

21

John 6

Jesus Declares, "I Am the Bread of Life"

As we move into John 6, Jesus' teachings and miraculous healings attract a very large crowd that follows him as he travels through the countryside. Jesus feeds this crowd of thousands with five barley loaves and two small fish. This miracle amazes the crowd, so much so that many of them perceive that this miracle was a sign of the **prophet** who was to come into the world.

Some thirteen hundred years earlier, Moses foretold of a prophet (that would be like himself) that God would raise up from amidst the Israelites. God would put his words in the mouth of this prophet, and the prophet would speak unto them all that God should command him. God foretold through Moses that anyone who did not hearken unto the words that the prophet spoke in his name would be judged (see Deuteronomy 18:15-19).

Now, many in this crowd suspect that Jesus is this anticipated prophet. One of the noteworthy things that transpired while Moses led the Israelites through the wilderness for forty years was the miraculous "manna" that God provided each morning for the people to eat (see Exodus 16).

In Exodus 16:4, God said to Moses, "Behold I will rain bread from heaven for you, and the people shall go out and gather a day's portion every day." This manna (along with quail in the evening) sustained the food needs of the Israelites for forty years as they wandered through the desert. The Israelites associated this miracle with the leadership of Moses.

Now that the crowds have seen Jesus miraculously feed the thousands, they interpret this event as a sign that he is the prophet that Moses spoke of. They are, in fact, correct in interpreting this sign, but they are incorrect in that they assume Jesus intends to be an earthly king.

In fact, the crowd becomes intent on making Jesus their king. Jesus must elude the crowd and withdraws to a nearby mountain by himself. The fact that Jesus can miraculously feed them has them determined to follow him. After all, if this man can do miracles including feeding thousands, how much more could he do for them if he were indeed inaugurated as the prophet and made a king? The excitement among the thousands that pursue him is palpable.

During the night, Jesus crosses the sea to Capernaum along with his disciples. This is, in itself, a miraculous event but has nothing to do with *zoe*, so we are going to skip discussing this journey. The next morning, the crowd realizes that Jesus and his disciples have left, so they commandeer a number of boats and cross the sea to follow Jesus to Capernaum. When they find Jesus, they begin to question him about when he managed to get to this side of the sea. Jesus' reply (as we shall see) was not what they were expecting.

This sets up the crowd for "paradigm shift" teaching by Jesus. Jesus uses the miraculous feeding done the day before as a metaphor to lead them into deeper instruction. In this encounter, just as in John 5, most of his listeners will not accept his teaching. In this chapter, Jesus uses an incredibly strong metaphor that most of the crowd will not understand. I would encourage you to read all of John 6. It is very informative and powerful. But, again, in the interest of staying on course in this section, I am focusing on the verses that have to do with *zoe*.

We are going to pick up in John 6:25, the following day after Jesus has fed the thousands.

> **John 6:25-27** *And when they found him on the other side of the sea, they said to him, "Rabbi, when did you get here?" Jesus replied to them and said, "Truly, truly I say to you, you seek me not because you saw signs, but because you ate of the loaves and were satisfied! Do not work for the food that perishes, but the food that remains to **eternal life (zoe),** which the Son of Man will give to you. For God the Father has set his seal on this one." (LEB)*

Jesus confronts this crowd that followed him to Capernaum and tells them that they are seeking him not because they saw the miracles, but because they ate the bread and were filled. He challenges them not to work for food that perishes but for food that remains unto eternal *zoe*.

Jesus uses the crowd's focus on food to segue into that which is of vital importance. This is similar to the segue that Jesus used with the woman at the well, in John 4. She was drawing water from the well, which was a daily burden for her, when Jesus challenged her to ask him for "water that wells up to eternal life." Jesus applies similar teaching here but is about to introduce a stronger metaphor.

> **John 6:28-29** *So they said to him, "What shall we do that we can accomplish the works of God?" Jesus answered and said to them, "This is the work of God: that you believe in the one whom that one sent." (LEB)*

The crowd asks Jesus what they must do, in order to accomplish the works that God requires. Jesus' reply is simple and to the point: "The work of God is this: believe in the one that he has sent."

I'd like to share my experience with this verse when I was young. I often struggled with the question of what I should be doing to please God. At times, I would wonder if I should be doing more of this or that. This verse is magnificent because it shows the grace of God in its simplicity.

The work that God requires is this: believe in Jesus, as the Son of God, the Messiah, the promised one. Believe in the work that Jesus accomplished in his death on the cross, when he took your death penalty and mine upon himself. When we actively count on that fact, we have believed on the one that God sent.

Secondly, the Greek word for "sent" implies a commission. God has commissioned Jesus for a mission. He has not been randomly sent out. Jesus has a distinct and vital purpose. We will see Jesus gradually reveal his mission in its entirety by John chapter 10.

> *John 6:30-31 So they said to him, "Then what sign will you perform, so that we can see it and believe you? What will you do? Our fathers ate the manna in the wilderness, just as it is written, 'He gave them bread from heaven to eat.' (LEB)*

The crowd then replies, "What sign will you show us that would give us reason to believe in you?" They go on to challenge Jesus, "Can you do what Moses did and provide us with manna from heaven to eat?" This is a two-fold challenge. First, they are asking Jesus to do something miraculous that compares with what Moses did. Jesus has already performed multiple miracles, including healing the diseased and feeding the five thousand. This should be adequate proof for them.

Jesus exposed their ulterior motive earlier in 6:26. Ultimately, they are looking for a king who can be a provider. They want someone to feed them. So, they are not just looking for confirmation. They want to see if he can continue to miraculously feed them.

This seems a bit odd to me as someone from a part of society where I take my next meal for granted. I usually have plenty of food in my pantry. Therefore, I admit that I have a hard time relating to the crowd's focus on this. But, my experience is not like theirs at all. Just as getting water was a daily burden for the woman at the well in John 4, finding enough daily food to eat was a significant challenge for these people.

*John 6:32-33 Then Jesus said to them, "Truly, truly I say to you, Moses did not give you bread from heaven, but my Father is giving you the true bread from heaven! For the bread of God is the one who comes down from heaven and gives **life (zoe)** to the world." (LEB)*

Jesus replies to their question about manna by correcting them.

He instructs them that, indeed, it wasn't Moses who gave them manna but his Father. He declares that now his Father will give them the **true bread from heaven** (Jesus uses this metaphor to allude to himself). Jesus uses the phrase **true bread from heaven** here to emphasize the surpassing importance of this bread of life (*zoe*) and its huge implications (in contrast to the manna).

Jesus defines this **true bread from heaven** as:

1. He that comes down from Heaven (referring to himself).

2. This true bread from heaven gives life (*zoe*) to the world.

Next, we see the crowd's response:

John 6:34 So they said to him, "Sir, always give us this bread!" (LEB)

Jesus segue into the **true bread from heaven** that gives life (*zoe*) to the world has drawn the crowd's attention to the vital truth he is about to reveal using a stronger metaphor. Be sure to not miss this, Jesus is starting to set up a powerful **contrast** between the "manna" that the Israelites ate in Moses day, and the "true bread" from heaven (himself).

He is also about to clarify this true bread, by identifying himself as the bread of zoe. This clarification focuses on what this bread will do for those who eat this bread. Jesus uses *eating* as a metaphor for believing in Him. The effect of eating this bread is quite different from the manna that the Israelites ate some 1300 years before.

Jesus' "I Am" Statements

This sets up the first of the seven famous "I Am" statements that Jesus makes in John's gospel. Would it surprise you to know that every one of the "I Am" statements is directly tied to *zoe*?

In fact, if you don't understand what Jesus means when he is referring to *zoe*, the intended thrust of each "I Am" statement will be obscured at best and totally misunderstood at worst.

I Am the Bread of Life (Zoe).
"I Am" Statement 1

> *John 6:35 Jesus said to them, "I am the bread of **life (zoe).** The one who comes to me will never be hungry, and the one who believes in me will never be thirsty again. (LEB)*

Jesus declares that he is the bread of life (*zoe*). At this point, the conversation between Jesus and the crowd becomes very strained. First of all, many know his background and his family history, so they question how he can claim to come down from heaven. Secondly, Jesus begins to say some very bizarre things in relation to the metaphor about him being the bread of life.

However, so far, the metaphor is fairly simple to follow. We can see that by coming to him, we will never be hungry and that by believing in him, we will never be thirsty. Going forward, the metaphor becomes much more difficult.

The Key to Understanding John 6

The key to understanding the rest of chapter is to remember that Jesus is using the concept of bread and eating as a metaphor. He speaks about eating his flesh and drinking his blood. Many in the crowd that day are offended as they take what he is saying **literally**. Jesus often spoke in parables and metaphors, which were sometimes difficult to understand. Nowhere is this more apparent than in John 6.

Jesus Contrasts the Bread of Zoe with Manna

Don't let this confusion of the crowd distract you. Jesus is using the metaphor of himself being the bread of zoe, to show it's surpassing greatness over the manna. The reason it surpasses the manna is because those who ate the manna are now dead. Jesus is going to explain that those who eat his flesh will live forever.

This is the main point of John chapter 6. This idea was so bizarre, that most of the crowd left Jesus after this teaching. However, this metaphor is critical to understand. This section may leave you with questions, just as it did those in the crowd. Please hang in there with me as we continue through John chapter 6. John will clear this up progressively as we continue through John.

This exchange with the crowd becomes more challenging as it goes back and forth. Let's pick up about halfway through the conversation in 6:47, where Jesus repeats, "I am the bread of life."

> *John 6:47-51 Truly, truly I say to you, the one who believes has **eternal life (zoe)**. I am the bread of **life (zoe)**. Your fathers ate the manna in the wilderness and they died. This is the bread that comes down from heaven so that someone may eat from it and not die. I am the living bread that came down from heaven. If anyone eats from this bread, he will live forever. And the bread that I will give for the life of the world is my flesh." (LEB)*

"Bread of Life" Defined by Jesus

Let's break John 6:47-51 into six critical concepts defined by Jesus:

1 - He who believes in Jesus receives Eternal *Zoe*.

> *Truly, truly I say to you, the one who believes has **eternal life** (zoe)*

Jesus repeats that he who believes in him has eternal life (*zoe*).

2 - Jesus is the metaphorical bread of *Zoe*.

> *I am the bread of **life** (zoe).*

Jesus repeats that he is the bread of **life (*zoe*)**.

3 - The manna did not prevent their ancestors from dying.

What Jesus says here is totally unexpected, but it is this contrast that is Jesus' ultimate emphasis for this encounter.

> *Your fathers ate the manna in the wilderness, and they **died**.*

This statement by Jesus is shocking and bizarre, but it is intended to draw the crowd's attention to a critical truth.

Jesus tells the Jews that their ancestors indeed ate the manna in the wilderness, **but that they died**.

Let that soak in for a minute. The fact that the Israelites that ate manna thirteen hundred years earlier have died seems a bit obvious, doesn't it? But, Jesus' intent in this conversation is to get the crowd to focus on the difference between the manna and its inability to prevent the Israelites from dying and contrast that with the **true bread from heaven** that a person *may eat of and not die*.

4 - I am the bread from heaven, that a person may eat of, and not die.

I mentioned earlier in this book that John's purpose in writing this book was to reveal Jesus' teaching about *zoe*. However, up until now, Jesus has not mentioned the ultimate purpose of *zoe*. We have seen that *zoe* gives eternal life, which is its ultimate effect on the believer. **But, there is a purpose for *zoe* that is just as important as its effect.** That is what Jesus introduces here and will elaborate on in the next five chapters of John.

So, it is here in John 6:50 where Jesus introduces the ultimate purpose of *zoe*.

> *John 6:50 This is the bread that comes down from heaven so that someone may eat from it and not die (LEB)*

Jesus says that he is the bread that comes down from heaven that a man may eat of it and *not die!*

Jesus saying that he is the bread that a person "can eat of and not die" is indeed a bizarre statement. There are two aspects to this statement that this crowd struggles with.

First is the concept that Jesus wants the people to eat him. This gets even more bizarre in the next few verses in John 6. Jesus extends this metaphor of eating himself to include drinking his blood. The crowd is so disturbed by this thought that many will no longer follow him after this encounter.

Second, Jesus tells them that if they do eat him, they will not die. The first part of the statement about eating him derails the crowd so much that most don't get far enough to choke (no pun intended) on the second bizarre component of this statement where Jesus says those that eat this bread *will not die*.

As it turns out, "not dying" is the whole point of John 6. The crowd gets so hung up taking Jesus' statement about "eating" him literally (when it was a metaphor) that most fail to see the significance of the purpose of the statement . . . *that they can avoid dying.*

5 - Whoever eats this bread will live forever.

I am the living bread that came down from heaven. If anyone eats from this bread, he will live forever.

Jesus emphasizes that he is the "living bread" that came down from heaven. He goes on to explain that whoever eats this bread will live forever. This is another way of saying that a person may eat of this bread and "not die." Only the bread of life (*zoe*) can enable a person to live forever.

6 - This bread is my flesh, which I will give for the life (*Zoe*) of the world.

*And the bread that I will give for the **life (zoe)** of the world is my flesh*

Jesus sums up the conversation to this point by tying it together with a *zoe* statement. Jesus gives us his flesh in order to save us from death. This is the connection between *zoe* and its ultimate purpose.

The Purpose of *Zoe* Is to Save Our *Psuche* from Death

Indeed, this is the ultimate purpose of *zoe*. Contained within the nature of *zoe* is immortality. Immortality is the essence of *zoe*. You and I don't have it as a part of our human nature. Immortality is not innately a part of *psuche*. *Psuche* is never associated with immortality or eternal life.

If you recall, "eternal life" is "*zoe* unto the ages." The Greek phrase "unto the ages" is never associated with *psuche*. *Psuche* is mortal and already on the path to death, unless it is preserved by the gift of eternal *zoe*. Jesus has already defined that we already exist in a state of death. This is what Jesus has come to redeem us from. This is only possible if we depend on him for *zoe*.

We consume Jesus (the bread of *Zoe*) by believing in him and depending on him as the giver of *zoe*. It is through our active dependence on the sacrifice of his flesh (via his death upon the cross) that we metaphorically eat his flesh. Jesus gave us his flesh when he willingly allowed his body to be crucified.

We "consume" Jesus metaphorically when we actively accept and depend on his "death" as a substitue for our sentence of death (that we are already existing in). When we believe in Jesus, we cross over from this sentence of death (that we already exist in), into a status of "zoe".

Note: Zoe and Death are polar opposites. You might be saying, "Duh, life and death are always polar opposites!"

Well, not exactly. To clarify, our psuche is alive even though we are in a state of death. (i.e., we are under a sentence of death). Jesus also tells us that our psuche can be killed in Gehenna.

On the other hand, this state of death is instantly removed when we believe. We cross over at the point of belief from a status of death into zoe.

It is zoe, via the gift of the indwelling Holy Spirit, that a person is born a second time, this time of God's spirit, and they become a child of God.

Zoe is always contrasted with death. Zoe (as Jesus consistently uses this word), never dies, in fact zoe is incapable of death. Zoe is life as God has it, zoe is immortal.

Understanding: The Bread of Life Metaphor

We consume (eat) Jesus when we believe
in him and depend on him as the giver of *Zoe*.
It is through our active "dependence" on
the sacrifice of his body (flesh) that we
metaphorically eat his flesh.

This active dependence would also be known as
trusting in what Jesus did on the cross

Jesus gave us his flesh when he willingly
allowed his body to be crucified

Rather than perishing, our *psuche* is preserved for eternal *zoe*. It is the impartation of *zoe* into the *psuche* of the believer that saves him or her forever. Jesus offers this gift to the world, but a person has to believe in him in order to receive it.

Remember Jesus' statement in John 5:

> **John 5:21** *For just as the Father raises the dead and* **makes them alive (root word is zoe),** *thus also the Son* **makes alive (root word is zoe)** *whomever he wishes. (LEB)*

Ever since Adam and Eve were cast from the Garden of Eden and thus prevented from having access to the tree of life, mankind has faced the certainty of death. The fruit of the tree of life would have enabled Adam and Eve to live forever. God warned Adam that if he were to eat of the tree of knowledge of good and evil, that he would surely die.

Indeed, Adam did die. His access to the tree of life was taken away from him. Adam exchanged immortality for mortality. We will see this as a powerful teaching not only from Jesus. The apostle Paul hammers on this as a core issue of Christianity. We will look at his writings on this shortly.

If man were to ever have hope of immortality again and restore that level of intimate fellowship with God the Father, we would need intervention on our behalf. God indeed had a plan of intervention. His plan was his son, Jesus, and the restoration of *zoe*. But, there was a problem.

The problem was the penalty for Adam's sin has remained imposed on all mankind since that day. We have all been born under that curse. We do not have *zoe*, and we have no access to *zoe*. We are destined to be born and die. Our *psuche* has no hope of immortality. The penalty has been decreed and cannot be revoked. The penalty of death has remained and will forever remain. We have no hope of removing this penalty ourselves. Our death is certain unless someone intervenes.

Someone has . . .

God's plan of our redemption has been revealed over thousands of years through his word in the Bible. Jesus would come as the Son of God, live a perfect life, and take the penalty of death for all mankind—for you and for me. Anyone who accepted this redemption by believing the truth about Jesus, that he is their substitute for their death, could receive the gift of eternal *zoe*.

Death would be vanquished. We can avoid the penalty. We can walk out of death row right now from the prison of certain death. But, this is only possible because someone divine (Jesus), who has *zoe* within himself as part of his divine nature, has gone to the gallows in our place. He has redeemd us from our sentence of death. We can now exchange our mortality for immortality that only comes via the imputation of *zoe*.

There is no other **way** than this for man to be saved. There is no other **truth**. If all of mankind's needs, problems, and struggles could be boiled down and refined to one need and one truth about the solution to that need, it would be this. The problem is death. Jesus is the truth of the only way to overcome death and receive this *zoe*. Jesus is the giver of *zoe*. There is no other avenue, no other way to access *zoe*.

Further Defining the Bread of Life Metaphor

The crowd is disturbed by this notion of Jesus giving them his flesh to eat.

When Jesus said the bread he would give them to eat was his flesh, the Jews began to argue among themselves: "How can this man give us his flesh to eat?"

> *John 6:53 Then Jesus said to them, "Truly, truly I say to you, unless you eat the flesh of the Son of Man and drink his blood, you do not have **life (zoe)** in yourselves!" (LEB)*

As the crowd begins to murmur about eating his flesh, Jesus emphatically restates what he said previously. He prefaces the statement this time with, "Truly, truly I tell you." Then, he goes on to say, "Unless you eat the flesh of the Son of Man and drink his blood you have no life (*zoe*) in you." It seems that Jesus is indeed making sure the crowd understands that he meant what he said. In addition to that, he now adds the part about drinking his blood.

Note: *The Greek text actually says, "You will have no life (zoe) in yourselves." This sounds just like the opposite of what Jesus said about his Father and himself. God the Father and God the Son do indeed have zoe in themselves. We don't have zoe innately as humans, but we can receive it as a gift . . . **if we believe in Jesus***.

> *John 6:54-55 The one who eats my flesh and drinks my blood has **eternal life (zoe)**, and I will raise him up on the last day. For my flesh is true food, and my blood is true drink. (LEB)*

Just when his disciples were probably hoping Jesus would say something like, "Wow, did I just say that? What I really meant to say was . . . " But, that doesn't happen. Instead, Jesus continues with this metaphor about eating his flesh and drinking his blood.

> **John 6:56** *The one who eats my flesh and drinks my blood resides in me and I in him. (LEB)*

This concept of residing in Jesus comes from the Greek word *meno*, meaning "abide," "remain," or "reside." It is by our continual dependence upon Jesus' sacrifice of his body and blood (through his death on the cross), that we reside (remain) in Jesus, and he in us. In other words, we abide in Jesus by always trusting in his identity as the son of God, and what he has done for us through his death upon the cross. Jesus then resides in us, via his zoe indwelling us through his Holy Spirit. The Holy Spirit indwells the believer, conveying immortal zoe. More on this later.

> **John 6:57** *Just as the living Father sent me, and I **live (root word is zoe)** because of the Father, so also the one who eats me—that one will **live (root word is zoe)** because of me. (LEB)*

Jesus explains that just as the Father sent him and he lives because of the Father, so the one who feeds on him will live because of him.

Important Note: *it is vitally important to understand the "type" of life that Jesus is talking about, when he refers to zoe. He emphatically states that he "lives" (root is zoe), because of the Father, and that the person who feeds on him (Jesus) will also live. Now, it goes without saying, that the people Jesus is talking to are already physically alive. Their psuche (although it is under a sentence of death), is currently alive.*

So when Jesus says that he "lives" because of the Father, he is not talking about psuche. Jesus is speaking specifically about immortality. Jesus has life (zoe) as God has it, which is at it's core "immortal".

Zoe cannot die, period. Psuche on the other hand can die, and in fact will die forever, if that person rejects Jesus. A person's psuche is not inherently mortal. Immortality only comes from zoe.

> Jesus has Life (Zoe) as God has it,
>
> which is at it's core "immortal".
>
> **Zoe cannot die, period.**
>
> Psuche on the other hand can die,
>
> and in fact will die forever,
>
> if that person rejects Jesus.
>
> A person's psuche is not inherently mortal.
>
> **Immortality only comes from Zoe**

Why Did the Crowd Misunderstand the Metaphor?

As Jesus tells the crowd they must eat his flesh and drink his blood, they struggle with what he is saying for a couple of reasons. First of all, they are prone to taking what he says literally (not metaphorically). This seems really bizarre to them. They think, "This guy wants to me eat his flesh? Really?"

Secondly, this process of Jesus giving his flesh for us does not occur until his crucifixion, which, at the time Jesus is speaking here in John 6, is still in the future. Many of the parables and metaphors that Jesus taught had to do with his crucifixion and resurrection. Even his closest apostles did not fully understand most of these teachings until sometime after Jesus had been killed and then resurrected.

Important: Had Jesus not died and then resurrected, his teachings on having zoe within your psuche, and thus not dying, would be entirely meaningless. It is indeed his resurrection that punctuates the entire problem that mankind that has faced since Eden, i.e., death. Jesus came to give us zoe, in lieu of death. Zoe is immortal, it is life as God has it. Therefore if we have been given eternal zoe, we have been given immortality (which we did not have prior to being given zoe).

We have crossed over from a status of death, to zoe. Jesus is emphasizing that if we do not believe in what he has done for us, by taking our death penalty for us, and then subsequently rising from the dead, then ultimately we will not have zoe in ourselves. His resurrection is paramount to all of these teachings.

After his apostles understood these things, spreading this truth would become their lifelong purpose. They themselves would be transformed by the truth of Jesus' teachings, but only after Jesus was resurrected from the dead and the Holy Spirit was bequeathed to them by Jesus.

The Spirit then helped them to recall his teachings and understand them. These transformed men then went into the world, taking the message with them. They gave the rest of their lives to spreading this gospel ("gospel" means "good news") throughout the nations. In fact, all but two of the apostles died as martyrs for preaching about Jesus. Would you like to take a guess as to which one of them died of old age? I will let you know toward the end of this chapter.

Eating Jesus and Drinking His Blood . . . What It Means

It is when we believe in Jesus and consciously depend on the sacrifice of his death on the cross for us that we metaphorically eat his flesh and drink his blood.

Eating Jesus' Flesh

His flesh is figuratively referring to his body that was crucified on the cross. Earlier, we learned that we consume Jesus (the bread of *zoe*) by believing in him and depending on him as the giver of *zoe*. It is by our active dependence on the sacrifice of his body (flesh) that we metaphorically eat his flesh.

Drinking Jesus' Blood

His blood is **directly** referring to his actual blood that he bled out during his crucifixion. However, the phrase "drinking his blood" is metaphorical, in the sense that we drink his blood by actively depending on his blood to cover (or forgive) our sins.

Remember, Jesus had just answered the question that the crowd asked him, "what must we do to be doing the work that God requires?" Jesus answered, "Believe in the one he has sent".

Throughout the Old Testament, there is a strong connection of the shedding of blood with forgiveness. In Hebrews 9, the author goes into historical detail about how Jesus' sacrifice of his own blood was superior to the animal sacrifices performed by priests. I would recommend reading Hebrews 9:11-28 for an in-depth understanding of this concept, but for brevity I am only showing 9:22 below.

> *Heb. 9:22 Indeed, nearly everything is purified with blood according to the law, and apart from the shedding of blood there is no forgiveness. (LEB)*

In addition, in John 1, John the Baptist called Jesus the "Lamb of God."

> *John 1:29 On the next day he saw Jesus coming to him and said, "Look! The Lamb of God who takes away the sin of the world! (LEB)*

The term "Lamb of God" is referring to the lamb that was sacrificed during Passover. Historically, Passover occurred about fifteen centuries before Jesus' teaching. Passover was the final plague on the Egyptians that precipitated the "exodus" of the Israelites from Egypt.

During the Passover plague, any household that had the blood of a lamb painted above and to the sides of the door would be spared from the death of their firstborn. The angel of death would "pass over" that home, sparing any firstborn. Moses had given the Israelites instructions on how to prepare the lamb for the night of that Passover.

God later instructed Moses to establish an annual Passover memorial commemorating the original Passover for all time. This annual memorial included the sacrifice of the "Passover lamb" as an annual memorial commemorating God's deliverance of the Israelites.

Note: Jesus was crucified during this annual memorial feast of the Passover. His death occurred on Passover day at approximately the same time as the lamb that was slain for the Passover memorial. John again refers to Jesus as the "Lamb of God" three separate times in the book of Revelation (13:8, 14:1, 15:3).

Time does not permit us to go into detail on all the significance of the "blood" of Jesus, but there is plenty. Look at Paul's reference to this in the verse below.

> *Rom. 5:9-10 Therefore, by much more, because we have been declared righteous now by his blood, we will be saved through him from the wrath.For if, while we were enemies, we were reconciled to God through the death of his Son, by much more, having been reconciled, we will be saved by his life (zoe). (LEB)*

Summary: Eating Jesus' Flesh and Drinking His Blood

If we believe Jesus is the Son of God and lay hold of his sacrifice on the cross by accepting his death as payment for our own death sentence, and we depend on his blood for the forgiveness of our sin, we are **figuratively feeding** on Jesus.

> Reminder: This Is a Metaphor!
>
> Believing in him, trusting him, and depending on him for what he has done for us on the cross **"is"** the metaphorical eating and drinking of Jesus.

There is nothing literal about what he is saying here. Don't get hung up on literally eating and drinking Jesus. These verses have no direct connection with partaking (eating) of the Lord's Supper or believing that a cracker miraculously turns into his body (the notion of transubstantiation), etc.

Note: Jesus does later institute the memorial known as the Lord's Supper in the gospels (Matthew 26:26-29, Luke 22:14-20, Mark 14:22-25) the night before he is crucified. But, even in these instances, it is not commanded or portrayed as a literal eating of Jesus' flesh and blood. Jesus says to do this "in remembrance of me."

*Partaking of the bread and wine is a symbolic remembrance (**memorial**) of what he has done. In 1 Corinthians 11:23-26, the apostle Paul says we not only do this to commemorate Jesus' death and resurrection but also to proclaim his **death** and **resurrection** until he returns. Jesus death and resurrection is fundamental to all of his teachings on zoe. Without zoe, none of us have hope of resurrection.*

Whoever Feeds On This Bread Will Live Forever

John 6:58 *"This is the bread that came down from heaven, not as the fathers ate and died. The one who eats this bread will live forever." (LEB)*

Jesus again contrasts the difference between the manna that their ancestors ate with the bread from heaven (himself). The difference is that those ancestors died, while those who feed on the "true bread" from heaven will live forever. Please do not overlook this contrast. This is the main point of Jesus' dialogue in this section.

> Jesus makes a stark contrast between their ancestors who ate the manna and then eventually died, and those who feed on the "true bread" from heaven who **will live forever.**
> This is Jesus' main point in this section.

John 6:60 *Thus many of his disciples, when they heard it, said, "This saying is hard! Who can understand it?" (LEB)*

It is not only the crowd that struggles with this metaphor. His disciples who have accompanied him for much of his ministry (including the twelve apostles) struggle with understanding and accepting this metaphor as well.

*John 6:61-63 But Jesus, because he knew within himself that his disciples were grumbling about this, said to them, "Does this cause you to be offended? Then what if you see the Son of Man ascending where he was before? The Spirit is the one who gives **life (zoe)**; the flesh profits nothing. The words that I have spoken to you are spirit and are **life (zoe)**. (LEB)*

Jesus gives another important clarification here. He explains that it is the Spirit that gives life (*zoe*).

Note: The Greek word for "spirit" is *pneuma*, which is also translated as "breath" or "wind."

*The Spirit is the one who gives **life (zoe)**; the flesh profits nothing*

The flesh is of no help when it comes to getting *zoe*. Some English versions translate this as "the flesh counts for nothing." It is just part of the bodily experience and can do nothing to help a person gain eternal life (*zoe*).

However, the body is definitely part of the *psuche* experience. In fact, much of what we enjoy in the *psuche* realm has to do with the senses God gives us through our body. But, the body is only flesh. It is destined to decay and perish. A person's *psuche* is in a status of death unless the person becomes a believer. Only *zoe* has an eternal aspect to it.

Jesus reiterates this in the very next verse.

*The words that I have spoken to you are spirit and are **life (zoe)**.*

He exclaims, "The words I am speaking to you, they are spirit and life. In other words, don't get hung up on the flesh and body stuff. I am speaking to you using a metaphor with worldly terms that are illustrating a spiritual truth." It is as if Jesus is saying, "Everything I have been saying to you is about what the Spirit will do in the believer. It will impart *zoe* into the believer, so that the believer will not die. The believer crosses over from death to life (*zoe*)."

Holding on to What You Know and Believe

*John 6:66-69 For this reason many of his disciples drew back and were not walking with him any longer. So Jesus said to the twelve, "You do not want to go away also, do you?" Simon Peter answered him, "Lord, to whom would we go? You have the words of **eternal life (zoe)**. And we have believed, and have come to know, that you are the Holy One of God." (LEB)*

Jesus knew these people in the crowd were going to leave. Now, he challenges his disciples, testing their tenacity. At some point in our human lifetimes, we are going to run into confusion or difficult times that may be very hard for us to understand. These difficulties can sometimes last for a season of life and can be very dark and confusing.

But, we can choose to be like Peter and say, "Where else can we go? You have the words of eternal life (*zoe*). We have come to believe and to know that you are the Holy One of God."

That's it: hold on to what you know, even if everything else is confusing. Hold on to Jesus. He has the words of eternal *zoe*. There is no other way to *zoe*.

Summary of Definitions in John 6

There are several major definitions from Jesus in John 6. He introduced these concepts in previous chapters of John, but now he gives us deeper insight.

- Death is the problem.

- There is a solution that will keep a person from dying. It is the bread of life, which a person can consume figuratively (by believing in Jesus and counting on his death on the cross as payment for their own penalty of death).

- It is the Spirit of God that gives (imparts) *zoe*.

What Is Left to Define?

Jesus has introduced and begun defining what he identifies as the problem of mankind and his solution. The problem is death due to sin. His solution is *eternal zoe* for those who will put their trust in him.

But, at this point we do not have Jesus' complete definition of death. What does it mean to be in a state of death, and what does that look like for our *psuche* after we die on earth?

Jesus will unfold this over the next five chapters. When we finally understand just what it is that he is saving us from, Jesus' mission will be totally apparent to us.

Without a clear understanding of death as defined by Jesus, we are left with a blurry interpretation of the message of salvation, resulting in inaccurate doctrine.

Now, for the answer to the earlier question about which apostle died of old age: the apostle John, who wrote the gospel according to John, died in AD 102. In addition to the gospel according to John, he also wrote 1st, 2nd, and 3rd John and the Book of Revelation.

There was one other of the original twelve apostles who did not die as a martyr or of old age: Judas Iscariot. Judas hung himself after he betrayed Jesus to the Jewish leaders, which led to Jesus' crucifixion.

Milestones

Key Concepts Defined

Let's review several key concepts that have been defined in preceding chapters of John. These are vital to understanding Jesus' message going forward.

➢ *Zoe* is defined by Jesus as "life as God has it." *Zoe* is a divine nature possessed by God the Father and Jesus the Son. *Zoe* is an intrinsic aspect of who they are.

➢ *Zoe* is always associated with Eternal *Zoe*. One essential aspect of *Zoe* is its immortality.

➢ As humans, we possess *psuche*. Mortal life is the inherent nature of *psuche*. We do not have *Zoe* inborn within us. *Zoe* is the inherent nature of God.

➢ As humans, we are in an initial state of death. We do not have *Zoe*. It is only at the moment when we believe that we cross over from this status of death to a status of life (*Zoe*).

➢ It is the Spirit of God/Jesus that conveys *Zoe*. Jesus has explained that the Spirit will impart *Zoe* to us if we will believe. If we do not believe, then we remain in the state of death that we were born into.

22

John 8—I Am the Light of the World

As we move into John 8, we come to a flash point between Jesus and the Jews—even between Jesus and many of the Jews who have believed in him thus far. Jesus is trying to break through beliefs and traditions that the Jews have strongly adhered to for millennia. He is not willing to patronize them just to maintain their loyalty.

He knows he is only with them for short time. Jesus must challenge them to see the truth, to come to his light, to come to him for *zoe*, even at the risk of offending them. This is not a debate for the curious observer. Jesus pushes everyone to the limit of their beliefs and understanding. He offers them the opportunity **to be set free**. Those who choose to be offended will be left in slavery.

John 8 is literally a do-or-die chapter. This chapter is a clash between eternal truth and long-held lies, between life (*zoe*) and death. Those with the fortitude to hold on to Jesus' teaching through this struggle of wills and precepts shall become children of God.

I Am the Light of the World.

"I Am" Statement 2

Jesus begins this conversation in 8:12 with another "I Am" statement.

> **John 8:12** *Then Jesus spoke to them again, saying, "I am the light of the world! The one who follows me will never walk in darkness, but will have the light of life (zoe)." (LEB)*

Light of the World is Inseparably Tied to *Zoe*

This light comes from the indwelling *zoe*, which believers receive upon being born again (born of the spirit of God). It is not available through any other means.

There are Two Aspects to this Light

First – Zoe Saves Us From the Darkness of Death. All mankind is currently living in the darkness of sin and death. Jesus brings the light of *zoe*, into this dark realm, thus bringing the certainty of *zoe* to all who otherwise face certain death. Remember, believers cross over from death to *zoe*.

Isaiah prophecies of the birth of Jesus into this land of darkness:

> **Isaiah 9:2** *The people who walked in darkness have seen a great light... (LEB)*

> **Isaiah 9:2** *The For a child has been born for us; a son has been given to us. And the dominion will be on his shoulder, and his name is called Wonderful Counselor, Mighty God, Everlasting Father, Prince of Peace (LEB)*

John the Baptist was born about 6 months prior to Jesus' birth. His father Zechariah who had been mute during his wife's pregnancy, begins speaking the following prophetic words about his son John after his birth. Zechariah is quoting from Isaiah as he makes this prophecy. He is prophecying about his son John (you will go before the Lord to prepare his ways), and then prophecies about Jesus. When he speaks of the sunrise and light he is referring to Jesus. Notice the connection between darkness and the "shadow of death".

> *Luke 1:76-79 And so you, child, will be called the prophet of the Most High, for you will go on before the Lord to prepare his ways, to give knowledge of salvation to his people by the forgiveness of their sins, because of the merciful compassion of our God by which the dawn will visit to help us from on high, to give light to those who sit in darkness and in the shadow of death, to direct our feet into the way of peace (LEB)*

Note: *Mankind lives in the shadow of death. This certainty and permanence of death that looms over all men casts a dark shadow. The traditional view does not understand this significance, and underplays the role of death in the destiny of man. In fact, the traditional view practically ignores the significance of death, due to it's fascination with it's straw man - "Hell". It should be noted that neither John nor Paul, ever uses the Greek word Gehenna (most often translated as Hell) in any of their 18 books of the New Testament. If Hell was the issue, they would have mentioned it.*

Second – The Light of Zoe Illuminates the Path of Believers
Believers have the *zoe* of Jesus within them via the indwelling Holy Spirit. Believers do not have this light of *zoe* available from within themselves or any other source other than the *zoe* offered by Jesus.

This insight is not available from human wisdom or any philosophy of man. It is not a matter of having a high IQ or a good education. This is not merely a statement where Jesus suggests that his wisdom is better than that which the world gives.

Jesus is categorically stating that he is truly the only light of the world. He is using the metaphor of light to illustrate a vital reality. Without his light, your world is dark, metaphorically speaking. You don't have the tools to navigate the realities that exist all around you because you can't see them. The only way to have this light is via the enlightening that flows from the indwelling Holy Spirit.

23

John 8 — Dying in Sin

Dying in Sin

In 8:21, Jesus warns those listening about the consequences of failing to believe that he is the Messiah. The consequences: **they will die in their sin.**

> *John 8:21-24 So he said to them again, "I am going away, and you will seek me and will **die in your sin**. Where I am going you cannot come!" Then the Jews began to say, "Perhaps he will kill himself, because he is saying, 'Where I am going you cannot come.'" And he said to them, "You are from below; I am from above. You are from this world; I am not from this world. Thus I said to you that **you will die in your sins**. For if you do not believe that I am he, **you will die in your sins**. (LEB)*

Jesus' stern warning: If we don't believe he is the Messiah, then we will die in our sins. Jesus tells them three times in this text that they will die in their sin.

What Does Jesus Mean By, "You Will Die in Your Sins?"

Obviously, this concept of dying in our sins is very significant. Even if we may not completely understand what Jesus means, it is certain that no one would want to die in their sin.

So, just exactly what does Jesus mean by the term "die in our sins?" At this point in our study, which of the following choices do you think best describes what Jesus is saying **here**?

- When we die, we won't go to heaven.

- When we die, we will end up in Hell.

- My sins will end up killing me because they are bad for my health.

- My sins have such a grip on me that I cannot seem to get away from them, and I will end up dying in this condition.

- I am already in a state of death according to Jesus (due to sin). Therefore, if I don't believe in him, my status of death will remain unchanged. In effect, I am already destined to die in my sin. I need a savior to save me from my current fate.

Let's see if we can zero in on what Jesus is saying. Earlier, in John 5:24, Jesus said that those who have believed have crossed over from **a status of death . . . to a status of life (*zoe*)**. Here in John 8, Jesus merely restates the exact same precept but points out the **negative** consequence instead of just focusing on the new life (*zoe*). He is using the carrot and the stick approach. Up until now in his teachings, Jesus has primarily focused on the positive aspect of receiving *eternal zoe* if we believe. Now, he is hitting the self-righteous, judgmental Pharisees with the stick.

A Modern Day Metaphor of a Savior: A Fireman

By not believing Jesus, a person stays stuck in the condemned sentence (of death) that they have been living under due to the consequences of sin. This would be like refusing to accept the hand of a fireman who can pull you out of a burning building. You would be, in effect, destined to die, since you are already in the burning building. You face certain death unless you take the hand of the fireman. Your status doesn't change if you refuse to take the fireman's hand, because you were going to die anyway before the fireman showed up. However, if you take the fireman's hand, your status changes from one of certain death to one of being saved. You have received your life back, so to speak.

If a person chooses to believe in Jesus, they cross over from death to life. The status of death is due to sin. So, if a person chooses not to believe, they merely remain in a status of death. If they never believe, then they will ultimately die in their sin.

> If a person chooses to believe in Jesus, they cross over from death to life. If a person never believes, they merely remain in a status of death and will ultimately die in their sin.

Application

The following is essentially what happens when we believe. Our *psuche* is saved from certain impending death by the amazing gift offered to the world to those that believe: the gift of eternal *zoe*. Our *psuche* is preserved (saved from death) by the impartation of eternal *zoe* (living forever). Although this gift is offered to all mankind for no more than believing with all their heart (it is free), it came with the ultimate price. **Jesus paid for this by laying down his own *psuche*.**

Jesus clearly predicts his death (of his *psuche*) in John 10. Jesus willingly allows himself to be tortured nearly to the point of death and subsequently be killed by crucifixion. There is no question about this; Jesus' *psuche* is going to be killed. He is going to die.

Why would Jesus willingly do this? Because he knew that the penalty of sin (since the fall of Adam) was the impending death of **our** *psuche*. The Father's plan was to redeem all mankind who would believe by sending his Son to die in our place. Jesus took our death penalty upon himself. If we but accept the crucifixion of his body for us, accept the spilling of his blood in lieu of ours, and follow him with all our heart, we not only get our status of death removed, but we also receive *zoe*, enabling us to become children of God and live forever.

The **immediate benefits** of this gift are the blessings that we begin receiving at the moment of belief. We do not have to wait until our physical death to reap the benefits of participating in the divine nature. This gift of *zoe* not only allows us to live forever; it allows us to enjoy sweet fellowship with the Father and the Son in the here and now. The Spirit will flow from within us today to give us the opportunity of understanding, insight, and greater faith, resulting in the bearing of the fruit of the Spirit (see Galatians 5:22-23).

Note: It's possible you may be a bit confused at this point with all this talk about the penalty of death, dying in sin, having an initial status of death, crossing over to life (zoe), and so forth. I'm just giving you a heads up. It is going to continue to be a bit confusing until we get through a few more chapters. Jesus is about to talk about never dying, which is going to seem even more confusing.

Some of this confusion is due to the incorrect paradigm about death that so strongly influences current Christian thought.

What I can tell you at this point, which may help some with the confusion, is that Jesus is not concerned with saving you from your earthly death. He is very intent, however, in saving you from the second death. It is the second death that is at the core of what Jesus has been talking about this whole time in the gospel according to John. In fact, Jesus will clearly state this as his purpose for coming to earth in John 10.

Jesus will thoroughly define this issue in the next few chapters.

Life
Defined

24

John 8—Jesus Indicts Satan

Jesus Indicts Satan for the Death of Adam and Eve

John 8:31-42 Then Jesus said to those Jews who had believed him, "If you continue in my word you are truly my disciples, and you will know the truth, and the truth will set you free." They replied to him, "We are descendants of Abraham and have not been enslaved to anyone at any time. How do you say, 'You will become free'?" Jesus replied to them, "Truly, truly I say to you, that everyone who commits sin is a slave of sin. And the slave does not remain in the household forever; the son remains forever. So if the son sets you free, you will be truly free. I know that you are descendants of Abraham. But you are seeking to kill me, because my word makes no progress among you. I speak the things that I have seen with the Father; so also you do the things that you have heard from the Father." They answered and said to him, "Abraham is our father!" Jesus said to them, "If you are children of Abraham, do the deeds of Abraham! But now you are seeking to kill me, a man who spoke to you the truth which I heard from God. This Abraham did not do. You are doing the deeds of your father!" They said to him, "We were not born from sexual immorality! We have one father, God!" Jesus said to them, "If God were your father, you would love me, for I have come forth from God and have come. For I have not come from myself, but that one sent me. (LEB)

As we continue in John 8, the crowd insults Jesus by accusing him of being an illegitimate child.

In their anger, the crowd throws this accusation in his face right after Jesus challenges their self-righteousness (which is based on the fact that they claim Abraham as their father).

We are going to pick back up in 8:43, as Jesus ignores their insult. Now, he takes the argument a step further by not just saying Abraham is **not their Father** but rather Satan is.

> *John 8:43-47* *"Why do you not understand my way of speaking? Because you are not able to listen to my message. You are of your father the devil, and you want to do the desires of your father! That one was a murderer from the beginning, and does not stand firm in the truth, because truth is not in him. Whenever he speaks the lie, he speaks from his own nature, because he is a liar and the father of lies. But because I am telling the truth, you do not believe me. Who among you convicts me concerning sin? If I am telling the truth, why do you not believe me? The one who is from God listens to the words of God. Because of this you do not listen—because you are not of God." (LEB)*

There are a lot of points that could be made here. Jesus doesn't respond tit-for-tat with this crowd. He doesn't say that their father is the devil just to retaliate to their insult. He points out that they cannot understand what he is saying because they belong to the devil, who fathers their deception. In turn, there are those in the crowd who will want to murder Jesus, following in the steps of their father (Satan), who was a murderer from the beginning.

But, for our purpose, we are focusing on what Jesus said about Satan (the devil).

Jesus Explains Several Facts about Satan

- He was a murderer from the beginning.

- He does not hold to the truth.

- There is no truth in him.

- Lies are his native language.

- He is the father of lies.

Genesis 3:1-6

When Jesus says Satan was a "murderer from the beginning," he is referring to the account of Adam and Eve in the book of Genesis (the Hebrew word *genesis* means "beginning").

> *Gen. 3:1-6 Now the serpent was more crafty than any other wild animal which Yahweh God had made. He said to the woman, "Did God indeed say, 'You shall not eat from any tree in the garden'?" The woman said to the serpent, "From the fruit of the trees of the garden we may eat, but from the tree that is in the midst of the garden, God said, 'You shall not eat from it, nor shall you touch it, lest you die'." But the serpent said to the woman, "You shall not surely die. For God knows that on the day you both eat from it, then your eyes will be opened and you both shall be like gods, knowing good and evil." When the woman saw that the tree was good for food and that it was a delight to the eyes, and the tree was desirable to make one wise, then she took from its fruit and she ate. And she gave it also to her husband with her, and he ate. (LEB)*

Satan lied to Eve, leading her to stray from the truth, convince Adam to go along with her, and sin. The result was death. Jesus indicts Satan for the death of Adam and Eve at the beginning. On the day that Adam and Eve disobeyed God and ate of the forbidden tree, they were cast out of the Garden of Eden.

They died a spiritual death that day, since they no longer had access to the tree of life, which provided them immortality. By losing access to immortality, they eventually died a natural death of their *psuche*.

The resulting banishment from the tree of life in the Garden of Eden left Adam and Eve with the certain impending death of their *psuche*. This action has resulted in all mankind living in a state of certain death.

Satan continues to attempt to deceive you and me every day, trying to sway us from the truth or prevent us from understanding the truth, in hopes that he can keep us in a state of death. He was a murderer from the beginning, and he continues to be. He is intent on murdering you! In fact, he has basically already accomplished this. You are trapped in your mortality unless you accept Jesus' gift of eternal *zoe*.

This state of death (the absence of *zoe*) is the condition that all mankind has found itself in to this day. We desperately need a solution to this death sentence. **We need a Savior**.

The resulting banishment from the **Tree of Life** in the Garden of Eden left Adam and Eve with the certain impending death of their *Psuche*. This action has resulted in all mankind living under a state of certain impending death.

We need a **Savior**

Satan Is Still At Work in the *Psuche* of Unbelievers

The apostle Paul describes how Satan is at work in the sons of disobedience. Unless we are walking in the light by becoming children of God, Satan will continue to have his way with us by deceiving us and enslaving us with our own desires.

Paul also points out to the believers he is writing to that they were once dead due to their sin.

> ***Eph. 2:1-5*** *And you, although you were **dead in your trespasses and sins**, in which you formerly walked according to the course of this world, according to the ruler of the authority of the air, the spirit now working in the sons of disobedience, among whom also we all formerly lived in the desires of our flesh, doing the will of the flesh and of the mind, and we were children of wrath by nature, as also the rest of them were. But God, being rich in mercy, because of his great love with which he loved us, and **we being dead in trespasses, he made us alive together with Christ** (by grace you are saved) (LEB)*

But, God, in his rich mercy, made them alive with Christ, even when they were dead in their trespasses. It is by grace that we have been saved. We have been made alive, crossing over from a status of "death" to a status of "zoe", by the impartation of *zoe* into the psuche of the believer, via being born again (this time not of the flesh, but of the Holy Spirit). It is through the indwelling of the Holy Spirit that *zoe* is deposited into the psuche of the believer, giving them eternal life.

The apostle Paul explains this process very clearly in two of his letters to the early church. We will segue briefly in the next chapter, to examine what Paul had to say about life, and death.

Life
Defined

25

Paul's Teachings on Death

Paul's Teachings on Death from 1 Corinthians

The apostle Paul addresses the matter of death coming to all men through Adam in two of his letters to the early churches. Paul wrote the first letter to the church at Corinth about two decades after Jesus' resurrection. He wrote the letter to the church at Rome a few years later.

In these letters, Paul points out stark contrasts between Adam and Jesus.

The brackets have been inserted by me to point out the reference to Adam or Jesus.

We will first look at Paul's explanation in 1 Corinthians 15.

> *1 Cor. 15:21-22 For since through a man came death, also through a man came the resurrection of the dead. For just as in Adam all die, so also in Christ all will be made alive. (LEB)*

Paul begins this section on the resurrection by introducing that death came to all mankind through Adam. By contrast, the resurrection of the dead comes through Jesus.

> *1 Cor. 15:45 Thus also it is written, "The first man, Adam, became a living soul" (psuche) the last Adam became a life-giving (zoe-root) spirit. (LEB)*

Adam was created as a soul (*psuche*). He had been granted access to the tree of life, but immortality was not part of his basic nature. He would live forever as long as he continued to have access to the tree of life. But, when he and Eve were driven from the Garden of Eden, they lost all access to the tree of life. The emphasis of the

143

contrast here between Adam and Jesus is that Adam was merely a man with *psuche*.

> Adam was created as a soul (*psuche*). He had been granted access to the **tree of life**, but immortality was not part of his basic nature.

Jesus, on the other hand, has *zoe* (life as God has it) within himself, thus he is the **zoe-giving spirit**. In fact, if you look at the Greek-English Interlinear for this verse, it clearly describes Jesus as the **"spirit making live"** (*zoe* is the root). It is the Spirit of Christ (the Holy Spirit) that conveys *zoe* into the believer.

This is Jesus' purpose: to give life (*zoe*) to believers. We will see Jesus state this as his purpose when we get to John 10.

> *1 Cor. 15:47-49 The first man is from the earth, made of earth; the second man is from heaven. As the one who is made of earth, so also are those who are made of earth, and as the heavenly, so also are those who are heavenly. And just as we have borne the image of the one who is made of earth, we will also bear the image of the heavenly. (LEB)*

Notice that, as humans, we initially bear the image of the first man (Adam). We have human DNA; we possess *psuche*. *Psuche* is our earthly nature, and that is all we have.

If we believe, we are born again of the Spirit of God. We then become children of God. At that point, we begin to bear the image (spiritually) of Jesus because the Spirit of God indwells us. One way this image is manifested in the believer is via the fruit of the Holy Spirit that is displayed in their life.

There will be a final stage of this image that will be revealed when we have our new resurrected bodies, which will be imperishable.

At that point, the believer will fully bear the image of Christ, in that they will have an imperishable body in like nature to that of Jesus.

1 Corinthians 15 (selected verses)

*25 For it is necessary for him to reign until he has put all his enemies under his feet. 26 The last enemy to be abolished is **death.***

32 If the dead are not raised, let us eat and drink, for tomorrow we die.

50 But I say this, brothers, that flesh and blood is not able to inherit the kingdom of God, nor can corruption inherit incorruptibility. 51 Behold, I tell you a mystery: we will not all fall asleep, but we will all be changed, 52 in a moment, in the blink of an eye, at the last trumpet. For the trumpet will sound, and the dead will be raised imperishable, and we will be changed. 53 For it is necessary for this perishable body to put on incorruptibility, and this mortal body to put on immortality. 54 But whenever this perishable body puts on incorruptibility and this mortal body puts on immortality, then the saying that is written will take place:

"Death is swallowed up in victory.

55 Where, O death, is your victory?

Where, O death, is your sting?

56 Now the sting of death is sin, and the power of sin is the law. 57 But thanks be to God, who gives us the victory through our Lord Jesus Christ! (LEB)

Let's take a brief look at some key points in this passage.

The last enemy for Jesus to destroy is death. Does this sound familiar? Jesus has been telling his followers in the gospel according to John that those who believe in him will not die and will never die. We will see a more exact definition of this as we move forward in our study of John.

- Jesus vanquishes death by his own resurrection from the dead. If Jesus had not risen from the dead, then we would have no hope of resurrection. In Revelation, John speaks of death being finally destroyed.

- Flesh and blood cannot inherit the kingdom of God. Again, this sounds familiar, because we saw in John 3:3-8 that Jesus used the metaphor of being born again to explain to Nicodemus that a man must be born again of the Spirit in order to enter the kingdom of God.

- The believer will be resurrected imperishable and immortal. We will exchange mortality for immortality.

- Death will be vanquished for the believer.

The Sting of Death is Sin!

In other words, sin's sting is a lethal venom that has resulted in death for all men since Adam. But, this deadly sting is overcome by the spirit of God, which gives eternal *zoe* to the believer.

Paul's Teachings on Death from the Book of Romans

> **Rom. 5:9** *Therefore, by much more, because we have been declared righteous now by his blood, we will be saved through him from the wrath. (LEB)*

There are two interesting points Paul makes here. First, we have been justified (declared righteous) by Jesus' blood. Remember in John 6:53, Jesus said, "Very truly I tell you, unless you eat the flesh of the Son of Man and drink his blood, you have no Life in you." That was a metaphor for depending upon the righteous blood of Jesus that paid for our sins to justify us before God the Father.

Secondly, Paul mentions God's wrath and how much more we shall be saved from this wrath. If you remember, in John 3:36, John the Baptist mentioned the wrath of God. "Whoever believes in the Son has eternal life (*zoe*), but whoever rejects the Son will not see life (*zoe*), for God's wrath remains on them."

When we previously looked at this verse, we tied the state of death that we are initially under to this wrath and the fact that we do not have *zoe* within us initially.

> **Rom. 5:10** *For if, while we were enemies, we were reconciled to God through the death of his Son, by much more, having been reconciled, we will be saved by his **life (zoe)**. (LEB)*

Don't miss the the key point that Paul is making here. Before we can talk about *zoe*, we have to deal with the sin issue. Sin makes us enemies of God, and the sentence of sin against God is death. If we do not deal with this issue, there can be no discussion of life (*zoe*). It is by the death of Jesus on behalf of the believer that our death has been paid for, reconciling us with God the Father. This is the first aspect of our salvation, redeeming the believer from death.

It is only after being reconciled with God through the death of his Son that we can begin to discuss the second aspect of our salvation. Then and only then, can we lay hold of the fact that the final aspect of our salvation is that we have been given eternal zoe, which comes from Jesus via the Holy Spirit. It is only by this infusion of Jesus' *zoe* into the psuche of the believer, that the believer will themselves be resurrected from death. This *zoe* begins to indwell the believer at the point of the believer's saving faith while they are still alive in this present life. Eternal *zoe* will ultimately be manifested when the believer is resurrected from the dead with a new impersishable body. There are many wonderful benefits of the indwelling *zoe* in the psuche of the beleiver while they are still alive in this present world. We will cover these potential benefits in detail later in the chapter on the three stages of *zoe*.

The key is to not just merely believe (Jesus said that even the demons believe, and they tremble at the thought of him), but to believe by entrusting our psuche to Him.

To truly believe means to place trusting faith in Jesus. This includes a complete trust in his sacrifice on the cross for us and dependence on his spirit for life (*zoe*) and the light that comes with it, so that we may walk in the fullness of this life. With this trust comes obedience to his leading us as Lord of our lives. This is a lifelong endeavor, as Jesus strips away our pride, sin, fears, selfishness, and self-reliance step by step—one precept, one stronghold at a time.

> **Rom. 5:12-15** *Because of this, just as sin entered into the world through one man, and death through sin, so also death spread to all people because all sinned. For until the law, sin was in the world, but sin is not charged to one's account when there is no law. But death reigned from Adam until Moses even over those who did not sin in the likeness of the transgression of Adam, who is a type of the one who is to come. But the gift is not like the trespass, for if by the trespass of the one, the many died, by much more did the grace of God and the gift by the grace of the one man, Jesus Christ, multiply to the many. (LEB)*

Sin and death came to all mankind, since the sin of Adam. It was through Adam that this consequence of sin came upon all men. It is through Jesus that life (*zoe*) becomes available to all men who will believe.

*Rom. 5:17-21 For if by the trespass of the one man, death reigned through the one man, much more will those who receive the abundance of grace and of the gift of righteousness reign in **life (zoe)** through the one, Jesus Christ. Consequently therefore, as through one trespass came condemnation to all people, so also through one righteous deed came justification of **life (zoe)** to all people.*

*For just as through the disobedience of the one man, the many were made sinners, so also through the obedience of the one, the many will be made righteous. Now the law came in as a side issue, in order that the trespass could increase, but where sin increased, grace was present in greater abundance, so that just as sin reigned in death, so also grace would reign through righteousness to **eternal life (zoe)** through Jesus Christ our Lord. (LEB)*

Sin and death came to all mankind, since the sin of Adam. It was through Adam that this consequence of sin came upon all men. It is through Jesus that life (*zoe*) becomes available to all men who will believe.

> Just as sin has reigned in death since Adam's fall,
> Grace now reigns through righteousness to bring
> Eternal Life (Zoe) through Jesus Christ
> to those with trusting faith

*Rom. 6:23 For the compensation due sin is **death**, but the gift of God is **eternal life (zoe)** in Christ Jesus our Lord. (LEB)*

This verse summarizes what Paul has been talking about in Romans 5 and 6. Can this message be any more concise? This is the message of the gospel plain and clear.

Can you see why it is so vital that we understand what Jesus and Paul were saying when they spoke of death and life?

If we try to redefine "life and death" by twisting it to fit some outside agenda or preconceived doctrine, then we will obscure and distort the original message.

Thus, we may be preaching that Jesus saves, which is entirely true. But, we end up conveying an incorrect interpretation of the gospel as to the message of what we are being saved "from" and what we are being saved "to."

Note Regarding the Tree of Life

The tree of life imparted unto man immortality; it allowed him to live forever. Access to the tree of life was cut off intentionally when Adam and Eve were driven from the garden. Being banned from the garden was, in fact, their sentence of death.

The Bible never speaks again of the tree of life until the very end, in the last chapter of the book of Revelation. In Revelation 20, John speaks about the day of judgment. On the day of judgment, those whose names are found in the book of life (*zoe*) will be given Eternal Life.

Then, in John 21, John speaks of a new heaven and a new earth. There will be a holy city of God that comes down out of heaven unto the new earth, and God will dwell there with mankind. There will be no more death, for the old order of things will have passed away.

Finally, in Revelation 22, John speaks of a river of life that will flow through this new kingdom. Straddling the river, there will be a tree, whose leaves are for the healing of nations. It is the tree of life (*zoe*). The tree of life marks the beginning and the end of God's word.

The Bible does not speak again of the Tree of Life (that mankind was banned from in the Garden of Eden) until the very last chapter of the book of Revelation. In chapter 22, John speaks of a river of Zoe that will flow through the new kingdom. Straddling the river, there will be a tree, whose leaves are for the healing of nations.

It is the **Tree of Zoe**. This **Tree of Life** marks the beginning and the end of God's word.

Jesus is the alpha and omega

Jesus is the Alpha and Omega

*Revelation 21:5-6 And the one seated on the throne said, "Behold, I am making all things new!" And he said, "Write, because these words are faithful and true." And he said to me, "It is done! **I am the Alpha and the Omega, the beginning and the end**. To the one who is thirsty I will give water from the spring of the water of **life (zoe)** freely. (LEB)*

Just as the *Tree of Zoe* marks the beginning and end of God's word, we can see that Jesus (the source of *zoe*) is also called the alpha and omega, (the beginning and the end of the Greek alphabet). Here we can see the direct connection of *zoe* to that statement.

The Power of a Paradigm

A paradigm is an established perspective by which each of us interprets those things we experience. Your paradigm develops and changes over time through your experiences, by what you have seen and learned. Some have compared a paradigm to the color of glasses you wear. Your paradigm colors how you see things and how you interpret what you see and hear. Our paradigms strongly influence the way we think and react to what is going on around us.

While a paradigm can be very strong, at the same time, it can have a great weakness. In fact, the stronger a paradigm is, the greater its weakness may be. If the paradigm encounters something that is outside of its perspective or experience, it will seek to shape the experience to make it conform or reconcile to its standard. A paradigm can be so strong that it can prevent a person from correctly interpreting reality.

As we have progressed through this study, we have seen where Jesus' teachings definitely challenged the paradigms of those he was speaking to. In many cases, the people ended up walking away disillusioned or angry with Jesus. Some dismissed him as being demon possessed because they either could not accept or understand the things he was teaching.

Jesus once used a metaphor to describe this "paradigm conflict" as pouring new wine into an old wineskin (Luke 5:36-39). He said you must pour new wine into a new wine skin; otherwise, the old wine skin will burst, losing the wine. He was using this metaphor to refer to people's hearts, their attitudes, and their inability to flex enough to embrace his teaching.

Paradigms can also be dangerous. The Pharisees and scribes ended up killing Jesus because his claims were totally outside of their paradigm. Their hearts had become hardened like an old wineskin. There was no room for Jesus' teaching in their paradigm.

Jesus depicts a "paradigm conflict" as pouring new wine into an old wineskin. He said you must pour new wine into a new wine skin, otherwise the old wine skin will burst losing the wine.

He was using this metaphor to refer to people's hard hearts, their attitudes, and their inability to flex enough to embrace his teaching.

As we have progressed through this book, it is possible that your own paradigm has been challenged. Let's look at some of the common paradigms that can shape interpretations of the Bible today.

The following statements represent paradigms that have been firmly entrenched for over fifteen hundred years. These powerful paradigms are very influential:

- Every person is born with an immortal soul.

- If a person has a saving faith in Jesus, that person's soul will go to heaven for eternity.

- If a person is not a believer, that person's soul will spend eternity in Hell.

- The penalty for sin is death. This "death" is defined as a permanent separation from God. This includes suffering in Hell for eternity.

As you move ahead in this book, examine how your own paradigms may be limiting how you interpret what Jesus is saying. Just because we are separated from his original listeners by millennia, **the issue of how we listen** remains the same. The quest here is for clarification and truth.

26

The Spirit's Role in Overcoming Death

Interchangeable Terms for the Holy Spirit

The Holy Spirit, Spirit of God, Spirit of Christ, and the Spirit of the Son are interchangeable names for the Spirit throughout the New Testament. These are referring to the same Spirit. For an example, see the following verse. Notice that it is the spirit that conveys *zoe* to humans. Eternal *Zoe* comes from the indwelling spirit of Christ Jesus.

> ***Rom. 8:9-11*** *But you are not in the flesh but in the **Spirit**, if indeed the **Spirit of God** lives in you. But if anyone does not have the **Spirit of Christ**, this person does not belong to him. But if Christ is in you, the body is dead because of sin, but the **spirit is life (zoe)** because of righteousness. And if the **Spirit** of the one who raised Jesus from the dead lives in you, the one who raised Christ Jesus from the dead will also make **alive (zoe)** your mortal bodies through **his Spirit** who lives in you. (LEB)*

Transitioning from Death into a New Creation

> ***2 Cor. 5:17*** *Therefore if anyone is in Christ, he is a new creation; the old things have passed away; behold, new things have come. (LEB)*

It could be said that we now bear the DNA of God, as a figure of speech. This process begins as soon as we are born again (it is at that point that the Holy Spirit indwells us). That is, when we believe, we cross over from a status of death to life (*zoe*), because we have been given *zoe* via the indwelling Holy Spirit.

We are now a new creation, born of God, becoming a child of God. We now possess a dual nature: one of the flesh and one of the Holy Spirit.

To be clear, we enter life when we receive *zoe* (life as God has it). This happens at the moment we believe, when we cross over from the status of death into life (*zoe*).

Remember the verse that was giving me problems at the beginning of this book? I could not make sense of it because it said it was possible to enter life without a hand or eye.

> **Matt. 18:8-9** *And if your hand or your foot causes you to sin, cut it off and throw it[c] from you! It is better for you to enter into **life (zoe)** crippled or lame than, having two hands or two feet, to be thrown into the eternal fire! And if your eye causes you to sin, tear it out and throw it from you! It is better for you to enter into **life (zoe)** one-eyed than, having two eyes, to be thrown into fiery hell! (LEB)*

My confusion at that time had to do with the misunderstanding that entering life was synonymous with entering heaven. I could not reconcile that notion with the idea of entering heaven missing body parts.

Now I understand that, in Matt 18:8-9, Jesus is talking about something we enter while we are still walking physically on this earth.

As believers, we transition into the status of life (*zoe*) as we are born again of the Holy Spirit. It is the Spirit that conveys *zoe* into the *psuche* of the believer.

Therefore, we do indeed enter life (*zoe*) while we are yet mortals living on this earth when we believe the truth about Jesus. We participate in immortality in the present, because it has been given to us. It dwells within us via the *zoe*-giving Holy Spirit.

We will not enter eternal life (*zoe*) physically, so to speak, until we are resurrected into our new imperishable body on the day of resurrection. But, we have indeed already entered life (*zoe*). Or, to put it more accurately, *zoe* has entered us.

From Mark 10:30, we can see that we receive eternal *zoe* in the age to come.

> **Mark 10:29-30** *Jesus said, "Truly I say to you, there is no one who has left house or brothers or sisters or mother or father or children or fields on account of me and on account of the gospel who will not receive a hundred times as much now in this time—houses and brothers and sisters and mothers and children and fields, together with persecutions—**and in the age to come, eternal life (zoe)**. (LEB)*

Our Guarantee of What Is to Come

Even though eternal *zoe* is yet to be manifested, we are guaranteed of this by the indwelling of God's Holy Spirit. See the following verses in Ephesians and 2 Corinthians. Some translations use the phrase "the Holy spirit who is the **guarantee** of our inheritance". The idea is that the Holy Spirit's indwelling of the believer is their assurance or seal (guarantee) of their redemption.

> **Eph. 1:13-14** *In whom also you, when you heard the word of truth, the gospel of your salvation, in whom also when you believed you were **sealed** with the promised **Holy Spirit**, who is the **down payment of our inheritance,** until the redemption of the possession, to the praise of his glory. (LEB)*

> **2 Cor. 1:21-22** *Now the one who establishes us together with you in Christ and who anoints us is God, who also **sealed** us and gave the **down payment of the Spirit** in our hearts. (LEB)*

We are now participating in the divine nature. We have not yet been resurrected unto eternal *zoe*, but we do now have *zoe* living within us, regenerating our *psuche* to make it alive with Christ.

We are now experiencing the life (*zoe*) of Christ within us. We are children of God in the present day and age.

There are some who say we don't enter eternal life until the day of resurrection, and this is true. But, we must not miss the fact that believers already possess *zoe* and participate in *zoe* **now** . . . *zoe*, which, by its very nature, is eternal.

We just have not been resurrected yet into the new imperishable bodies, which will occur on the resurrection day.

> Believers can **now** participate in the divine nature. We have not yet been resurrected unto Eternal Zoe, but we do **now** have Zoe living within us, having regenerated our Psuche from a status of death to a status of Life (Zoe)

27

Jesus Says Death Can Be Avoided

If you recall from John 6, Jesus identified death as the problem that all mankind faces. He began a stark contrast by pointing out that the Jew's ancestors ate the manna (bread) but eventually died.

> *John 6:47-49 "Truly, truly I say to you, the one who believes has **eternal life (zoe). I am the bread of life (zoe)**. Your fathers ate the manna in the wilderness **and they died**."* (LEB)

He is specifically referring to the Israelites who died during the period of forty years of wandering in the desert. He makes the contrast between the manna that they ate (and yet died) with the true bread that comes down from heaven (himself).

Jesus said that if a person eats of this living bread (referring to himself) he will not die, in fact that person will live forever.

> *John 6:50-51 "This is the bread that comes down from heaven so that someone may eat from it **and not die**. I am the living bread that came down from heaven. If anyone eats from this bread, he will live forever. And the bread that I will give for the **life (zoe)** of the world is my flesh."* (LEB)

Never See Death?

As we now return to John 8, Jesus continues with teaching about death. He now tells the Jewish crowd that if they obey his word, they will never see death.

John 8:51 *"Truly, truly, I say to you, if anyone keeps my word,* ***he will never see death."*** *(ESV)*

This claim escalates an already tense confrontation, as it is way outside of the Jews' paradigm. They resort to calling him demon-possessed because they see his statement as extremely outrageous.

Those in the crowd should be asking themselves this question: "Could this possibly be true?" But, their paradigm prevents them from ever getting to that point. Jesus tries to strip away their misconceptions and educate them on the truth. He is more concerned that they understand the truth than he is about offending them.

Let me ask you, the reader: Is there any way this could possibly be true?

Could it be true that a person who obeys Jesus' word will **never** see death? Does this line up with what Jesus has already taught thus far in the gospel according to John?

As we progress through John, we will see Jesus continuing to press this topic of death. We will come to understand that it is one of the primary components of his message. This should not surprise us, as it is tied directly to his message of *zoe*.

> We will see Jesus continuing to press this
> topic of **death** and understand that it is
> a key component of his message.
> This should not surprise us, as it is tied
> directly to his message of **Zoe**.

This is not the message of a deranged man but of the Son of God, who knows exactly what his purpose is. He reveals this concept precisely and bit by bit, to those who will listen. Jesus will revisit this concept of never dying again when we get to John 11. There, he goes into more detail on this concept and even defines it by demonstrating his power over death.

In John 11, we will encounter some very difficult and obscure statements by Jesus at one of the most vital points in his ministry. However, if you continue with this study, when we get to John 11, these statements will hopefully become crystal clear for you.

However, for now we must return to John 8. This chapter is absolutely foundational to understanding what Jesus tells us in John 11. We cannot lightly pass through this chapter.

We now proceed to these very important verses.

> *John 8:48-53 The Jews answered him, "Are we not right in saying that you are a Samaritan and have a demon?" Jesus answered, "I do not have a demon, but I honor my Father, and you dishonor me. Yet I do not seek my own glory; there is One who seeks it, and he is the judge. **Truly, truly, I say to you, if anyone keeps my word, he will never see death.**"*
>
> *The Jews said to him, "Now, we know that you have a demon! Abraham died, as did the prophets, yet you say, 'If anyone keeps my word, he will never taste death.' Are you greater than our father Abraham, who died? And the prophets died! Who do you make yourself out to be?" (ESV)*

We are going to take a very close look at the following snippet (8:51) from the verses above. I believe there is a crucial component in this verse that has been missed, that is absolutely fundamental to understanding Jesus' message. Please take an earnest look at this with me.

> **John 8:51** *"Truly, truly, I say to you, if anyone keeps my word, he will never see death." (ESV)*

Pause with me for just a second. Would you agree this statement was way outside the crowd's paradigm? I dare say this is way outside my paradigm, and probably yours as well. I have never personally known someone who has never died, so this statement would be very hard for me to accept. Why would Jesus make such an outlandish claim?

As you consider this verse, remember that earlier in this conversation (8:24), Jesus told the crowd that if anyone did not believe in him, they would die in their sins.

> **John 8:24** *I told you that you would die in your sins, for, unless you believe that I am he you will die in your sins. (ESV)*

These two verses are part of a continuous conversation that took place in one encounter. The crowd is still pondering what Jesus said only a minute or two before in 8:24 when he makes the statement in 8:51. Only by keeping this in mind can we even begin to understand what Jesus is saying now in 8:51.

It's as if Jesus is saying, "I told you that if you do not believe in me, you will indeed die in your sins. But, I want to tell you what will happen if you do believe in me and hold to my teachings! Not only will you not die in your sins, but you will also never see death!"

In No Case Shall You Be Beholding Death in the Eon

At first glance, this statement seems difficult to understand or believe.

It is hard to understand because of one of two reasons:

- Either this verse has been incompletely translated,

- Or we don't clearly understand Jesus' definition of death.

Jesus' definition of life (*zoe*) is the main emphasis of John's gospel. And, in the last few chapters of John, Jesus makes a strong contrast between life (*zoe*) and death. With that in mind, keep an open mind that Jesus may define death in a unique way just as he has done for life (*zoe*).

Think about this. Even Jesus died on the cross. In fact, in John 10, Jesus predicts that he will give up his *psuche* (thereby dying). We will get to John 10 soon. However, first we need to digest John 8 in order to understand the upcoming chapters.

Remember that John put these sections in a particular sequence, so that we could gradually understand Jesus' teachings, one precept at a time, until we can grasp the whole picture. Keep in mind that even John did not totally understand what Jesus was teaching while Jesus was still alive. It was only after Jesus' death and resurrection, with the power of the Holy Spirit gifting John with understanding, that John totally understood the entirety of Jesus' teaching. It is with this understanding that John is now gradually unwrapping Jesus' teaching for us in his gospel.

So, just what did Jesus mean when he said, "Whoever believes my word will never see death?" Ten of the twelve apostles were killed for preaching Jesus' words in the decades immediately following Jesus' own death upon the cross. **So, obviously, Jesus could not have meant that those whose hold to his teaching would "never see death."**

Obviously, the Jews that heard him say this were offended by what he said because it was so preposterous to them. But, is it possible that our English translation has missed a key part of his statement that would have been just as outlandish and offensive but more clearly tied to what Jesus has been teaching?

This is a possibility, one that we will explore in the next few chapters of John. On the other hand, what if the expression "never see death" is actually be the best translation of the Greek. This is a distinct possibility as well, one that we will also explore.

> It's as if Jesus is saying...
>
> "I told you that if you do not believe in me, you will indeed die in your sins. But, I want to tell you what will happen if you do believe in me and hold to my teachings! Not only will you not die in your sins, but you will also never see death!"

Another English Translation

In the LEB translation, notice the different rendering of this verse.

> *John 8:51 Truly, truly I say to you, if anyone keeps my word,* **he will never experience death forever.***" (LEB)*

I like how this reads much, much better. I believe it is very close to being correct. But I believe the English wording still misses the critical point that Jesus is emphasizing. We need to *clearly* understand what Jesus is saying.

Interlinear Greek-English New Testament

Greek-English Interlinear New Testaments have been used as reference material for generations by serious biblical scholars. The online access to this resource is a wonderful study tool.

Look at the original Greek verse (John 8:51) on the following page. It is from a Greek-English Interlinear New Testament, which can be found online at the following link:

http://www.scripture4all.org/OnlineInterlinear/NTpdf/joh8.pdf)

The benefit of an Interlinear translation is that it shows the original Greek word with an appropriate English word below. You do not have to be a Greek scholar to see that a key aspect of this original Greek text has been omitted from the English translation. As you can see, the Greek text here does not "exactly" say that "whoever obeys my word shall **never** see death".

See the screen shot below:

8:51	AMHN	AMHN	ΛΕΓω	YMIN	EAN	TIC	TON	ΛΟΓΟΝ	EMON
	amEn	amEn	legO	humin	ean	tis	ton	logon	emon
	G281	G281	G3004	G5213	G1437	G5100	G3588	G3056	G1699
	Hebrew	Hebrew	vi Pres Act 1 Sg	pp 2 Dat Pl	Cond	px Nom Sg m	t_ Acc Sg m	n_ Acc Sg m	ps 1 Acc Sg
	AMEN verily	AMEN verily	I-AM-sayING	to-YOU(p) to-ye	IF-EVER	ANY anyone	THE	saying word	MY

	THPHCH	ΘΑΝΑΤΟΝ	OY	MH	ΘΕωΡΗCΗ	EIC	TON	ΑΙωΝΑ
	tErEsE	thanaton	ou	mE	theOrEsE	eis	ton	aiOna
	G5083	G2288	G3756	G3361	G2334	G1519	G3588	G165
	vs Aor Act 3 Sg	n_ Acc Sg m	Part Neg	Part Neg	vs Aor Act 3 Sg	Prep	t_ Acc Sg m	n_ Acc Sg m
	SHOULD-BE-KEEPING	DEATH	NOT	NO	he-SHOULD-BE-beholdING	INTO	THE	eon

51 . Verily, verily, I say unto you, If a man keep my saying, he shall never see death.

Copyright 2010 Scripture4all Foundation – www.scripture4all.org

Look carefully at the last 3 words in this verse. The last 3 words are "eis ton aiOna", meaning "into the eon".

Do you see this phrase "into the eon" (or anything resembling this) in the English translation shown in the right-hand margin adjacent to the Greek text? Did you see this expression in the text of John 8:48-53 that was previously displayed a few pages earlier?

This phrase "into the eon" is missing entirely in the English translation. So, I ask you, if it were included, could it possibly change the meaning of this text?

From the screenshot above, you can see the Greek roughly reads something like this:

"Amen, Amen, I am saying to you, if ever anyone my word should be keeping, death not no should he be beholding into the eon." (my paraphrase)

Jesus' use of the phrase "into the eon" shares the same root word as the word he has been using for "Eternal Life" throughout John and the other gospels. Jesus is using the same terminology for death as he did for life (*zoe*) throughout the gospel according to John. Both are "into the eon," or eternity.

Another difficulty in the translation comes with the use of two negatives—"not no"—that occur in the Greek immediately prior to the phrase "he should be beholding into the eon." This is the combination of the two Greek words *"ou mE"*.

According to *Strong's Greek Dictionary* (see website link below), the double negative *ou mE* should be read as an extra emphatic "not even a possibility" or "in no case" or "never." So, the word "never" that we see in the English translation could be deemed appropriate, but may fail to emphasize the the gist of "not even a possibility". The idea is that there is absolutely no way that is going to happen.

http://Biblehub.com/greek/3364.htm

Into the Eon

In addition, could the omission of "into the eon" be an error? If so, it could significantly change the meaning of 8:51.

Let's take a look at some different possible outcomes of this translation.

First, let's look at the English translation as it is most often seen.

> *"Very truly I tell you, whoever obeys my word will never see death." (ESV)*

Next, let's look at using the double negative interpreted as "in no case" and include the phrase "into the eon" (following the Interlinear translation).

> *"Very truly, I am saying to you, if ever anyone my word should be keeping, death in no case should he be beholding into the eon." (my paraphrase)*

Lastly, let us use the word "experience" in lieu of "should be holding" but still include the phrase "into the eon."

> *"Very truly I am saying to you, if anyone my word should be keeping, in no case (not even a possibility) shall he be experiencing death into the eon." (my paraphrase)*

Can you see the significant difference between the first translation and the last two?

Does "never see death" mean the same thing as "death in no case should he be beholding into the eon?"

I liked the word "experiencing" that the LEB tranlsation used.

I believe the gist of this verse is:

"Very truly, I am saying to you, if anyone keeps my word, then in no case shall that person experience death into the eon." (my paraphrase)

> John 8:51 should be read as...
>
> "Very truly, I am saying to you, if anyone keeps my word, then in no case shall that person experience death into the eon."

Dear reader, if you don't get this, you have just missed the whole journey. That is why Jesus came. He came to save you from death into the ages... staying dead forever. Jesus sacrificed his psuche via his death upon the cross, and God raised his psuche from the dead via the zoe infusing power of the Holy Spirit.

He has come to offer you this zoe-giving power that will resurrect you from the dead to a life of immortality, also known as eternal zoe.

On the other hand

On the other hand, what if Jesus actually intended to just imply that "whoever obeys my word will never see death." Either way you want to translate this verse (and similar verses coming up), we have to get a clear understanding of the message that Jesus is trying to convey about avoiding death.

Obviously, he is not referring to someone dying a bodily, physical death that has occurred to everyone that has ever lived (believers or not) in the millennia since his death and resurrection. He has to be talking about something else, or he has to be referring to "death in no case shall he be experiencing into the eons."

But again, either way we have to zero in on Jesus' message about avoiding death and what that means.

Remember, in John 6, Jesus told the crowd that a person could eat of this bread (himself) and not die. That was very straightforward. There are no extra words to include or omit there. So, what did Jesus mean when he said that? Obviously everyone that was there that day, including believers, has died a physical, bodily death. So, that cannot be what he was talking about.

One more question to ponder: Is it possible that a very strong paradigm can influence how Greek words are translated? Or even . . . omitted?

Milestones

Let's Review

We have uncovered something about Jesus' description of death that we have to admit, at this point, we do not totally understand. So, this would be a good place to review what we do know thus far about death from Jesus' teaching in the gospel according to John.

What we know about death so far:

> ➤ We are initially in a status of death and remain that way unless we believe in Jesus.

> ➤ If we do not believe, we will die in our sins.

> ➤ When we believe in Jesus, we cross over from a status of death, to possessing life (Zoe).

> ➤ *Zoe* is defined as "life as God has it" and provides us "*Zoe* unto the eons" (Eternal Life).

What we are still working on:

> ➤ What does Jesus mean by the phrase "death in no case shall he be experiencing into the eon?"

What does Jesus mean by the phrase "death in no case shall he be beholding into the eon?"

We have to remember that when Jesus talks about death, he is referring to death of one's *psuche*. **Death is never associated with zoe.**

Zoe is the opposite of death, and Jesus frequently contrasts *zoe* against death. *Zoe* is defined by the way Jesus uses the word. We have seen that Jesus defines *zoe* as "life as God has it." God is immortal. Therefore, *zoe* does not die, period. *Zoe* is forever. *Zoe* is always associated with eternal life (*zoe*).

Take a closer look at this especially since you have been studying what Jesus said about *psuche*, *zoe*, and death. Remember what Jesus said about those who believe in him? Those believers will receive eternal life.

> We have to remember that when Jesus talks about death, he is referring to the death of one's *Psuche*. Death is never associated with Zoe.
> **It is impossible for Zoe to Die**
> Jesus frequently contrasts Zoe against Death

Ask yourself: what is the opposite of Eternal Life (*Zoe*)?

Think about this. The opposite of Eternal Life is not "never dying."

The opposite of Eternal Life is Eternal Death, staying dead forever . . . exrperiencing death into the eon.

This makes sense with everything Jesus has taught so far about life (*zoe*), *psuche*, and death. In fact, Jesus contrasts life (*zoe*) with death frequently, as we have seen throughout the gospel according to John. This is just the first time that you and I have sought to define what Jesus means when he speaks about death.

In fact, the first time we see Jesus discuss this, it is in John 3:15-16. In these verses, Jesus does not use the word death but rather a word that is translated into English as "**perish**."

The actual Greek word *apoletai* means "destroy utterly." This is actually helpful in defining what Jesus means when he speaks of death or dying.

See the screen capture on the following page from John 3:15-16:

3:15 — That whosoever believeth in him should not perish, but have eternal life.

Greek	Translit	Strong's	Parsing	Meaning
INA	hina	G2443	Conj	THAT
ΠAC	pas	G3956	a_Nom Sg m	EVERY
O	ho	G3588	t_Nom Sg m	THE
ΠICTEYWN	pisteuOn	G4100	vp Pres Act Nom Sg m	one-BELIEVING / one-believing
EIC	eis	G1519	Prep	INTO
AYTON	auton	G846	pp Acc Sg m	Him
MH	mE	G3361	Part Neg	NO
AΠOΛHTAI	apolEtai	G622	vs 2Aor Mid 3 Sg	SHOULD-BE-beING-destroyED / should-be-perishing
AΛΛ	all	G235	Conj	but
EXH	echE	G2192	vs Pres Act 3 Sg	MAY-BE-HAVING
ZWHN	zOEn	G2222	n_Acc Sg f	LIFE
AIWNION	aiOnion	G166	a_Acc Sg f	eonian

3:16 — For God so loved the world, that he gave his only begotten Son, that whosoever believeth in him should not perish, but have everlasting life.

Greek	Translit	Strong's	Parsing	Meaning
OYTWC	houtOs	G3779	Adv	thus
ΓAP	gar	G1063	Conj	for
HΓAΠHCEN	EgapEsen	G25	vi Aor Act 3 Sg	LOVES
O	ho	G3588	t_Nom Sg m	THE
ΘEOC	theos	G2316	n_Nom Sg m	God
TON	ton	G3588	t_Acc Sg m	THE
KOCMON	kosmon	G2889	n_Acc Sg m	SYSTEM / world
WCTE	hOste	G5620	Conj	AS-BESIDES / so-that
TON	ton	G3588	t_Acc Sg m	THE
YION	huion	G5207	n_Acc Sg m	SON
AYTOY	autou	G846	pp Gen Sg m	OF-Him
TON	ton	G3588	t_Acc Sg m	THE
MONOΓENH	monogenE	G3439	a_Acc Sg m	ONLY-generated / only-begotten
EΔWKEN	edOken	G1325	vi Aor Act 3 Sg	He-GIVES
INA	hina	G2443	Conj	THAT
ΠAC	pas	G3956	a_Nom Sg m	EVERY
O	ho	G3588	t_Nom Sg m	THE
ΠICTEYWN	pisteuOn	G4100	vp Pres Act Nom Sg m	one-BELIEVING / one-believing
EIC	eis	G1519	Prep	INTO
AYTON	auton	G846	pp Acc Sg m	Him
MH	mE	G3361	Part Neg	NO
AΠOΛHTAI	apolEtai	G622	vs 2Aor Mid 3 Sg	SHOULD-BE-beING-destroyED / should-be-perishing
AΛΛ	all	G235	Conj	but
EXH	echE	G2192	vs Pres Act 3 Sg	MAY-BE-HAVING
ZWHN	zOEn	G2222	n_Acc Sg f	LIFE
AIWNION	aiOnion	G166	a_Acc Sg f	eonian

The utter destruction (*apoletai*) that Jesus speaks of in John 3:15-16 (shown on the previous page) would be the utter destruction of a person's *psuche*.

Destroy both Body and Psuche

Jesus describes this destruction in Matthew 10:28 as well:

> *Matt. 10:28 And do not be afraid of those who kill the body but are not able to kill the **soul (psuche)**, but instead be afraid of the one who is able to destroy both **soul (psuche)** and body in hell (Gehenna). (LEB)*

See the screen capture of Matthew 10:28 from the Greek-English Interlinear Bible on the following page:

28 And fear not them which kill the body, but are not able to kill the soul: but rather fear him which is able to destroy both soul and body in hell.

10:28

KAI	kai	G2532	Conj — AND
MH	mE	G3361	Part Neg — NO
ΦΟΒΗΘΗΤΕ	phobEthEte	G5399	vm Aor pasD 2 Pl — BE-BEING-afraid be-ye-being-afraid !
ΑΠΟ	apo	G575	Prep — FROM
ΤΩΝ	tOn	G3588	t_ Gen Pl m — THE
ΑΠΟΚΤΕΙΝΟΝΤΩΝ	apokteinontOn	G615	vp Pres Act Gen Pl m — ones-FROM-KILLING ones-killing
ΤΟ	to	G3588	t_ Acc Sg n — THE
ΣΩΜΑ	sOma	G4983	n_ Acc Sg n — BODY
ΤΗΝ	tEn	G3588	t_ Acc Sg f — THE
ΔΕ	de	G1161	Conj — YET
ΨΥΧΗΝ	psuchEn	G5590	n_ Acc Sg f — soul
ΜΗ	mE	G3361	Part Neg — NO
ΔΥΝΑΜΕΝΩΝ	dunamenOn	G1410	vp Pres midD/pasD Gen Pl m — OF-beING-ABLE being-able
ΑΠΟΚΤΕΙΝΑΙ	apokteinai	G615	vn Aor Act — TO-FROM-KILL to-kill
ΦΟΒΗΘΗΤΕ	phobEthEte	G5399	vm Aor pasD 2 Pl — BE-BEING-afraid be-ye-being-afraid-of !
ΔΕ	de	G1161	Conj — YET
ΜΑΛΛΟΝ	mallon	G3123	Adv — RATHER
ΤΟΝ	ton	G3588	t_ Acc Sg m — THE
ΔΥΝΑΜΕΝΟΝ	dunamenon	G1410	vp Pres midD/pasD Acc Sg m — One-beING-ABLE one-being-able
ΚΑΙ	kai	G2532	Conj — AND
ΨΥΧΗΝ	psuchEn	G5590	n_ Acc Sg f — soul
ΚΑΙ	kai	G2532	Conj — AND
ΣΩΜΑ	sOma	G4983	n_ Acc Sg n — BODY
ΑΠΟΛΕΣΑΙ	apolesai	G622	vn Aor Act — TO-destroy
ΕΝ	en	G1722	Prep — IN
ΓΕΕΝΝΗ	geennE	G1067	n_ Dat Sg f — GEHENNA

The Second Death

Jesus points out that a person's **body and *psuche*** may be destroyed in *Gehenna*. Jesus used *Gehenna* as a metaphor to refer to the second death. *Gehenna* does not mean "Hell," as the term is commonly understood in our English culture today. I dedicate a chapter to the true etymology of Gehenna in Part 3 of this book.

John speaks of the second death several times in the book of Revelation. (Revelation 2:11, 20:6, 20:14, and 21:8). This concept is actually in total agreement with everything Jesus says in the gospel according to John. For example, when someone dies, it is their *psuche* that dies. If they are a believer, their *psuche* is saved (preserved) by the impartation of eternal *zoe* (*zoe* unto the eon).

In other words, a believer's *psuche* will not remain dead unto the eon. If a person is not a believer, they do not have this hope.

Think about this. Even Jesus died. In John 10, Jesus explains that he will lay down his *psuche* for his sheep (not his *zoe* but his *psuche*!).

Jesus' *psuche* will be killed when he is crucified, but he will be able to take it up again. More on this later.

> When someone dies, it is their *Psuche* that dies.
> If they are a believer, their *Psuche* is saved by the
> impartation of Eternal *Zoe* (Zoe unto the eon).
> Zoe is imparted into the believer's Psuche
> by the indwelling Holy Spirit.

Final Analysis of John 8

Why is it important that we have a clear understanding of Jesus' use of these words?

Well, it's important if we want to have clear doctrine as to what Jesus' message was. What message did he devote his entire ministry trying to convey?

Is it important that we clearly understand the message that he died for? Or is it okay that we confuse what the issues really are? How will that affect our lives? How will that affect our message and our emphasis?

The question boils down to this: what is Jesus identifying as mankind's problem? What does he say the real issue is? What is man's predicament and status prior to believing in Him? What is the result of sin?

If we believe in him in order that we might be saved . . . just what are we being saved *from*?

What's the Real Problem?

What is the **real** problem that Jesus has identified in the gospel according to John?

Is it Hell? Did you know that Jesus is never recorded using the word *Gehenna* in the gospel according to John? In fact, John never uses the word *Gehenna* in any of his writings (John wrote the gospel according to John, 1 John, 2 John, 3 John, and the Book of Revelations). The apostle Paul never used the word *Gehenna* in any of his writings either.

However, John does use the word *Hades* four times in the book of Revelation. But, *Hades* should never be translated as "Hell" or confused with *Gehenna*. Jesus and the New Testament authors had a unique definition of *Hades* that sets it totally apart from *Gehenna*.

For that matter, *Gehenna* should not be translated as "Hell" either. Hell is actually a pagan word that was used to replace the word *Gehenna* centuries after Jesus used the word *Gehenna*. *Gehenna* was the proper name of a location just outside of Jerusalem that in Jesus' day, had an infamous history associated with apocalyptic judgement and destruction.

Jesus uses the word Gehenna eleven times in the synoptic gospels, but it is not used in the gospel according to John or any of Paul's letters. More on the concept of *Gehenna* and *Hades* will be covered in in Part 3 of this book.

Now Is the Time to Believe

Jesus' warning in 8:21-24 is not just to those Jews who were present.

> *John 8:21-24 So he said to them again, "I am going away, and you will seek me and will die in your sin. Where I am going you cannot come!" Then the Jews began to say, "Perhaps he will kill himself, because he is saying, 'Where I am going you cannot come.'" And he said to them, "You are from below; I am from above. You are from this world; I am not from this world. Thus I said to you that you will die in your sins. For if you do not believe that I am he, you will die in your sins." (LEB)*

This warning is just as relevant today as it was then. Jesus states that he is going away and that when he is gone, they will vainly look for him and not find him. When the opportunity comes for us to believe in and accept Jesus as our Savior, we cannot assume that this opportunity will always be there for us. Procrastination can be deadly. In the future, we may not take the time again to reflect on his truth.

Later in John 12:35-36, Jesus makes another similar warning.

John 12:35-36 So, Jesus said to them, "The light is among you for a little while longer. Walk while you have the light, lest darkness overtake you. The one who walks in the darkness does not know where he is going. **While you have the light, believe in the light, that you may become sons of light**." *(ESV)*

The world is full of darkness. Satan is very real, and his only tool is deception. Darkness is not an entity in and of itself. It is only defined as the absence of light. But, the consequences of living in darkness are quite tangible. In this darkness, Satan can keep us quite content with untruths (lies) about who Jesus is. Or he can just keep us distracted with all the stress and busyness of things going on in our world. Jesus' warning to listen and believe before darkness overtakes you is a dire warning indeed. Jesus desires for you to escape the lies of Satan, come to the light, escape the fruitless, harmful effects of living in darkness, and ultimately escape the penalty of all sin, which is death of your *psuche* . . . your death.

If you hear Jesus' words resonating today, do not harden your heart. Do not glaze your mind over and say to yourself, "Oh, another time. I'll look at this another day."

Dear friend, there may not be another time! That is the point Jesus is making here. He is telling these people that he is going away. He is urging them to make a decision on who he is. He is warning them that when he is gone, there may not be another opportunity for them to listen to his words again.

Life

Defined

28

John 10 – The Good Shepherd

In John 10, Jesus begins a long metaphor involving sheep, the gate to the sheep pen, and shepherds. This extensive metaphor contains two of his famous "I Am" statements. The first has to do with the gate to the sheep pen.

First, a little background will be helpful. Shepherds out in the countryside often brought their sheep together into a communal sheep pen during the night in order to keep the sheep safe while the shepherds slept. One shepherd would be on watch as the gatekeeper. Thus the sheep pen provided protection for the sheep during the night. The gate was the only way in or out of the pen.

Anyone who attempted to remove the sheep other than through the gate would be regarded as a thief. The only one who could enter by the gate was the shepherd of the sheep. When the gatekeeper opened the gate for the shepherd, the shepherd would then call out to his sheep. His sheep would recognize the voice of their shepherd and quickly find their way out of the large group of sheep in order to follow their shepherd.

Sheep will only follow the voice of their shepherd. The sheep will not follow the voice of a stranger; in fact, the sheep will run from a stranger. It is using this scenario that Jesus makes the first "I Am" statement that takes place in this metaphor.

I Am the Gate for the Sheep.

"I Am" Statement 3

This is Jesus speaking in John 10:

> **John 10:1-9** *"Truly, truly, I say to you, he who does not enter the sheepfold by the door but climbs in by another way, that man is a thief and a robber. But he who enters by the door is the shepherd of the sheep. To him the gatekeeper opens. The sheep hear his voice, and he calls his own sheep by name and leads them out. When he has brought out all his own, he goes before them, and the sheep follow him, for they know his voice. A stranger they will not follow, but they will flee from him, for they do not know the voice of strangers."*
>
> *This figure of speech Jesus used with them, but they did not understand what he was saying to them. So, Jesus again said to them, "Truly, truly, I say to you,* **I am the door of the sheep**. *All who came before me are thieves and robbers, but the sheep did not listen to them.* **I am the door. If anyone enters by me, he will be saved and will go in and out and find pasture.***" (ESV)*

Using the metaphor of being the door (or gate) for the sheep, Jesus emphasizes that whoever enters the sheep pen through him will be saved. This is the primary point Jesus is making in John 10:1-9. It is only through Jesus that anyone can be saved. **There is no other way (or door/gate) that leads to salvation**. (See more on the "way" in the section on John 14).

Also, his sheep will be able to come and go from the sheep pen and will find pasture. This is a reference to Psalm 23, when King David says, "The Lord is my shepherd. He leads me to green pastures." The Jews would have instantly picked up on this reference and the fact that Jesus is referring to himself as this shepherd. He will continue with this shepherd metaphor throughout John 10.

Jesus States His Purpose

Next comes 10:10, when Jesus states his purpose for coming into the world. This verse is the crux of John 10 and is one of the most critical verses in the New Testament. Let's take a closer look.

> **John 10:10** *The thief comes only to steal and kill and destroy. I came that they may have* **life (zoe)** *and have it abundantly. (ESV)*

Analyzing the First Sentence

The thief comes only to steal and kill and destroy

Jesus says the thief comes only to steal, kill, and destroy. This is a direct reference to Satan and Satan's objective to distort the truth, thereby stealing the hearts and minds of man. By luring the sheep away with his voice of lies, Satan steals the sheep in order to keep them from being saved. Satan seeks the death and destruction of the sheep. Jesus will refer to this death and destruction again later in this chapter (10:28).

Keep in mind that Jesus has been contrasting *zoe* with death for the last several chapters in John. It is Jesus' purpose (mission) to save the sheep by giving them life (*zoe*), thereby saving them from destruction.

Analyzing the Second Sentence

The **good news** comes in the second sentence in John 10:10. Jesus clarifies his entire purpose for coming to earth in the form of a man.

I came that they may have **life (zoe)** *and have it abundantly.*

He says that he has come that the sheep (those people who will believe in him) might have **life (zoe)** . . . and have this life (*zoe*) **abundantly** (to the fullest).

183

Don't Miss Jesus' Powerful Contrast

Jesus makes a very powerful contrast in this chapter. He has been making contrasts repeatedly throughout the Gospel of John as we have already seen, contrasting death with zoe.

In verse 10:19 Jesus contrasts what Satan has come to do, versus what he has come to do.

The simple but powerful contrast is this:

- Satan has come to kill and destroy the sheep
- Jesus has come to save them by giving them zoe

There is no mention of eternal suffering or everlasting torment. The ultimate fate of the sheep is clearly contrasted: Life or Death.

The simple but powerful contrast is this:

- **Satan has come to destroy the sheep**

- **Jesus has come to give them Zoe**

There is no mention of eternal suffering.

The ultimate fate of the sheep is clearly

contrasted as: **Life or Death**

Jesus' Purpose: That the Sheep Might Have Life (Zoe)

He says that he has come that the sheep (those people who will believe) might have **life (zoe)**. We have covered zoe thoroughly thus far, so I don't want to belabor this point. But, it is here that Jesus emphatically states his purpose for coming to earth as a man. He did not come to give us *psuche*; we already have that. He came to give us *zoe*, **in order to save our *psuche* forever.**

Note: Notice that there is no way whatsoever to glean this from the English translation. By reading the English translation, you have no true idea of what Jesus just said or its significance.

> Jesus did not come to give us *Psuche*.
>
> We already exist as *Psuche*.
>
> (Humans are psuche, that is our inherent nature)
>
> Jesus came (his stated purpose) to give us *Zoe*,
>
> in order to save our *Psuche* forever.

One more note: *Jesus makes purpose statements in the other gospels as well. But they all boil down to the same thing, Jesus has come to save the lost. He has come to give eternal zoe to those who will trust and believe in him as the Son of God, and Savior of the world. The lost are in a state of death. John's purpose statement only varies from the other gospel statements because John focuses more on man's state of death.*

For example, see Jesus statement in Mark 10:45. A first glance it may seem to indicate a different purpose, but upon closer inspection, it is saying the exact same thing as John 10. Jesus came to give his psuche as a ransom for the many who will believe.

> **Mark 10 :45** *"For even the Son of Man did not come to be served but to serve, and to give his **life (psuche)** as a ransom for many" (ESV)*

What is Abundant Zoe?

Let's be very clear as to what Jesus is saying here. Jesus is talking about *zoe*, not *psuche*!

So, what does it mean to have "abundant *zoe*?" The Greek wording indicates that he came to give believers *zoe* "super-abundantly" or "excessively."

Jesus' purpose is to give us **unbridled** access to the Father, himself and the Holy Spirit. They will abide within believers, giving the believers' hearts and minds understanding and encouragement. Believers can now cry out "Abba Father" as God's spirit within them gives them the confidence that they are now children of God. Jesus said he is the Light of the World. This light comes to indwell the believer.

Take a quick look at the following verses from 1 John. John makes several statements about zoe and the Holy Spirit *abiding* in a believer. When a person is born again, of God's seed (the Holy Spirit, the Spirit imparts zoe into that person (into their psuche).

> *1 John 3:14-16 We know that we have passed out of **death into life (zoe)**, because we love the brothers. Whoever does not love **abides in death**. Everyone who hates his brother is a murderer, and you know that no murderer **has eternal life (zoe) abiding in him**. By this we know love, that **he laid down his life (pusche) for us**, and we ought to lay down **our lives (pusche)** for the brothers. (ESV)*

> *1 John 3:24 Whoever keeps his commandments abides in God, and God in him. And by this we know that he abides in us, by the Spirit whom he has given us. (ESV)*

> *1 John 5:11-12 And this is the testimony, that God gave us **eternal life (zoe),** and this **life (zoe)** is in his Son. Whoever has the Son has **life (zoe)**; whoever does not have the Son of God does not have **life (zoe)**. (ESV)*

Application of the Abundant Zoe

After we receive the gift of *zoe*, we need to focus on abiding in Jesus. As we live by abiding in God's word and the assurance of his love and forgiveness, as well as faithfully seeking him in prayer, the fruit of the Spirit will become manifest in our lives.

The fruit of the Spirit . . . love, joy, peace, patience, kindness, goodness, faithfulness, gentleness and self-control come from the Spirit living itself out in our lives. These characteristics are no more than the character of God himself. Jesus displayed these attributes in his life on earth. They are ours to live out as well, if only we will.

__Note__: The impartation of zoe into the believer when they believe is a done deal. It is accomplished at the moment of true belief.

However, the light and abundance of zoe that is available in order for us to discern our lives, enjoy sweet fellowship with Abba Father, and to bear the fruit of the Holy Spirit, is dependent upon us abiding in Jesus! To the extent that we walk by the Spirit, we will bear its fruit.

If we choose to, we can just as easily live a carnal life and not bear this fruit. That does not necessarily mean a person is not saved (does not have zoe). Rather, it may just indicate they are not living their lives by the Spirit (i.e., abiding in Christ). This is indeed the daily struggle for all believers.

As believers, we keep one foot in this world and one in the world to come. It is like a dance where we continually move two steps one way, then a step or two back. We must daily redirect our hearts and minds to Christ and not allow the distractions of this world and the deceptions of Satan to draw us toward the forgery of temptations, doubts, fears, and diversions that seek to hinder our walk with the Spirit.

> To the extent that we walk with and
> in dependence upon the Holy Spirit,
> we will bear its fruit.

Tying Zoe to Psuche

Just as he has for the last few chapters in John, Jesus continues to contrast death with *zoe*. He also contrasts Satan's intent to kill man's *psuche* with Jesus' intent to save man's *psuche*.

Up until this point, I've attempted to keep all of the John verses in sequence, but I need to break with that convention at this point. Please look ahead with me for just a minute at John 12:25. We briefly looked at this in an earlier chapter. Since it is so relevant to John 10:10, we need to look at it again now.

> *John 12:25 "Whoever loves his **life (psuche)** loses it, and whoever hates his **life (psuche)** in this world will keep it for **eternal life (zoe)**." (ESV)*

> *John 12:25 "The one who loves his **life (psuche)** loses it, and the one who hates his **life (psuche)** in this world **preserves** it for **eternal life (zoe)**." (LEB)*

The only way to save a person's *psuche* is to impart *zoe* into that person. It is *zoe* (life as God has it, which includes immortality) that preserves (keeps or saves) a person's *psuche* for eternal *zoe*. When a person believes (has saving faith), they receive the gift of *zoe*, via the indwelling Holy Spirit. At that point, zoe abides within the believer. They are still psuche, but now have zoe as a gift. This gift of zoe, is their assurance of immortality on the resurrection day.

On the day they are resurrected, they will be raised to eternal zoe. They will in effect "keep" their psuche, because God had given them "life' as he has it, as a gift. It is in fact the indwelling Holy Spirit that is a guarantee of our resurrection.

Man does not have *zoe* in and of himself (remember that man's initial state since Adam and Eve were driven from the garden is a state of death). *Zoe* only comes as a gift from God to those who believe in Jesus as the Son of God, the Messiah, and understand that he paid the penalty of **their** death (due to sin) by giving **his** *psuche* for them.

A bit later in this chapter Jesus will plainly state that he is going to sacrifice his *psuche* for his sheep. He is predicting his death.

Thus, Jesus has clarified his purpose for coming from heaven to earth and being born as a man.

He came to give his *psuche* for us, stepping in and taking our death sentence for us. Then, in addition to taking away our death sentence, he comes to give us *zoe*.

That's it. It is as profound as it is simple. It is not difficult to understand. And, to make it even better, after being given *zoe*, we then have *zoe* to the fullest, more than we can imagine. When we receive *zoe*, there is so much that comes with it.

> Jesus came to sacrifice his *Psuche* for us, thus stepping in and taking our death sentence for us
>
> Then, (don't miss this!) in addition to taking away our death sentence, he comes to give us Eternal *Zoe*

Abundant Life: Clarifying what it is <u>not</u>

We have just identified what Jesus meant when he spoke of "*zoe* to the fullest." Unfortunately, we must now clarify what Jesus did **not** mean by this expression. This verse has been misunderstood and misrepresented perhaps more than any other verse in the Bible.

Basically, abundant life is not "abundant *psuche*"; rather it is specifically "abundant *zoe*." There is a huge difference!

Abundant *psuche* is what many preachers talk about when they preach that Jesus came to make them successful, wealthy, healthy, etc.

Possibly the reason that many of them misrepresent the truth is because they either don't know there is a difference in the Greek words that Jesus has been defining, or they don't want to hear that.

> Abundant Life is not "abundant *Psuche.*"
>
> Rather, it is specifically "abundant *Zoe.*"
>
> There is a huge difference!

The gospel according to health and wealth does not come from Jesus, period!

Imagine the believing woman who watched her children being tortured and killed at the hands of the Roman emperors in the second and third centuries AD. Also consider the believing women who watched the exact same thing occur in 2015 and 2016, when ISIS invaded the cities of Iraq. Those women had just as much *zoe* and abundantly, as a believer living on Wall Street or driving an expensive car in Beverly Hills.

In fact, those women likely had a greater of a measure of *zoe*, as the only way they could persevere through something like that (long enough to be killed themselves) was to hold on to Jesus' promises very tightly.

A person who is suffering with terminal cancer, or has a physical disability, or a person living in poverty can absolutely have *zoe* in abundance. Abundant *zoe* has nothing to do with a person's financial status, social status, health, or physical life expectancy. Thank God for that! Let's quit beating ourselves up for not keeping up with the financial, physical, or social success of others and then blaming ourselves for not being good enough.

> **Abundant Zoe** has nothing to do with a person's financial status, social status, health, or physical life expectancy

Let's get rid of the self-blame that is put on those Christians who have a terminal disease and are not only dealing with the pain and struggle of the disease but also the blame that their church culture casts upon them due to the prevailing notion that their failure to be healed is due to their own lack of faith. Shame on those who preach this lie, and add to the pain and isolation of these dear believers!

Let's get rid of the horrid lie of "abundant *psuche*"! This does not come from Christ. If it doesn't come from Jesus, then take a wild guess where it comes from, based on what Jesus says in John 8 and 10.

I Am the Good Shepherd.

"I Am" Statement 4

Back to John 10 . . . I Am the Good Shepherd

Continuing the sheep metaphor, Jesus now swings his attention to the shepherd. In another "I Am" statement, Jesus claims that he is the "Good Shepherd." This is an indirect claim that he is God. The Jews would again have understood his reference to Psalm 23 and the inference that God is the good shepherd. He has already alluded to the shepherd that leads the sheep, much as described in Psalm 23. Now, he is claiming to be the "Good Shepherd".

To the Jews, this would be a blasphemous statement, but Jesus has already gotten away with several extreme statements and is still alive. They are no doubt perplexed about the seeming blasphemy—that he, a man, is claiming to be God—but that point seems to get muted by what he says next.

> **John 10:11-18** *"**I am the good shepherd**. The good shepherd lays down his **life** (psuche) for the sheep. He who is a hired hand and not a shepherd, who does not own the sheep, sees the wolf coming and leaves the sheep and flees, and the wolf snatches them and scatters them. He flees because he is a hired hand and cares nothing for the sheep. I am the good shepherd. I know my own and my own know me, just as the Father knows me and I know the Father; and I lay down my **life** (psuche) for the sheep. And I have other sheep that are not of this fold. I must bring them also, and they will listen to my voice. So, there will be one flock, one shepherd. For this reason the Father loves me, because **I lay down my life** (psuche) **that I may take it up again**. No one takes it from me, but I lay it down of my own accord. **I have authority to lay it down, and I have authority to take it up again**. This charge I have received from my Father." (ESV)*

> **John 10:17-18** *Because of this the Father loves me, because I lay down my **life (psuche)** so that I may take possession of it again. No one takes it from me, but I lay it down voluntarily. **I have authority to lay it down, and I have authority to take possession of it again.** (LEB)*

Let's focus on what Jesus says the good shepherd is prepared to do. This good shepherd is willing **to lay down his life (*psuche*)** for his sheep (not his *zoe* but his *psuche*). There is a huge difference, as you should know by now.

> This good shepherd (Jesus) is going to
> sacrifice his life (psuche) for his sheep.
> (Not his zoe, but his psuche)
> There is a huge difference

Jesus contrasts himself as the good shepherd with the hired hand who does not care for the sheep. Instead, Jesus states that as the "Good Shepherd," he is going to lay down his *psuche* for the sheep. **Jesus is going to be killed.**

> Jesus states that as the "Good Shepherd," he is
> going to lay down his *psuche* for the sheep.
> Jesus is going to be killed

Jesus Predicts His Death and Resurrection

Jesus says the good shepherd will lay down his *psuche* for the sheep. And then he will take it up again. In saying this, he proclaims not only his own death, but his resurrection. He explains that he has the authority to lay his *psuche* down and then to take it back up again.

Continuing Contrast between Zoe and Destruction

Sometime later in John 10, Jesus is at the Festival of Dedication in Jerusalem. He is confronted there by several Jews who question him about his identity.

Jesus resumes his conversation, using the metaphor of the shepherd and the sheep. In 10:28, Jesus makes a defining statement about eternal *zoe* and its polar opposite.

Remember, earlier in John 10:10, Jesus contrasted the fact that he came to give the sheep life (*zoe*), whereas the thief comes to kill and destroy.

> **John 10:10** *"The thief comes only to steal and kill and destroy. I came that they may have **life (zoe)** and have it abundantly." (ESV)*

Now, in 10:28, Jesus contrasts *zoe* again but uses slightly different wording. He now contrasts eternal *zoe* against "perishing".

> **John 10:27-30** *"My sheep hear my voice, and I know them, and they follow me. **I give them eternal life (zoe), and they will never perish**, and no one will snatch them out of my hand. My Father, who has given them to me, is greater than all, and no one is able to snatch them out of the Father's hand. I and the Father are one. " (ESV)*

Jesus reiterates that he will give eternal *zoe* to his sheep and that they will never perish. "Perish" and eternal life are polar opposites! It is implicit that by giving his followers eternal life, they are saved from perishing.

> **John 10:28** *I give them **eternal life (zoe)**, and they will never perish, and no one will snatch them out of my hand. (ESV)*

> **John 10:28** *And I give them **eternal life (zoe)**, and they will never perish <u>forever</u>, and no one will seize them out of my hand. (LEB)*

He explains that his sheep listen to his voice (they are believers), and no one can snatch or steal his sheep from him. They are secure in his Father's hands, and no one is greater than God the Father.

Taking a Closer Look at "Perish"

The next thing he says gives us more clarity about the fate of those that do not believe. Jesus says his sheep will never perish. If you recall from John 8, these "never" verses don't exactly say "never."

Notice that the LEB version includes the word forever. This is more accurate, but still a bit hard to understand, in my opinion.

We also need to know the word Jesus uses for "perish."

The Greek word *apolontai* comes from *apollumi* and means "utterly destroy." It is frequently translated into English as "perish" or "destroy."

The definition for *apollumi* can be found at http://Biblehub.com/greek/622.htm

Look at the Interlinear Greek-English verse on the next page.

Read the English word for word translation below the Greek (John 10:28). Does it say "never perish?"

28 And I give unto them eternal life; and they shall never perish, neither shall any [man] pluck them out of my hand.

KAΓW	ZWHN	AIWNION	ΔIΔWMI	AYTOIC	KAI	OY	MH
kagO	zOEn	aiOnion	didOmi	autois	kai	ou	mE
G2504	G2222	G166	G1325	G846	G2532	G3756	G3361
pp 1 Nom Sg Con	n_Acc Sg f	a_Acc Sg f	vi Pres Act 1 Sg	pp Dat Pl m	Conj	Part Neg	Part Neg
AND-I	LIFE	eonian	AM-GIVING	to-them them	AND	NOT	NO

AΠOΛWNTAI	EIC	TON	AIWNA	KAI	OYX	APΠACEI	TIC
apolOntai	eis	ton	aiOna	kai	ouch	harpasei	tis
G622	G1519	G3588	G165	G2532	G3756	G726	G5100
vs 2Aor Mid 3 Pl	Prep	t_Acc Sg m	n_Acc Sg m	Conj	Part Neg	vi Fut Act 3 Sg	px Nom Sg m
THEY-SHOULD-BE-beING-destroyED	INTO	THE	eon	AND	NOT	SHALL-BE-SNATCHING	ANY anyone

AYTA	EK	THC	XEIPOC	MOY
auta	ek	tEs	cheiros	mou
G846	G1537	G3588	G5495	G3450
pp Acc Pl n	Prep	t_Gen Sg f	n_Gen Sg f	pp 1 Gen Sg
them	OUT	OF-THE	HAND	OF-ME

If you combine the English words below the Greek, the verse will read something like this: "Not No they should be being destroyed into the eon." The double negative leading phrase "not no" can be read as "in no case."

This results in the verse reading as:

"in no case should they be being destroyed into the eon"

What Does "Perish" or "Destroy" Mean?

If this verse doesn't mean death into the eons, then how do you define it without going into some twisted explanation?

If you choose to define perishing as "permanent separation from God while undergoing eternal torment in Hell," you cannot support that from any of Jesus' teachings in the gospel according to John or from any of John's other books (1, 2 or 3 John or the book of Revelation) nor can you support that from any of the apostle Paul's writings.

We will take a detailed look at the New Testament's use of this word in Part 3 of this book.

Life

Defined

29

John 11

This Will Not End in Death

John 11 starts out with Jesus receiving an urgent message from a family that is very dear to him. The brother, Lazarus, is deathly ill. His two sisters, Mary and Martha, are caring for him, and they have sent an urgent message to Jesus notifying him that Lazarus is dangerously ill.

This family is devoted to Jesus, and they are faithful believers. The sisters have seen Jesus heal many types of disease and illness and are confident that Jesus can save their brother. But, this occasion is extremely urgent as Lazarus is deathly ill. When Jesus hears of Lazarus's illness, he makes a very strange statement. He states that this sickness will not *end in death*, **when in fact he knows Lazarus is going to die.**

Indeed, Jesus intentionally stays where he is for two more days **to make absolutely sure that Lazarus will die**. He does not want to rush to Bethany at the request of the sisters in time to save Lazarus.

After remaining where he is for two more days, Jesus tells his disciples, "Let's back go Judea." He explains to his disciples that their friend Lazarus is ill and has fallen asleep. Jesus says that he is going back to Bethany (where Lazarus lives) to wake him.

The disciples reply to Jesus that if Lazarus is sick, sleeping will help him to get better. Jesus used the term "asleep" to describe the state of Lazarus's death, but the disciples still think of it as literal sleep at this point.

So then, Jesus tells them plainly that Lazarus is dead.

Jesus has been complicit (sovereignly) in orchestrating Lazarus's death in order to demonstrate that he (Jesus) has power over death. John 11 is the pinnacle of everything that Jesus has taught up until this point. Up until now, it has been just that . . . talk. But now, Jesus is going to powerfully demonstrate both who he is and his purpose.

John 11:1-16 Now, a certain man was ill, Lazarus of Bethany, the village of Mary and her sister Martha. It was Mary who anointed the Lord with ointment and wiped his feet with her hair, whose brother Lazarus was ill. So the sisters sent to him, saying, "Lord, he whom you love is ill." But when Jesus heard it, he said, "This illness does not lead to death. It is for the glory of God, so that the Son of God may be glorified through it."

Now, Jesus loved Martha and her sister and Lazarus. So when he heard that Lazarus was ill, he stayed two days longer in the place where he was. Then, after this, he said to the disciples, "Let us go to Judea again." The disciples said to him, "Rabbi, the Jews were just now seeking to stone you, and are you going there again?"

Jesus answered, "Are there not twelve hours in the day? If anyone walks in the day, he does not stumble, because he sees the light of this world. But, if anyone walks in the night, he stumbles, because the light is not in him."

After saying these things, he said to them, "Our friend Lazarus has fallen asleep, but I go to awaken him." The disciples said to him, "Lord, if he has fallen asleep, he will recover." Now Jesus had spoken of his death, but they thought that he meant taking rest in sleep.

Then Jesus told them plainly, "Lazarus has died, and for your sake I am glad that I was not there, so that you may believe. But let us go to him." So Thomas, called the Twin, said to his fellow disciples, "Let us also go, that we may die with him." (ESV)

Taking a Closer Look

> **John 11:4** *But, when Jesus heard it, he said, "This illness **does not lead to death**. It is for the glory of God, so that the Son of God may be glorified through it." (ESV)*

Jesus knew that Lazarus was about to die. Jesus was not lying or intentionally misleading his disciples. Jesus' intent can be understood in the phrase "does not lead to death."

Ultimately, this will not end in death, as Jesus will demonstrate when he gets to Lazarus's hometown of Bethany. There is something to be aware of at this point in Jesus' ministry. Jesus is either partially or totally sovereign. His close relationship with God his Father enables him to either foresee or even possibly orchestrate this event. But, to be sure, the events in this chapter are totally orchestrated by God to bring clarity as to Jesus' purpose and who he is.

Everything in John's gospel thus far has been preparing us for the clarifying moment that will occur in the next few verses.

Your Brother Will Rise Again

Jesus and his disciples arrive in Bethany four days after Lazarus has died. As they approach Lazarus' home, Martha (Lazarus's sister) runs out to meet Jesus. Martha is broken hearted, and she pours out her heart to Jesus about her beloved brother, Lazarus. She is confident that if Jesus had been there, he could have cured Lazarus and prevented him from dying. She cannot understand why Jesus did not come to his rescue.

After all, they had sent word to Jesus that Lazarus was sick. In the midst of her devastating disappointment and confusion, she still reaches out to Jesus for some type of hope, even though she is not sure what to hope for. She does not understand why Lazarus had to die. In spite of her despair and confusion, she lets Jesus know that she still believes in him.

In this very intimate conversation between Jesus and Martha, John provides the final clarification on *zoe*. If you blink, you will miss the whole thing. But, it is the skilled and inspired hand of the author (John) who places this clarifying statement not in the midst of a large group of half-hearted believers, curious onlookers or murderous critics . . .

But, rather, it is a soft-spoken statement made by Jesus as he tenderly lifts the fallen face of one who has wholeheartedly believed in him, followed him, and served him. Looking directly into the eyes of this dear, broken-hearted sister, he whispers truth and hope to her.

Truth and hope that now resonate throughout the world and have done so for two millennia.

That is how life and death works though, isn't it? It is indeed a very personal thing. You may fear losing a dearly loved one or maybe even fear death for yourself. It is not the message that is spoken to crowds that will bring you comfort in the end. At the end, it is knowing that Jesus is looking into your eyes and speaks truth, hope, and love, that he will take you home to where you belong, in God's family.

John 11:17-32 *Now, when Jesus came, he found that Lazarus had already been in the tomb four days. Bethany was near Jerusalem, about two miles off, and many of the Jews had come to Martha and Mary to console them concerning their brother.*

So when Martha heard that Jesus was coming, she went and met him, but Mary remained seated in the house. Martha said to Jesus, "Lord, if you had been here, my brother would not have died. But, even now, I know that whatever you ask from God, God will give you."

Jesus said to her, "Your brother will rise again." Martha said to him, "I know that he will rise again in the resurrection on the last day." Jesus said to her, "I am the resurrection and the life. Whoever believes in me, though he dies, yet shall he live, and everyone who lives and believes in me shall never die. Do you believe this?"

She said to him, "Yes, Lord; I believe that you are the Christ, the Son of God, who is coming into the world." When she had said this, she went and called her sister Mary, saying in private, "The Teacher is here and is calling for you." And when she heard it, she rose quickly and went to him. Now, Jesus had not yet come into the village, but was still in the place where Martha had met him.

When the Jews, who were with her in the house consoling her, saw Mary rise quickly and go out, they followed her, supposing that she was going to the tomb to weep there.

Now, when Mary came to where Jesus was and saw him, she fell at his feet, saying to him, "Lord, if you had been here, my brother would not have died." (ESV)

Taking a Closer Look

John 11:21-22 *Martha said to Jesus, "Lord, if you had been here, my brother would not have died. But, even now, I know that whatever you ask from God, God will give you." (ESV)*

Martha holds on to what she knows from the things she has seen Jesus do, as well as what she has heard him teach. She has no doubt that he is the Messiah and the son of God and that God will do whatever he asks. While she is confessing her unwavering faith in Jesus, she appears, at the same time, to hint that she knows that Jesus can raise her brother from the dead.

John 11:23-24 *Jesus said to her, "Your brother will rise again." Martha said to him, "I know that he will rise again in the resurrection on the last day." (ESV)*

Jesus assures her that her brother will rise again. Martha expresses that she understands Jesus' teachings about Eternal Life. She also knows her brother was a believer, which explains her confidence of his resurrection at the last day. Martha has obviously been following Jesus' teachings for a long time and has a good understanding of his teachings on *zoe*, including the resurrection.

Jesus' Reply to Martha

Jesus' next statement is the crux of this chapter and the key point that this sovereign act was meant to so powerfully illustrate. Jesus now responds to Martha's statement, where she says that she knows that her brother will rise again in the resurrection at the last day.

Jesus' response to Martha incorporates another of his "I Am" statements. This statement summarizes Jesus primary purpose and God's solution to the problem of death. This the most purposeful verse in the gospel according to John.

Indeed, this statement is the fulfillment of the whole Bible.

I Am the Resurrection and the Zoe

"I Am" Statement 5

---

*John 11:25-26 Jesus said to her, "I am the **resurrection** and the life (zoe). Whoever believes in me, though he dies, yet shall he live, and everyone who lives and believes in me shall never die. Do you believe this?" (ESV)*

Jesus is making a factual statement to reassure Martha, clarifying who he is and helping her understand what is about to happen.

We are on the cusp of getting the final clarification we have been waiting for. However, for most of us at this point in our journey, even though this understanding can be life changing, this is just academic knowledge.

But, for Martha and Lazarus, this is very personal—the most powerful moment in their lives.

I Am the Resurrection and the *Zoe*

> John 11:25 Jesus said to her, "I am the **resurrection** and the **life (zoe)**. (ESV)

Jesus replies to Martha's statement that she knows Lazarus will rise again in the resurrection on the last day. It is like Jesus is holding her gaze, looking into her eyes, and gently speaking the following:

"Martha, do you realize who you are talking to? **I am the resurrection you speak of. I am the *zoe*, which makes resurrection possible**. You are talking to the one individual in the universe that can make resurrection happen." Jesus clarifies, "I am Lazarus's resurrection, and it is through me and because of the *zoe* that I give that Lazarus will rise again."

Jesus gives believers life (*zoe*) via the impartation of the indwelling of the Holy Spirit into the psuche of the believer in order that they might be resurrected to eternal life (*zoe*).

So, when Jesus says "I am the resurrection and the *zoe*," he is being profoundly accurate.

Whoever Believes, Though He Dies, Yet Shall He Live

> John 11:25-26 Jesus said to her, "I am the resurrection and the life (zoe). Whoever believes in me, though he dies, yet shall he live . . ." (ESV)

While Jesus comforts and encourages Martha, he also clarifies her understanding. The clarification is that any person who believes in Jesus has *zoe*. It is this simple truth that drives everything else in these verses. Since Lazarus was a believer, Martha can have confidence that even though Lazarus has died, he will live (the root word here is *zoe*).

Conclusion: The one who believes in Jesus as the Messiah, the Son of God, can in confidence know that even if they die a bodily death they will live. That is, they will rise againfrom the dead.

> Anyone who believes in Jesus as the Messiah, the Son of God, can confidently know that even if they die a bodily death they will live (root zoe). That is, they will rise again from the dead.

What better way to drive this point home than to raise Lazarus from the dead? We are about to witness Jesus finally demonstrating who he is and his authority to make the claims he has been making all through the gospel according to John.

Note: *We are about to look at the third and final statement that Jesus makes in these two verses. However, the next statement will be the most difficult that we have encountered thus far in our study. In most English translations, the next verse appears to actually contradict what Jesus just said in the previous sentence.*

Yet, it is this last component of these two verses that is the culmination of all that John has been carefully preparing us for: the ultimate purpose of Jesus and zoe.

Whoever Lives (*Zoe*) and Believes in Me Shall Never Die

This last sentence of Jesus' reply to Martha is the final clarification that John provides for us into the purpose of *zoe*. This is the pinnacle that the gospel according to John has been leading us to.

Jesus defines this vital truth of life (*zoe*) here:

> **John 11:26** . . . *and everyone who lives [root word is zoe] and believes in me* **shall never die.** *(ESV)*

Jesus begins this sentence by summarizing what he said in the previous sentence. He is doing this for emphasis and to clarify the resulting effect of the truth in the previous sentence. In other words, Jesus is now identifying the person from the previous sentence as "the person who lives (that has zoe abiding with them) and believes".

Next he makes the profound statement about the result that "this person who lives and believes" can and should confidently expect. This is the final clarifying point that we have been looking for.

Jesus is saying that this person **shall never die**.

A perspective from the the LEB

Earlier in this book when we looked at the verse from John 8:51, we took note of the English translation from the Lexham English Bible. I'd like to point out this version again, this time with John 11:25-26

*John 11:25-26 Jesus said to her, "I am the resurrection and the life. The one who believes in me, even if he dies, will live, 26 and everyone who lives and believes in me **will never die forever**. (LEB)*

I like this English translation better, but verse 26 could be worded a bit differently in my opinion. "Will never die forever" does a better job of conveying what Jesus actually said here, but is still hard to understand. Could there be a clearer way to translate this sentence that accurately reflects what Jesus is intently teaching here?

Does it really say "Shall Never Die?"

Before we move on, we need to take one more look at 11:25-26, this time analyzing the Greek text (refer to the Greek text on the next page).

From the Greek text on the following page, we can see that 11:25 might be read as:

John 11:25 I am the resurrection and the zoe. The one believing into me, even if ever he may be dying, he shall be living.

This makes complete sense with what we now know about *zoe*. Jesus says this as a prelude to what he is about to demonstrate to those who are present. Lazarus has died. Jesus is going to prove that he is indeed the resurrection and the *zoe* by resurrecting Lazarus. He is going to show them that he has power over death.

Now, to verse 26. If you remember from John 8, whenever the English translation reads "never die," it doesn't exactly state that in the original Greek. The Greek words that Jesus uses here are almost identical to the wording he used in John 8.

Carefully read the word-for-word translation that is shown below the Greek words for John 11:25-26 in the screen capture on the following page.

25 Jesus said unto her, I am the resurrection, and the life: he that believeth in me, though he were dead, yet shall he live:

26 And whosoever liveth and believeth in me shall never die. Believest thou this?

11:25

Greek	Translit	Strong's	Parsing	Gloss
EITEN	eipen	G2036	vi 2Aor Act 3 Sg	said
AYTH	autE	G846	pp Dat Sg f	to-her
O	ho	G3588	t_ Nom Sg m	THE
IHCOYC	iEsous	G2424	n_ Nom Sg m	JESUS
ECO	egO	G1473	pp 1 Nom Sg	I
EIMI	eimi	G1510	vi Pres vxx 1 Sg	AM
H	hE	G3588	t_ Nom Sg f	THE
ANACTACIC	anastasis	G386	n_ Nom Sg f	UP-STANDing / resurrection
KAI	kai	G2532	Conj	AND
H	hE	G3588	t_ Nom Sg f	THE
ZOH	zOE	G2222	n_ Nom Sg f	LIFE
O	ho	G3588	t_ Nom Sg m	THE
PICTEYON	pisteuOn	G4100	vp Pres Act Nom Sg m	one-BELIEVING / one-believing
EIC	eis	G1519	Prep	INTO
EME	eme	G1691	pp 1 Acc Sg	ME
KAN	kan	G2579	Cond Con	AND-[IF]-EVER / even-if-ever
APOOANH	apothanE	G599	vs 2Aor Act 3 Sg	he-MAY-BE-FROM-DYING / he-may-be-dying
ZHCETAI	zEsetai	G2198	vi Fut midD 3 Sg	SHALL-BE-LIVING

11:26

Greek	Translit	Strong's	Parsing	Gloss
KAI	kai	G2532	Conj	AND
PAC	pas	G3956	a_ Nom Sg m	EVERY
O	ho	G3588	t_ Nom Sg m	THE
ZON	zOn	G2198	vp Pres Act Nom Sg m	one-LIVING / one-living
KAI	kai	G2532	Conj	AND
PICTEYON	pisteuOn	G4100	vp Pres Act Nom Sg m	BELIEVING
EIC	eis	G1519	Prep	INTO
EME	eme	G1691	pp 1 Acc Sg	ME
OY	ou	G3756	Part Neg	NOT
MH	mE	G3361	Part Neg	NO
APOOANH	apothanE	G599	vs 2Aor Act 3 Sg	MAY-BE-FROM-DYING / may-be-dying
EIC	eis	G1519	Prep	INTO
TON	ton	G3588	t_ Acc Sg m	THE
AIONA	aiOna	G165	n_ Acc Sg m	eon
PICTEYEIC	pisteueis	G4100	vi Pres Act 2 Sg	YOU-ARE-BELIEVING
TOYTO	touto	G5124	pd Acc Sg n	this

If you assemble the words in 11:26, it will easily read as follows:

And every one living and believing into me, in no case may be dying into the eon.

I believe Jesus is merely clarifying his statement in 11:25 by further defining it. He is essentially saying that everyone who is a believer, thus having *zoe*, shall in no case remain dead into the eon.

This is a clear statement about **resurrection**.

> Jesus is stating that everyone who is a believer, thus having Zoe, shall in no case remain dead into the eon.
> This is a clear statement about **resurrection**.

We can be assured that if we are a believer we already have eternal *zoe* indwelling our *psuche*. This what Jesus is refering to by the phrase "he that lives and believes in me".

This fact guarantees that we will not **remain dead** into the eon. That is, Jesus assures us that he will resurrect us. We need have no fear of death, because we can rest assured he will raise us from the dead.

Taking another look at 11:26, let me ask you a few questions:

- Does this statement mean the same thing as "never die?"
- Does "never die" actually make any sense here whatsoever?
- In 11:25, Jesus said, "Even though a person dies, yet shall they live." He just said that people do indeed die. Would he in the next sentence say that a person will never die?

One other thing, the word "never" fails to deliver the emphatic context that Jesus uses when he makes this statement using the two Greek words "ou me", which are better translated as "in no case" or as "in no way possible".

Jesus uses this expression "ou me" to double down on what he just said in verse 25, by saying that there is no way possible that the person who lives (zoe) and believes in me, will be experiencing death into the eon. (Eternal death).

*And every one living and believing into me, **in no case** may be dying into the eon.*

In my opinion these two sentences are saying the following:

25 *-Jesus replied to Martha, "I am the resurrection and the zoe. The one who believes in me, even if he dies, he shall **live** (root word is zoe)*

Note: *Due to the root word here being zoe, Jesus is either:*

1- Making a resurrection statement by saying that this person will live again via zoe, (thus tying this sentence back to his statement that he is the resurrection and the zoe)

2- or Jesus could be saying that even though this person dies, he would in fact have zoe already abiding in him, so he is in effect still alive, his psuche being preserved by zoe. This would hold true whether you hold to "unconscious soul sleep" or believe the person is conscious in Hades.

26 *And everyone who is believing in me, thus having zoe, will in no way remain dead into the eon."*

In other words, Jesus is promising their resurrection!

Keep in mind, that the main focal point of this chapter is Jesus statement, "I am the Resurrection and the zoe."

Indeed these two verses are the crux of the gospel of John. We have just reached the pinnacle of the gospel of John, that John has been carefully revealing to us. Yet in most English translations this significance is totally obscured.

> Jesus replied to Martha, "I am the **Resurrection** and the **Zoe**. The one who believes in me, even if he dies, he shall be living (via Zoe). And everyone who is living (via Zoe) and believing in me, will in no way remain dead (be dying) into the eon

Main Emphasis of John 11

No matter the nuance of the interpretation of these two verses, the bottom line of John 11 can be summarized by the following points:

➤ He who believes in Jesus, even though he dies, already has the gift of *Zoe*. They previously crossed over from a status of death to zoe at the time of their belief.

➤ So, even though they may be dying a physical death now, they can be assured they will live (root zoe).

➤ The second verse clarifies that those who hold this status of *Zoe* can rest assured that they will not be experiencing death into the eon. (In other words, they are not going to remain dead, they will be resurrected).

➤ Jesus is guaranteeing the resurrection from the dead for all believers.

If you attempt to explain the phrase "shall never die" as some bizarre description of eternal torment in Hell, you have not only missed the epoch conclusion to Jesus' teaching on Resurrection and *Zoe*; you have also distorted his message into something tragically different and false.

Simple, Wonderful News

The power of this truth lies in its simplicity to understand and the reality of its result. In our weakness to do anything about our sentence of death, this is the wonderful news we have been looking for all of our life (*psuche*).

Jesus Raises Lazarus from the Dead

John 11:33-44 When Jesus saw her weeping, and the Jews who had come with her also weeping, he was deeply moved in his spirit and greatly troubled. And he said, "Where have you laid him?" They said to him, "Lord, come and see." Jesus wept. So the Jews said, "See how he loved him!"

But some of them said, "Could not he who opened the eyes of the blind man also have kept this man from dying?" Then Jesus, deeply moved again, came to the tomb. It was a cave, and a stone lay against it. Jesus said, "Take away the stone." Martha, the sister of the dead man, said to him, "Lord, by this time there will be an odor, for he has been dead four days." Jesus said to her, "Did I not tell you that if you believed you would see the glory of God?"

So they took away the stone. And Jesus lifted up his eyes and said, "Father, I thank you that you have heard me. I knew that you always hear me, but I said this on account of the people standing around, that they may believe that you sent me." When he had said these things, he cried out with a loud voice, "Lazarus, come out." The man who had died came out, his hands and feet bound with linen strips, and his face wrapped with a cloth. Jesus said to them, "Unbind him, and let him go." (ESV)

Taking a Closer Look

John 11:38-39 Then Jesus, deeply moved again, came to the tomb. It was a cave, and a stone lay against it. Jesus said, "Take away the stone." Martha, the sister of the dead man, said to him, "Lord, by this time there will be an odor, for he has been dead four days." (ESV)

What better way to prove that you are indeed the source of resurrection and life than to raise someone from the dead in the midst of a large group of people who knew this dead person and have been there several days mourning for him and supporting the family? This validates all that Jesus has taught throughout the gospel according to John. Raising Lazarus from the dead confirms **Jesus' authority as God's son to give *zoe*** to those who believe and to resurrect them from death.

You see, it is not the first death that Jesus intends to save us from. It is the second death. We are resurrected to eternal life (*zoe*). Remember that Jesus told his disciples earlier in this chapter that this would not "end" in Lazarus's death, even though Jesus knew Lazarus was already dead.

It is this **end** that we must all comes to grips with. Jesus does not intend to let any of us "end" in death. But, the choice is ours. We can receive his life (*zoe*) and preserve our *psuche* by believing in the truth about who he is, and what he has done for us . . .

Or, we can face the certainty of the perishing of our *psuche*.

Holding to Truth, Even When Hurt and Confused

Notice Martha's reply when Jesus asks her if she believes his statement about death and the resurrection and the life (*zoe*).

> *John 11:25-27 Jesus said to her, "I am the resurrection and the **life (zoe)**. Whoever believes in me, though he die, yet shall he live, and everyone who lives and believes in me shall never die. Do you believe this?" She said to him, "Yes, Lord; I believe that you are the Christ, the Son of God, who is coming into the world." (ESV)*

In the midst of Lazarus's death and Jesus' delay in coming, Martha is distressed, confused, disappointed, and hurt. As she looks to Jesus, her heart is filled with pain and a deep question: "Why did Lazarus have to die?" She believed in Jesus deeply; she trusted him. Now, she questions in her heart: Can she still trust him?

Her answer is profound.

John 11:27 She said to him, "Yes, Lord; I believe that you are the Christ, the Son of God, who is coming into the world." (ESV)

Her belief held fast, even though she did not understand all that was going on. Her statement was one of conviction. "No matter what, I am holding on to my belief that you are the Messiah, the one who is promised to come into the world. I don't understand what you are doing right now, but I believe you are in control. I don't understand why things are going the way they are, but I will hold onto you."

Jesus says that if we believe, we will see the glory of God. Faith often comes before complete understanding. In fact, sometimes we may never get the full understanding that we seek in this lifetime. Faith comes first. Holding on to the dear truth that we believe, even in spite of those things that cause us to doubt and question, is genuine faith. We will see Jesus' glory, sometimes dimly, but just enough to keep us going. Then, someday, we will see him in all his glory.

The Resurrection of Lazarus

John 11:41-42 So they took away the stone. And Jesus lifted up his eyes and said, "Father, I thank you that you have heard me. I knew that you always hear me, but I said this on account of the people standing around, that they may believe that you sent me." (ESV)

This resurrection of Lazarus was orchestrated by God the Father and Jesus his son. The purpose of the resurrection of Lazarus was to punctuate Jesus' teaching about life (*zoe*) and death by demonstrating his authority and power over death. It was done for the benefit of the people who were there, so that any doubts as to Jesus' credibility were removed. In fact, the word of Lazarus's resurrection spread like wildfire and caused many to believe in Jesus.

For this reason, the Pharisees sought not only to kill Jesus but Lazarus as well. See the verses below from John 12:

> **John 12:9-11** *When the large crowd of the Jews learned that Jesus was there, they came, not only on account of him but also to see Lazarus, whom he had raised from the dead. So the chief priests made plans to put Lazarus to death as well, because on account of him many of the Jews were going away and believing in Jesus. (ESV)*

30

Four Perspectives from John 11

Perspective 1

Mary and Martha are like you and me. If you live long enough on this earth, you will experience what Mary and Martha did when they saw their beloved brother dying. There will come a time, if there hasn't already, when you will struggle with the fact that someone you love is dying, and there doesn't seem to be anything you can do about it. The doctors have done all they can do, and you helplessly watch your loved one edge closer and closer to death. You cry out to God and plead with him to intervene.

You may ask him, "Why won't you help my loved one? They are a good person, and they deserve to be saved from this!"

We are going to ask for healing, and many, many times it is not going to come. We are going to question his love for us; we are going to cry out with the question, "Why didn't you come? You could have healed my brother if you had been here. But, even so, Lord, I know that he will be raised."

Perspective 2

Then, there is Lazarus. Whether or not you live long enough to see a loved one unexpectedly die, you will come to terms at some point with your own mortality. Lazarus himself must have wondered . . . will Jesus come to my aid? Will he get here in time?

Will he heal me? Does he care?

Perspective 3

Lastly, there is the crowd. They said, "Could not he who opened the eyes of the blind man have kept this man from dying?"

How many times have I said something just like this? I hear a news story about the child who ran out into the street in the path of an oncoming car, or I hear about the child who died from leukemia. For me, it is the children who die unexpectedly and what seems to me needlessly that cause me to ask, "Why, Father? Why did this child have to die, or suffer? Why? Where are you? Where were you? You are the one-of-miracles. Could you not have saved this little one from dying? From suffering? Could you not have cured them? Could you not have timed that differently, where they ran out into the street when no car was there?"

These questions are painful, and there are no easy answers. We see Jesus' response here, and there is undeniable comfort in his words and the results. But, these are still painful questions, and at times we think we only hear **silence**. But, Jesus is still there, and our *psuche* is in his hands.

Jesus himself asked this question in his last breaths upon the cross:

> **Matt. 27:45-46** *Now, from the sixth hour, there was darkness over all the land until the ninth hour. And about the ninth hour, Jesus cried out with a loud voice, saying, "Eli, Eli, lema sabachthani?"—that is, "My God, my God, why have you forsaken me?" (ESV)*

For three hours, Jesus labored in excruciating pain. He was exhausted, beaten, and pierced. With every breath, he caused himself immense pain by straining against the large spikes in his wrists and feet. He knew death was coming. He knew what was happening, and yet, there was a struggle within. He was literally and figuratively surrounded by darkness and evil. Where was his comforter; where was the touch that he needed then?

Was Jesus comforted by this question? Was God there for him? Quite frankly, no, God the Father was not there. It was God's intention for Jesus to die in this way, separated from God the

Father. It was God's purpose for Jesus to pay the death penalty that you and I are under. Jesus took our place.

God intentionally abandoned his own son at this moment; he turned his back on Jesus, symbolized by the darkness over all the land. He did not come to Jesus' rescue at that moment, any more than Jesus came to Lazarus's rescue when he was dying from the serious illness.

But, It is the End That Matters

Is this always going to be a comfort, an assurance? No, not necessarily. But, it is something that we can count on, just as Mary did in her own hurting and confusion. Mary held on to Jesus' words. **She held on to those things that she counted as fact about him**.

Perspective 4

Of the twelve apostles that accompanied Jesus throughout his ministry, ten of them willingly gave their lives to share Jesus' message with the nations. Over the next few decades, these men would be killed for continuing to share the message that Jesus died, was resurrected, and gives eternal *zoe*.

At any point, any one of them could have recanted their message, gone back home, and lived a normal existence.

Do you think they would have done this for someone they considered a lunatic? Or fraud? No, of course not. They continued with teaching the message of Jesus because they knew his teaching well and were witnesses of these things, including Lazarus's resurrection and, later, Jesus' own resurrection.

When you are confident that your God lives within you and will resurrect your *psuche* at the appointed day, you can face whatever end is in store for you. One of the last things that Jesus said to his apostles before he was crucified is recorded in John 16:33.

> **John 16:33** *"I have said these things to you, that in me you may have peace. In the world you will have tribulation. But, take heart; I have overcome the world." (ESV)*

31

Contrasting Zoe and Psuche

Contrasting Psuche and Zoe – Seeing the Clear Difference

I want to insert this small section here at the risk of appearing redundant, just to reiterate the significant difference that exists in Jesus' teachings (and the rest of the New Testament as well) with regard to psuche and zoe. Failing to recognize this important difference will impair your ability (practically blinding you) to understand the message of the gospels and the rest of the Bible.

If you miss this, you will miss the crescendo that is taking place in John 10 and 11. If you miss John 10 and 11, you might as well skip the whole book of John.

Read carefully below where Jesus states why he has come, and what he intends to do for his sheep. Both involve "life", but in sharply different ways, that are totally invisible in current English bibles.

> Read carefully below where Jesus states why he has come, and what he intends to do for his sheep. Both involve "**Life**", but in sharply different ways, that are **invisible** in current English bibles.

If you understand what Jesus is saying in these two verses, you will see the crux of the Bible. The concept unfolding in these next two verses is not isolated to these two verses. This concept involving psuche and zoe is prolific throughout the New Testament as already demonstrated in this book. But for this moment, we are focusing on these two verses because they so concisely explain Jesus' message and purpose.

We must see the original Greek words in order to understand how Jesus uses them (defines them) in order to accurately grasp this.

In John 10:10 we have already seen where Jesus states his purpose:

> *John 10:10 ... I came that they may have **life (zoe)** and have it abundantly. (ESV)*

Then in the very same breath Jesus says the following:

> *John 10:11 "I am the good shepherd. The good shepherd lays down his **life (psuche)** for the sheep. (ESV)*

Can you see the difference? ...and the powerful contrast?

First, Jesus has come to give his sheep Zoe!

This is because his sheep don't already have zoe. His sheep by their very nature are psuche, and are destined to die. He has come to give them eternal zoe, thus saving their psuche, instead of allowing Satan to kill and destroy them.

> Jesus has come to give his sheep Zoe!
> This is because his sheep don't have Zoe.
> His sheep by their very nature are psuche, and are destined to die if Jesus does not save them

Jesus reiterates this in John 10:28.

> *I give them (my sheep) eternal **life (zoe)**, and they will never **perish (appolumi)**, and no one (refering to Satan, who has come to kill and destroy) will snatch them out of my hand. (ESV)*

Next, Jesus say that he will lay down his psuche

Next notice what Jesus intends to do. He says the good shepherd (again powerfully alluding to himself) will lay down his psuche. **Not his zoe, but his psuche!** Jesus tells them he is going to die, following the plan given to him by the Father. He will obediently follow this plan to the cross, allowing himself to be killed on the cross.

Jesus' psuche will die. If you miss this, you miss the gospel.

> Notice what Jesus intends to do.
> He says the good shepherd
> will lay down his psuche.
> **Not his zoe, but his psuche!**
> Jesus is predicting his death

Why did Jesus have to die?

Mankind's psuche is in a status of death, and has been since Adam and Eve were cast out of the Garden of Eden, thus removing their from access to the Tree of Life.

Jesus came to save man, by sacrificing his own psuche, as a substitute for ours. This is exactly what he accomplished in his death upon the cross, he gave his psuche for ours. Thereby becoming a proxy for our own death sentence.

Notice what Jesus says about his psuche in John 10:18. This is a clarification by Jesus of what he has been talking about in this chapter.

> **John 10:18** *No one takes it (his psuche) from me, but I lay it down of my own accord. I have authority to lay it down, and I have authority to take it up again. This charge I have received from my Father. (ESV)*

Jesus knew he was going to die. But notice the caveat that he provides. He has the authority to take it up again.

What happened to Jesus when he died?

We will see later in the chapter on "What is Hades?," that God the Father would not abandon Jesus' *psuche* to Hades. In other words, God the Father is going to raise Jesus from the dead. Implicit in all of this, is that *zoe* that will ultimately resurrect Jesus from the dead as *zoe* is inherent within Jesus. God, the Father, will see to it that Jesus' *psuche* will live again.

Zoe does not die. *Zoe* is the "life as God has it" that saves man's *psuche* so that believers will ultimately live forever.

Jesus had to be killed. His *psuche* did indeed die. This is very clear. It is also just as clear, that his *pusche* was raised from the dead. That is why he was the perfect sacrifice. There is no one else who could be a victor over death, other than the very one known as the source of *zoe*.

Jesus predicts his death here in John 10. Later in Acts chapter 2, Peter explains that God did not leave Jesus' *psuche* in Hades (the place of the dead).

Jesus took the death sentence that has reigned over all mankind, thus redeeming all who will believe on him, saving them from this certain impending fate of death into the ages.

How did God raise Jesus from the dead? The verse below indicates it was the Spirit of God, (also called the Spirit of Christ) that raised Jesus from the dead.

Remember, Jesus had zoe in himself. Perhaps it was this inherent zoe within Jesus that somehow raised his psuche. (Remember he said he had the authority to take up his psuche again).

The Holy Spirit revitalized Jesus's psuche just as the Holy Spirit will bestow immortality (via zoe) to human believers on their day of resurrection. But without question, the immortal nature of zoe (life as God has it), which only comes from the indwelling Spirit of God, was instrumental in raising Jesus' psuche from the dead.

> *Rom. 8:9-11 But you are not in the flesh but in the **Spirit**, if indeed the **Spirit of God lives in you**. But if anyone does not have the **Spirit of Christ**, this person does not belong to him. **But if Christ is in you, the body is dead because of sin, but the spirit is life (zoe)** because of righteousness. And if the **Spirit** of the one who raised Jesus from the dead lives in you, the one who raised Christ Jesus from the dead **will also make alive (root is zoe) your mortal bodies** through **his Spirit who lives in you**. (LEB)*

Jesus' Resurrection is our Assurance

The clarity that this provides us with, is paramount.

Jesus came to save us from the second death, i.e., experiencing death unto the ages. Jesus death and resurrection, is the only solution to our status of death that we currently live under. His resurrection, is our assurance of our own resurrection.

We are clearly already in a state of death, and are clearly going to die. But Jesus assures believers that even though they may die an earthly death, they will live again. And that believers who currently live (being born again with the indwelling zoe), will in no way see death into the ages. That is, they can rest assured that in good time, Jesus will raise them from the dead, to live forever.

This clarity removes the confusion that surrounds the need and purpose for the death of Jesus

Life

Defined

32

Elaborating on *Zoe*

John 12

As we move into John 12, we now have a clear understanding of Jesus' teaching about life (*zoe*) and death. Now, we will look at some excerpts from the last few chapters of John, where Jesus continues teaching on *zoe*.

> *John 12:23-25 And Jesus answered them, "The hour has come for the Son of Man to be glorified. Truly, truly, I say to you, unless a grain of wheat falls into the earth and dies, it remains alone; but if it dies, it bears much fruit. Whoever loves his **life (psuche)** loses it, and whoever hates his **life (psuche)** in this world will keep it for **eternal life (zoe)." (ESV)*

Can you understand what Jesus is saying in the first paragraph above? Can you see how this makes sense with respect to *zoe*? Jesus is explaining the need for his death. He will resurrect from the dead because he has *zoe* within himself. Then, those who believe in him will have *zoe* (God's seed) given to them when they are born again, this time not of the flesh but of the Spirit of God.

In the second paragraph, Jesus emphasizes that the person who hates their *psuche* in this world will keep it for eternal *zoe*. Hating your own *psuche* is a way of saying that you are not seeking your own selfish, worldly desires and that you are not afraid of sacrificing your *psuche* if you are persecuted unto death. Your *psuche* will be preserved for eternal *zoe* by the fact that *zoe* indwells you, and Jesus will resurrect you for eternal *zoe*.

John 12:47-50 "*If anyone hears my words and does not keep them, I do not judge him; for I did not come to judge the world but to save the world. The one who rejects me and does not receive my words has a judge; the word that I have spoken will judge him on the last day. For I have not spoken on my own authority, but the Father who sent me has himself given me a commandment—what to say and what to speak. And I know that his commandment is* **eternal life (zoe)**." *(ESV)*

Jesus states his purpose here again but uses slightly different words. He did not come to judge the world. He came to save the world by giving believers eternal *zoe*. Whoever does not accept Jesus' words of salvation stands condemned.

Jesus explains that he followed his Father's commands in all that he has said and done. He knows the purpose of all that he has been commanded to say. His Father's commands show the way to eternal life.

I Am the Way, the Truth, and the Zoe.

"I Am" Statement 6

Here in John 14:6, we see another of Jesus' famous "I Am" statements. Jesus is spending his last evening with his disciples before he is crucified. The disciples are unaware that this is about to happen, as Jesus will not be betrayed until later in the evening. Jesus delivers his final teaching to his disciples in his last hours with them. He gives them words of direction and comfort that they will need to reflect on in the coming days, weeks, and years.

> **John 14:1-6** *"Let not your hearts be troubled. Believe in God; believe also in me. In my Father's house are many rooms. If it were not so, would I have told you that I go to prepare a place for you? And if I go and prepare a place for you, I will come again and will take you to myself, that where I am you may be also. And you know the way to where I am going."*
>
> *Thomas said to him, "Lord, we do not know where you are going. How can we know the way?"*
>
> *Jesus said to him, "I am the way, and the truth, and the **life (zoe)**. No one comes to the Father except through me." (ESV)*

Breaking This Down

➤ **Jesus is the only way** that God has provided for man to be saved from death and for man to be rejoined in fellowship with God for eternity.

➤ **Jesus is the truth.** That is, it is the truth about Jesus (who he is and his purpose) that one accepts to be saved. There is no other truth that will do this.

➤ **Finally, Jesus is the life (*Zoe*).** When someone believes in Jesus they cross over from death to *Zoe*. *Zoe* is deposited within the believer, bringing Eternal *Zoe* to that person's *psuche*. The believer is thus born again, a second time, this time by the Holy Spirit. The believer has literally become a child of the true God.

As Jesus continues encouraging his disciples on his last evening with them, he tells them about the Holy Spirit, which the Father will give to the disciples to indwell them. The terms Holy Spirit and Spirit of Christ (Jesus) are used interchangeably in the New Testament, and both refer to the Spirit of God.

> **John 14:15-17** *"If you love me, you will keep my commandments. And I will ask the Father, and he will give you another Helper, to be with you forever, even the Spirit of truth, whom the world cannot receive, because it neither sees him nor knows him. You know him, for he dwells with you and will be in you." (ESV)*

Notice that Jesus says the Spirit currently lives with them (through Jesus' presence) and will soon be in them (when Jesus bestows the Spirit upon them to indwell them). Jesus will do this after he is resurrected from the dead (this event is recorded in John 20:22). Jesus assures them that he will not leave them as orphans. This is only possible because of the indwelling presence that they will receive from him when he bestows the Spirit into them, which will remain with them when he leaves (dwelling within them).

> **John 14:17-19** *"You know him, for he dwells with you and will be in you. I will not leave you as orphans; I will come to you. Yet a little while and the world will see me no more, but you will see me. Because I live, you also will live." (ESV)*

Lastly, Jesus remarks to them that because he lives, they also will live. The root word to live is *zoe*. Only *zoe* would make sense here. Because *zoe* is an inherent part of who he is, Jesus is alive (immortal). Because Jesus has *zoe*, his disciples will also have *zoe*, since he gives this to them through the indwelling Spirit. Remember it is the Spirit of God that conveys *zoe*. The Holy Spirit is also called the Spirit of Christ and the Spirit of God. Notice that Jesus tells his disciples that, on the day that the Spirit is bestowed upon them, they will realize that Jesus is in the Father, that his followers are in him, and that he is in the disciples. This is through the indwelling Spirit.

> **John 14:19-20** *"Yet a little while and the world will see me no more, but you will see me. Because I live, you also will live. In that day, you will know that I am in my Father and you in me and I in you."* (ESV)

I Am the True Vine.

"I Am" Statement 7

In the following verses, Jesus uses the metaphor of himself as the vine and believers as the branches attached to the vine. The point he makes here is that the branches must "remain" in the vine. The branch is dependent upon the life flowing from the vine to keep it alive, help it grow, and ultimately bear fruit. Without this sustenance flowing from the vine, the branch has no hope of growing or bearing fruit.

> **John 15:1-8** *"I am the true vine, and my Father is the vinedresser. Every branch in me that does not bear fruit, he takes away, and every branch that does bear fruit, he prunes, that it may bear more fruit. Already, you are clean because of the word that I have spoken to you. Abide in me and I in you. As the branch cannot bear fruit by itself unless it abides in the vine, neither can you unless you abide in me.* **I am the vine; you are the branches**. *Whoever abides in me and I in him, he it is that bears much fruit, for, apart from me, you can do nothing. If anyone does not abide in me, he is thrown away like a branch and withers; and the branches are gathered, thrown into the fire, and burned. If you abide in me, and my words abide in you, ask whatever you wish, and it will be done for you. By this, my Father is glorified, that you bear much fruit and so prove to be my disciples." (ESV)*

The Greek word for "remain" is *meno*. This word means "abide, dwell within, or remain." It denotes one person dwelling or living within a home.

Jesus is instructing them to remain in his word, allowing his word to dwell in them. This metaphor is a perfect illustration of the life-giving sustenance of *zoe* within the believer. The very life (*zoe*) of the believer is dependent upon Jesus indwelling them through the

Holy Spirit. For the believer to grow and be fruitful, they must abide in his teachings, spending time each day mindfully meditating on the truth and application of God's word. This also entails prayer, watchful waiting, and dependence upon God. As we depend in this manner upon the "vine," The Holy Spirit, (Jesus' Spirit) flows into and through the believer, providing growth and fruit.

The final caveat that Jesus makes is that apart from him, we can do nothing. In other words, the branch cannot expect to survive, grow, and bear fruit unless it remains in the vine. We cannot resist sin or bear the fruit of the Spirit without continually abiding in Jesus.

Paul lists the fruit of the Spirit in Galatians 5:22-23.

> *Gal. 5:22-23 But, the fruit of the Spirit is love, joy, peace, patience, kindness, goodness, faithfulness, gentleness, self-control. (ESV)*

Neither can we experience Jesus' love or forgiveness unless we remain in him. All believers will continue to deal with their sinfulness to one degree or another. To the extent in which we abide in Jesus (keeping in step with the Spirit), we will be more like him. But even so, when we sin, it is this abiding that still provides comfort and assurance that we are still his, bathed in his forgiveness and never-ending love.

> *Gal. 5:25 If we live by the Spirit, let us also keep in step with the Spirit. (ESV)*

Lastly, Paul points out in 5:25 that it is by the Spirit that we have *zoe* (that we live, as opposed to remaining in a status of death). Since this is a fact, it behooves us to keep in step with the Spirit.

Have you ever tried dancing with a partner? Generally, one partner will lead, and the other has to keep in step with the one that is leading. That's what we do when we remain in Jesus. We are essentially keeping in step with the Spirit, allowing Jesus to lead us and staying in cadence with him.

It is never us leading; it is always us seeking to keep in step (cadence) with Jesus' gentle guidance through prayer and meditation on his word, seeking his guidance on how to apply it to our lives.

To the extent that we do this, we will bear his fruit. If we do not, then, at best, we will be a branch that survives but bears little or no fruit.

> Paul points out that since it is by the Spirit
> (God's Holy Spirit) that we live,
> then it behooves us to keep in step with this
> indwelling Holy Spirit that gave us Zoe.

John 16

John 16:7-15 *"But I tell you the truth, it is better for you that I go away. For if I do not go away, the Advocate will not come to you; but if I go, I will send him to you. And when he comes, he will convict the world concerning sin and concerning righteousness and concerning judgment: concerning sin, because they do not believe in me, and concerning righteousness, because I am going away to the Father and you will see me no more, and concerning judgment, because the ruler of this world has been condemned. I still have many things to say to you, but you are not able to bear them now. But when he—the Spirit of truth—comes, he will guide you into all the truth. For he will not speak from himself, but whatever he hears he will speak, and he will proclaim to you the things to come. He will glorify me, because he will take from what is mine and will proclaim it to you. Everything that the Father has is mine. For this reason I said that he takes from what is mine and will proclaim it to you. (LEB)*

While Jesus was with the apostles in person, the Holy Spirit was with the apostles (due to Jesus' presence). Jesus explains to them that when he leaves, he will send the Holy Spirit to them. The Holy Spirit will be his advocate, glorifying Jesus, and making known to them the truths that the Spirit receives from Jesus.

For all believers, the major acts of the Holy Spirit can be broken into at least three major components.

1. First, the Holy Spirit indwells the believer when they believe, giving them eternal *zoe*. This act bestows eternal life (*zoe*) in the believer, guaranteeing the preservation of their *psuche* for eternity (see also Ephesians 1:13-14).

   This first process is what Jesus referred to as being "born again" in John 3:16. This first process happens when a person believes wholeheartedly, as we discussed in the chapters on John 6 and John 8. The other components that I discuss below cannot happen if a person has not believed. Without being born again, a person will not have the Holy Spirit living within them.

2. Second, the Holy Spirit testifies to the mind of the believer the truth about who Jesus is, bringing light to the path of the believer in the midst of the world's darkness (he is Jesus' advocate). This also entails the Spirit bearing its fruit through the life of the believer. This fruit-bearing process is partially dependent upon the believer abiding in Christ (keeping in step with the spirit).

   To the extent that the believer abides, he/she will bear this fruit. The word for "abide" denotes a continuous presence of remaining or dwelling with another.

3. Unfortunately, believers will always be imperfect (we are weak) at this process. The Spirit will then also work within the *psuche* of the believer by introducing other people and events into the believer's life that will bring discipline, challenges, trials, and growth. This is lifelong process, which lasts until the earthly death of the believer. This is a wonderful aspect of the love, faithfulness, and grace of the Father, Son, and Holy Spirit working in perfect concert with one another for the good of the believer. See Romans 8:26-28 below.

   Rom. 8:26-28 Likewise, the Spirit helps us in our weakness. For we do not know what to pray for as we ought, but the Spirit himself intercedes for us with groanings too deep for words. And he who searches hearts knows what is the mind of the Spirit, because the Spirit intercedes for the saints according to the will of God. And we know that for those who love God all things work together for good, for those who are called according to his purpose. (ESV)

The advocate of Jesus is the Holy Spirit.

An advocate is one who speaks truth on behalf of someone else.

He will convince the world about sin, righteousness, and judgment.

The Spirit of truth will guide us into all truth.

He will only speak what he hears from Jesus.

He will glorify Jesus, as he makes **known** to us what he receives from Jesus.

He helps us in our weakness.

He intercedes for us according to the will of God the Father.

John 17

Jesus further defines "eternal *zoe*" as personally knowing the Father and the Son.

> **John 17:1-3** *Jesus said these things, and lifting up his eyes to heaven he said, "Father, the hour has come! Glorify your Son, in order that your Son may glorify you— just as you have given him authority over all flesh, in order that he would give **eternal life (zoe)** to them—everyone whom you have given him. Now this is **eternal life (zoe):** that they know you, the only true God, and Jesus Christ, whom you have sent. (LEB)*

In Jesus' prayer above, we can see that an intrinsic aspect of eternal *zoe* is knowing God on a personal, intimate basis. No longer will we rely on someone else to explain God to us, experiencing knowledge only through what we learn from others. Rather, we will come to know God experientially from his indwelling spirit within us.

It is through this indwelling spirit that we are brought into the family of fellowship with the Father, Son, and Spirit. We can personally know them, no longer just from the written pages or from the words of someone else.

In my opinion, this is the restoration of Eden. Man had an intimate knowledge of God while in the Garden of Eden. When Adam and Eve were driven out, this intimate level of knowledge was gone. It was God's intent to bring man back into this relationship.

In John 17:26, Jesus clarifies this process a bit more during his prayer. He has made the Father known to his apostles and will "continue" to make the Father known to them. This "continuing" process will come through the indwelling Spirit which is yet to come. Jesus makes it clear to the apostles that he is not leaving them as orphans but that he will come back to them via the indwelling spirit (this personal revelation of God has been emphasized by Jesus in the preceding chapters as well, as we have just seen in John 14:15-21 and John 16:7-14).

John 17:26 "I made known to them your name, and I will continue to make it known, that the love with which you have loved me may be in them, and I in them." (ESV)

Getting to know God on this personal level is lifelong process for the Christian. As we imperfectly listen and abide in Jesus, our intimate knowledge will wane and ebb. But, God is mercifully patient and loving and constantly woos us to be ever closer to him, if we but take the time to be still, abide, listen, and rest in Jesus.

John 20

Near the end of his gospel, John summarizes his intent for writing this narrative about Jesus. His heart's desire was that his readers might believe that Jesus is the Messiah, the Son of God, and that by believing that they might receive *zoe* though Jesus.

There is no other way to receive Eternal Life except through Jesus.

*John 20:30-31 Now, Jesus did many other signs in the presence of the disciples, which are not written in this book; but these are written so that you may believe that Jesus is the Christ, the Son of God, and that by believing you may have **life (zoe)** in his name. (ESV)*

33

Tying Zoe and Immortality Together

In Part Two, we have clearly seen Jesus explain and demonstrate the following connections between *zoe* and immortality:

> **John 1:4** *In him was **life (zoe)**, and the **life (zoe)** was the light of men. (ESV)*

Jesus has *zoe* (life) in himself.

> **John 5:24** *"Truly, truly, I say to you, whoever hears my word and believes him who sent me has **eternal life (zoe)**. He does not come into judgment but has passed from death to **life (zoe)**." (ESV)*

- Man's initial status is death.

- A believer crosses over from this penalty of death into *zoe*.

- From this, we can deduce that man does not have *zoe* in and of himself. Man is mortal and faces certain everlasting death.

> **John 5:26** *"For as the Father has **life (zoe)** in himself, so he has granted the Son also to have **life (zoe)** in himself." (ESV)*

Zoe is defined as "life like God has it." An inherent aspect of *zoe* is that it is immortal. Jesus also has this *zoe* as an inherent part of himself.

*John 3:16 For God so loved the world that he gave his only Son, that whoever believes in him should not **perish** but have **eternal life (zoe)**. (ESV)*

- A person is born again, when they believe. This second birth is not of the flesh but of God's Holy Spirit, making that person a child of God. They now have indwelling *zoe*.
- This eternal life (*zoe*) prevents the *psuche* from perishing (dying forever).

*John 6:63 "It is the Spirit who gives **life (zoe)**; the flesh is no help at all. The words that I have spoken to you are Spirit and **life (zoe)**." (ESV)*

It is the Holy Spirit that conveys *zoe*. This gift of eternal *zoe* takes place when someone believes in Jesus.

John 8:24 "I told you that you would die in your sins, for unless you believe that I am he you will die in your sins." (ESV)

If a person does not believe they will die in their sins (i.e., they will remain under the status [or sentence] of death).

Note: I am using my paraphrase (below) of John 11:25-27 (see my notes on John 11).

> *John 11:25-27 Jesus said to her, "I am the resurrection and the **life (zoe)**. The one who believes in me shall **live (zoe)**, even though they may be dying; and whoever **lives (zoe)** by believing in me will by no means die into the ages." (ESV)*

Immortality means that a person is not going to observe death into the ages. This is only possible because of the life-giving Holy Spirit that conveys *zoe* (*Zoe* is immortal by its very nature, as defined by the gospel according to John).

> *2 Tim. 1:10 And which now has been manifested through the appearing of our Savior Christ Jesus, who abolished death and brought **life (zoe)** and immortality to light through the gospel . . . (ESV)*

Paul summarizes this process in 1 Timothy 1:10:

- Jesus abolished death.
- Jesus brought *zoe* and immortality to light through the message of the gospel. Notice the link between *zoe* and immortality.
- Immortality is only possible via the gift of eternal *zoe*.

> Immortality is only possible because of the gift of Eternal Zoe (Zoe is immortal by its very nature). It is the Holy Spirit that conveys Zoe, that indwells a person receives when they are born again.

Life
Defined

34

The Three Stages of *Zoe*

I've heard some people say that a *psuche* cannot enter life until they are resurrected. I disagree. However, I do agree that the believer's *psuche* will not see the **final stage** of *zoe* (Stage Three) until they are resurrected with an imperishable, immortal body.

The concept of stages is not delineated in the Bible. I am merely using the idea of stages, to help describe the process of *zoe* within the believer.

Stage One

A believer's *psuche* enters life (*zoe*) at the time of their belief. One major aspect of *zoe* is its immortal (eternal) nature. Their *psuche* has been born again of the "*zoe*-giving" Holy Spirit and has already become a child of God. They have already crossed over from death to *zoe*. They are partakers of the divine nature (i.e., they have the gift of *zoe* dwelling within them.)

> *Matt. 18:8-9 And if your hand or your foot causes you to sin, cut it off and throw it from you! It is better for you to enter into **life (zoe)** crippled or lame than, having two hands or two feet, to be thrown into the eternal fire! And if your eye causes you to sin, tear it out and throw it from you! It is better for you to enter into **life (zoe)** one-eyed than, having two eyes, to be thrown into fiery hell! (LEB)*

When Jesus is speaking of entering **life (*zoe*)**, it is in this present age. This takes place at the instant a person wholeheartedly believes. Think of this as the first of three stages of the purpose of *zoe*.

*Eph. 2:1-5 And you, although you **were dead in your trespasses and sins**, in which you formerly walked according to the course of this world, according to the ruler of the authority of the air, the spirit now working in the sons of disobedience, among whom also we all formerly lived in the desires of our flesh, doing the will of the flesh and of the mind, and we were children of wrath by nature, as also the rest of them were. But God, being rich in mercy, because of his great love with which he loved us, and **we being dead in trespasses, he made us alive together with Christ** (by grace you are saved). (LEB)*

Note: It is zoe that makes a person's psuche alive with Christ.

In Stage One, God makes the believer alive with Christ. The believer (even though they were dead in their trespasses) crosses over from death to *zoe*.

A believing *psuche* enters eternal life (*zoe*) at the moment of their belief. At that point *zoe* indwells the *psuche* via the Holy Spirit. At this point of belief, the person's *psuche* is made alive (*zoe* root) with Christ. A person's *psuche* is saved and preserved by *zoe*.

The believer is already participating in immortality because their status has changed from death to *zoe*. They are no longer mortals; they become immortal as children of God. The final state (Stage Three) of this immortality will not appear until they have exchanged their mortal bodies for immortal. But, be assured of this, they have already entered **life (zoe)**.

*Note: Just to get rid of any confusion, a person's psuche before belief and their psuche after belief is the **same** psuche. The only difference is that upon saving belief, their psuche is indwelled by the Spirit of God, conveying zoe into their psuche. Their psuche has passed from death, into zoe (see John 5). Their psuche now has a dual nature: one that is human and one that has become an immortal child of God, participating in God's divine nature.*

248

Stage Two

During a believer's earthly existence, they are still stuck in this world, so to speak, with their mortal bodies, their fleshly desires, and the constant daily tug of war with sin. But, they have already entered life (*zoe*).

The believer's ability to bear the fruit of the Spirit during this time is dependent upon the believer keeping in step with the Spirit (this also known as abiding in Christ). It is living within the context of depending upon the *zoe* that is within them, which nurtures, sustains, comforts, and reassures the believer in whatever circumstances they find themselves in. This was covered in detail in the section on John 15.

Stage Three

> **Mark 10:29-30** *Jesus said, "Truly, I say to you, there is no one who has left house or brothers or sisters or mother or father or children or lands, for my sake and for the gospel, who will not receive a hundredfold now in this time houses and brothers and sisters and mothers and children and lands, with persecutions, and* **in the age to come eternal life (zoe)."** *(ESV)*

In the age to come, the believer will be resurrected with an eternal, imperishable body. Think of this as the third and final stage as the ultimate purpose of *zoe*. We won't see this final stage of *zoe* until we put on immortality with an imperishable body (at the time of the resurrection).

Important: Resurrection to eternal zoe, is the hope of the believer. Without confidence in the resurrection, there is no hope at all. The resurrection of the believer, based upon the fact that the Son of God has guaranteed our resurrection, by his own victory over death, and his impartation of zoe into the psuche of the believer, is not only the pinnacle of the entire Bible, but the basis of the entire storyline from Genesis to Revelation.

As humans, we are composed of body and *psuche*. We would lose our *psuche* (our *psuche* would die forever) if we had not been given eternal *zoe*. The believer's *psuche* is preserved (saved) by the gift of *zoe*. This effect begins while we are still living in our mortal bodies (Stage One). Yet, at the time of the future resurrection, our flesh-and-blood bodies must be changed to imperishable in order to dwell in the eternal kingdom of God (Stage Three).

Guarantee of Stage Three

> ***Eph. 1:13-14*** *In him you also, when you heard the word of truth, the gospel according to your salvation, and believed in him, were sealed with the promised Holy Spirit, who is the **guarantee** of our inheritance until we acquire possession of it, to the praise of his glory. (ESV)*

Even though this imperishable state of our bodies is yet to be manifested, we are guaranteed of this future event by the current indwelling of God's Holy Spirit.

The Holy Spirit is given to the believer at the time they become a believer. The Holy Spirit is the guarantee of our inheritance until we acquire possession of it.

> ***2 Cor. 1:21-22*** *And it is God who establishes us with you in Christ, and has anointed us, and who has also put his seal on us and given us his Spirit in our hearts as a guarantee. (ESV)*

So, what do we possess in this age?

We have the indwelling of *zoe* (which is immortal) at the time of our belief, making us children of God. We have crossed over from death to life (*zoe*) at the point of belief. We now participate in the divine nature. We then live in a dual nature simultaneously, living in the mortal flesh while also having the Spirit of God living within us, giving us immortality.

We do not acquire possession of our imperishable, immortal bodies (our inheritance in the age to come) until we are resurrected. But, we have assurance that this will indeed happen because we know we have been sealed with the promised Holy Spirit.

Part Three

Clarifying Hell

Important Note:

Parts 1 and 2 lay the foundation for understanding Part 3.

Please do not read Part 3, without reading Parts 1 and 2.

Thank You

Life

Defined

35

Obvious Questions That Arise

There has been a lot of debate regarding "Hell" over the centuries. However, there are some Christians who not only refuse to discuss this topic but also consider those who would even question the concept of "eternal torment in Hell" as heretics. This is unfortunate, as most believers on both sides of this issue are genuinely seeking to understand the truth in God's word. As such, we should extend grace to one another. One's understanding of "Hell" is not a "salvation" issue. However, there are some that hold to the traditional view who would appear in their fervency to defend their views, to portray that one's belief on this matter is a basis of fellowship and, in some cases, even imply it is a matter of salvation.

Due to this intimidation from many traditionalists, I have been hesitant to enter this fray. However, I believe a vital (and undeniable) aspect of Jesus' teaching on *zoe* is its direct connection and contrast to death (*Gehenna* and *Hades*). There is no way to have a clear understanding of Jesus' teaching on Hades and Gehenna, without understanding Jesus' teaching on psuche, zoe, and death. They are fundamentally and inextricably linked.

Understanding this connection is essential to understanding the purpose of Jesus, and the end state of man, yea, even the end state of the world. Yet, in many English Bibles, there is little to no distinction made between Hades and Gehenna, when in fact while they are both connected in stark contrast to zoe, their contrasts are distinctly and drastically different.

Failing to understand these connections will seriously handicap your ability to understand the importance and clarity of Jesus' message.

> A vital aspect of Jesus' teaching on *Zoe* is its direct contrast to death, Hades and Gehenna. They are fundamentally and inextricably linked

The study that we have been doing on *psuche* and *zoe* generates obvious questions about the afterlife.

As we have seen, Jesus often contrasted *zoe* with death. In fact, Jesus has shown us that it is indeed death that is the problem that all mankind faces. It is only by *zoe* that a person may escape death through the ages.

It is death's association with *Hades* and *Gehenna* (though in completely different ways) that makes this discussion about *Hades* and *Gehenna* unavoidable.

It is very important to understand the difference between *Hades* and *Gehenna* and the role that these two places/events hold for the destiny of mankind. Failing to understand these differences will likely leave you holding on to huge misconceptions as to what Jesus really taught. But, before we can discuss these ideas, we first need to have a better understanding of the concept of immortality.

> It is very important to understand the difference between *Hades* and *Gehenna* and the role that these two places/events hold for the destiny of mankind

The Second Death

In Revelation 20:14, John speaks of the "second death" that occurs when those whose names are not written in the book of *zoe* are thrown in to the lake of fire. The **traditional** belief in Christian circles today is that the "second death" is defined as eternal torment in Hell. This stance, by its very nature, would seem to be dependent upon the belief that every person has an "immortal soul."

But, Jesus clearly teaches that an unbeliever's *psuche* will be destroyed in *Gehenna*.

> *Matt. 10:28 And do not fear those who kill the body but cannot kill the* **soul** *(psuche). Rather fear him who can destroy both* **soul** *(psuche) and body in Hell (Gehenna). (ESV)*

If *psuche* is immortal, then how can it be destroyed?

And if one's *psuche* is destroyed, how could it continue with eternal torment?

God Alone Is Immortal

> *1 Tim. 6:15-16 . . . he who is the blessed and only Sovereign, the King of kings and Lord of lords,* **who alone has immortality,** *who dwells in unapproachable light, whom no one has ever seen or can see. To him be honor and eternal dominion, Amen. (ESV)*

1 Timothy 6:16 teaches that God alone is immortal. Man on the other hand, is not. Immortality is a gift bestowed upon the believer.

Rom. 2:4-8 Or do you presume on the riches of his kindness and forbearance and patience, not knowing that God's kindness is meant to lead you to repentance? But because of your hard and impenitent heart you are storing up wrath for yourself on the day of wrath when God's righteous judgment will be revealed.

*He will render to each one according to his works: to those who by patience in well-doing seek for glory and honor and **immortality**, he will give **eternal life (zoe)**; but for those who are self-seeking and do not obey the truth, but obey unrighteousness, there will be wrath and fury. (ESV)*

In Romans 2:4-8, Paul preaches that God's patience and kindness is meant to lead man to repentance. To those who by perseverance in well-doing seek for glory and honor and immortality, he will give eternal *zoe*.

If humans already have immortality, then why should they seek it? Why would God give eternal life (*zoe*) to humans, if they already possess it?

It is the gift of eternal life (*zoe*) that bestows immortality. Humans do not innately possess immortality.

It is the gift of Eternal *Zoe* (Life as God has it) that bestows immortality

Humans do not innately possess immortality

36

Defining "Perish" and "Destroy"

Strong's Concordance defines the Greek word *apollumi* to mean "to destroy, utterly destroy." The word occurs ninety-two times in various forms in the New Testament. There are well over twenty occurrences in the New Testament where this word or some derivation of it has been translated as "perish," "perishing," "perished," etc. It is also frequently translated as "destroyed" or "destruction."

Before we get much further, let's revisit a couple words that I will use from here on.

Traditional Viewpoint

The **"Traditional"** view is the belief that Hell is a place of everlasting torment, burning, darkness, and separation from God, where unbelievers will spend eternity. The Traditional view believes the **second death** does not mean death but rather signifies eternal spiritual separation from God. This would also include the everlasting suffering associated with that. The Traditional view explains that "perish" means "to ruin," as when Jesus describes the old wine skin that is "destroyed or ruined" when new wine is poured into it. Certainly "ruined" would be a suitable description of an inanimate wineskin that has been destroyed, from a practical perspective. But, does the concept of "ruin" describe how Jesus meant to use *apollumi* in John 3:16 when referring to the fate of unbelievers?

> **John 3:16** *For God so loved the world, that he gave his only Son, that whoever believes in him should not **perish** (apollumi) but have **eternal life** (zoe). (ESV)*

Jesus has contrasted life (*zoe*) with death and destruction throughout the gospel according to John. How could *apollumi*

257

mean anything other than death and destruction here in John 3:16?

Conditional Immortality

"Conditionalists" is the term associated with those Christians that hold to the belief that man is mortal. They believe the Bible does not teach that man "has a **soul**" but that man "is a **soul**" and that the soul (*psuche*) is mortal. Immortality is not an innate aspect of man's nature. They believe that a person receives **immortality** via the gift of eternal *zoe* when they wholeheartedly believe the truth about Jesus' identity and purpose.

> **Rom. 2:7** *To those who by patience in well-doing seek for glory and honor and* **immortality***, he will give* **eternal life** *(***zoe***). (ESV)*

They believe a person's immortality is **conditional** upon this gift of salvation. Immortality comes only from the impartation of the Holy Spirit into the believer. This deposit of the Holy Spirit imparts eternal *zoe*.

They believe that the unbeliever is destroyed (or perishes) in the lake of fire. This means that the unbeliever ceases to exist at some point after being thrown into the lake of fire, which is called the **second death** (see Revelation 20:12-15).

Thus, **Conditionalists** hold to the belief that when any person dies (passes away from their earthly life), that is their first death. They believe that unbelievers are cast into the lake of fire (the second death) and will, at some point, be annihilated (destroyed).

I would consider myself to be a Conditionalist. However, I would like to say this belief is not based solely upon my study of *Hades* and *Gehenna*. Rather, I came to my conclusions primarily from studying Jesus' teaching on *zoe*, *psuche*, death, and perishing.

> I came to my conclusions primarily from Jesus' teaching on *Zoe*, *Psuche*, death, and perishing

However, as we look closely at Jesus' teaching on *Hades* and *Gehenna*, we can see the New Testament teachings absolutely teach Conditionalism.

Let us look at a few of the scriptures where Jesus speaks of "perishing" and "destroying."

Luke 21:12-19 But before all this they will lay their hands on you and persecute you, delivering you up to the synagogues and prisons, and you will be brought before kings and governors for my name's sake. This will be your opportunity to bear witness. Settle it therefore in your minds not to meditate beforehand how to answer, for I will give you a mouth and wisdom, which none of your adversaries will be able to withstand or contradict. You will be delivered up even by parents and brothers and relatives and friends, and some of you they will put to death. You will be hated by all for my name's sake.

*But, not a hair of your head will **perish**. By your endurance, you will gain your **lives** (psuche).   (ESV)*

In Luke 21:12-18, Jesus explains to his followers that the day is coming when many of them will be betrayed, and some will be put to death. Jesus reassures them, however, that not a hair of their heads will **perish**.

Let's ask ourselves, just how does this make sense? If I was a believer listening to what Jesus just said, and I was concerned about being killed, would I seriously take comfort in the fact that my hair will not perish?

Obviously, Jesus was reassuring these believers of something much more significant. Jesus uses an understatement to emphasize that even if they are killed, they can have absolute assurance that their *psuche* will not be destroyed.

They can have certain hope that their *psuche* will be saved.

Refer to the screenshot of the Greek-English Interlinear from Luke 21:16-19 on the following page.

21:16

ΠΑΡΑΔΟΘΗΣΕΣΘΕ
paradothEsesthe
G3860
vi Fut Pas 2 Pl
YE-SHALL-BE-BEING-BESIDE-GIVEN
ye-shall-be-being-given-up

ΔΕ	ΚΑΙ	ΥΠΟ	ΓΟΝΕΩΝ	ΚΑΙ	ΑΔΕΛΦΩΝ	ΚΑΙ
de	kai	hupo	goneOn	kai	adelphOn	kai
G1161	G2532	G5259	G1118	G2532	G80	G2532
Conj	Conj	Prep	n_Gen Pl m	Conj	n_Gen Pl m	Conj
YET	AND also	by	parents	AND	brothers	AND

ΣΥΓΓΕΝΩΝ	ΚΑΙ	ΦΙΛΩΝ	ΚΑΙ	ΘΑΝΑΤΩΣΟΥΣΙΝ	ΕΞ	ΥΜΩΝ
suggenOn	kai	philOn	kai	thanatOsousin	ex	humOn
G4773	G2532	G5384	G2532	G2289	G1537	G5216
a_Gen Pl m	Conj	a_Gen Pl m	Conj	vi Fut Act 3 Pl	Prep	pp 2 Gen Pl
TOGETHER-generateds relatives	AND	FOND-ones friends	AND	THEY-SHALL-BE-(causing-to)-DIE they-shall-be-putting-to-death	OUT	OF-YOU(p) of-ye

16 And ye shall be betrayed both by parents, and brethren, and kinsfolks, and friends; and [some] of you shall they cause to be put to death.

21:17

ΚΑΙ	ΕΣΕΣΘΕ	ΜΙΣΟΥΜΕΝΟΙ	ΥΠΟ	ΠΑΝΤΩΝ	ΔΙΑ	ΤΟ	ΟΝΟΜΑ	ΜΟΥ
kai	esesthe	misoumenoi	hupo	pantOn	dia	to	onoma	mou
G2532	G2071	G3404	G5259	G3956	G1223	G3588	G3686	G3450
Conj	vi Fut vxx 2 Pl	vp Pres Pas Nom Pl m	Prep	a_Gen Pl m	Prep	t_Acc Sg n	n_Acc Sg n	pp 1 Gen Sg
AND	YE-SHALL-BE	beING-HATED	by	ALL	THRU because-of	THE	NAME	OF-ME

17 And ye shall be hated of all [men] for my name's sake.

21:18

ΚΑΙ	ΘΡΙΞ	ΕΚ	ΤΗΣ	ΚΕΦΑΛΗΣ	ΥΜΩΝ	ΟΥ	ΜΗ	ΑΠΟΛΗΤΑΙ
kai	thrix	ek	tEs	kephalEs	humOn	ou	mE	apolEtai
G2532	G2359	G1537	G3588	G2776	G5216	G3756	G3361	G622
Conj	n_Nom Sg f	Prep	t_Gen Sg f	n_Gen Sg f	pp 2 Gen Pl	Part Neg	Part Neg	vs 2Aor Mid 3 Sg
AND	HAIR	OUT	OF-THE	HEAD	OF-YOU(p) of-ye	NOT	NO	SHOULD-BE-belNG-destroyED should-be-perishing

18 But there shall not an hair of your head perish.

21:19

ΕΝ	ΤΗ	ΥΠΟΜΟΝΗ	ΥΜΩΝ	ΚΤΗΣΑΣΘΕ	ΤΑΣ	ΨΥΧΑΣ	ΥΜΩΝ
en	tE	hupomonE	humOn	ktEsasthe	tas	psuchas	humOn
G1722	G3588	G5281	G5216	G2932	G3588	G5590	G5216
Prep	t_Dat Sg f	n_Dat Sg f	pp 2 Gen Pl	vm Aor midD 2 Pl	t_Acc Pl f	n_Acc Pl f	pp 2 Gen Pl
IN	THE	UNDER-REMAINing endurance	OF-YOU(p) of-ye	YE-SHALL-BE-ACQUIRING	THE	souls	OF-YOU(p) of-ye

19 In your patience possess ye your souls.

Notice that the last verse contains the word *psuche*. By looking at the Greek text, we can see that this could be read as:

By your endurance you shall be acquiring your **psuche***.*

In other words, Jesus is telling these believers that even though you may be put to death, do not fear. He encourages them to stand firm (endure), assuring them they shall be acquiring (retaining or possessing) their *psuche*.

Certainly, this makes absolute sense from what we have learned about *psuche* and *zoe* from Jesus' teachings.

On the other hand, this makes no sense if you hold to the belief that perishing means the ruin of the person, who will end up in eternal flames of Hell. Honestly, if you hold to the belief that Jesus means the ruin of a person forever in the eternal torment and fires of Hell, then how do you explain this verse?

Would a believer find comfort in the words of Jesus saying, "Okay, you are going to be killed, but take assurance that not even a hair of your head will be going to Hell."

Really? Is that going to encourage a believer facing death? Maybe in a really morbid, fearful sort of way. In other words, if you hold to that belief, then you reduce what Jesus has said here to no more than this: "As a believer some of you are going to be killed, but persevere anyway, because you can be assured you are not going to be tormented in Hell forever."

Thankfully, that is not what Jesus is saying to these believers in any way whatsoever.

Jesus is saying that if one of these believers is killed, they will certainly not perish but will, with certainty, acquire (i.e., retain or keep) their *psuche*.

*Matt. 10:28 And do not fear those who kill the body but cannot kill the **soul** (psuche). Rather fear him who can destroy (apolesai) both **soul** (psuche) and body in Hell (**Gehenna**). (ESV)*

Jesus makes it clear that the unbeliever's *psuche* will be **destroyed** in *Gehenna*.

It is obvious that Jesus is referring to the "**killing**" or "**utter destruction**" of their *psuche*, as he connects this destruction of the *psuche* to the killing of the body in the first part of this verse. He makes the killing of the *psuche* equivalent to the killing of the body. The body is dead, not ruined. The body is dead, just as the *psuche* of the unbeliever will be after it is thrown into *Gehenna* and destroyed.

Jesus is clearly describing the death and destruction of a person's soul (*psuche*) in the lake of fire, which is the second death.

Could it be that this is why the apostle John, in the book of Revelation (through inspiration of the Holy Spirit), chose to call the lake of fire "the second death"?

John specifically chose this term, because that is exactly what he meant.

*John 10:10 The thief comes only to steal and kill and **destroy** (**apollumi**). I came that they may have **life (zoe)** and have it abundantly. (ESV)*

In John 10, Jesus explains that the thief comes to kill and destroy (*apollumi*) the sheep. Jesus' purpose, on the other hand, is quite different and directly opposed to that of the thief.

Jesus has come to rescue the sheep from this fate of death and destruction. Jesus has come to give them *zoe*.

Later in John 10:28, Jesus reiterates this statement:

*John 10:28 I give them **eternal life (zoe)**, and they will never **perish** (**apollumi**). (ESV)*

As you may recall from our earlier study of John, the English word "never" does not exactly reproduce the meaning in the original Greek (see the original Greek text on the following page)

The screen shot on the following page is a repeat of the Greek text in John 10:28 shown previously in the chapter on John 10.

Read the English word for word translation below the Greek (John 10:28). Does it say "**never perish?**"

10:28	ΚΑΓΩ	ΖΩΗΝ	ΑΙΩΝΙΟΝ	ΔΙΔΩΜΙ	ΑΙΩΝΑ	ΚΑΙ	ΑΥΤΟΙΣ	ΚΑΙ	ΟΥ	ΜΗ
	kagO	zOEn	aiOnion	didOmi	aiOna	kai	autois	kai	ou	mE
	G2504	G2222	G166	G1325	G165	G2532	G846	G2532	G3756	G3361
	pp 1 Nom Sg Con	n_ Acc Sg f	a_ Acc Sg f	vi Pres Act 1 Sg	n_ Acc Sg m	Conj	pp Dat Pl m	Conj	Part Neg	Part Neg
	AND-I	LIFE	eonian	AM-GIVING	eon	AND	to-them them	AND	NOT	NO

	ΑΠΟΛΩΝΤΑΙ	ΕΙΣ	ΤΟΝ		ΟΥΧ	ΑΡΠΑΣΕΙ	ΤΙΣ
	apolOntai	eis	ton		ouch	harpasei	tis
	G622	G1519	G3588		G3756	G726	G5100
	vs 2Aor Mid 3 Pl	Prep	t_ Acc Sg m		Part Neg	vi Fut Act 3 Sg	px Nom Sg m
	THEY-SHOULD-BE-*beING-destroy*ED	INTO	THE		NOT	SHALL-BE-SNATCHING	ANY anyone

	ΑΥΤΑ	ΕΚ	ΤΗΣ	ΧΕΙΡΟΣ	ΜΟΥ
	auta	ek	tEs	cheiros	mou
	G846	G1537	G3588	G5495	G3450
	pp Acc Pl n	Prep	t_ Gen Sg f	n_ Gen Sg f	pp 1 Gen Sg
	them	OUT	OF-THE	HAND	OF-ME

28 And I give unto them eternal life; and they shall never perish, neither shall any [man] pluck them out of my hand.

John 10:28 may actually be better translated as:

> *I give them **eternal life** (zoe), and they shall in no way be* **destroyed** *into the eon. (my paraphrase)*

Jesus contrasts what he said in the first half of the sentence with his statement in the second half. Jesus gives them eternal *zoe*. The result is that the sheep will in no way be destroyed into the eon.

If the unbelieving sheep (that are not of his flock) already possessed eternal life, why would it be necessary to give this to any sheep at all? If all of the sheep already possess immortality, why would they need "eternal *zoe*"? And if all the sheep already possess immortality, how can any of them be destroyed?

You can see how quickly this verse gets twisted up when the Traditional view attempts to make it say something beyond what is obvious. Jesus makes a clear, precise, simple contrast with opposites. His sheep will receive eternal *zoe* from him, and because of this, they will "in no way" exist in a state of being destroyed unto the eon. Even though they will die an earthly temporal death, they will not remain that way into the eon. They will be resurrected.

Tying This into Satan

Remember what Jesus said earlier about the thief who comes to steal, kill, and destroy? Jesus was referring to Satan, who intends to see all men destroyed.

Steal

Satan seeks to deceive all men into not believing the truth that God has set before them—in particular, the truth about who Jesus is and what he has done for them. Whenever Satan is successful, he has stolen the hearts and minds from the true intent that God had for all mankind. The result is death, and that is exactly Satan's end game. He wants the death and ultimate destruction of all mankind.

This first occurred in the Garden of Eden. Satan deceived Eve and Adam by convincing them that God had lied to them and that if they were to follow his (Satan's) advice, they would be able to decide for themselves what is good and bad and lead their lives as they wished. He told them that they would indeed not die, as God told Adam that they surely would if they ate of the tree of knowledge of good and evil.

So, Satan was successful in stealing the hearts and minds of Adam and Eve, turning them from wholeheartedly following God's desire and plan. He stole their affection for and their devotion to God. He entered the sheep pen not by the gate but by deception and outright lies (for more on this discussion, review the section on John 10).

Kill

As a result of believing in Satan's lies and not trusting and obeying God, Adam and Eve did indeed die on that day. God drove them from the Garden of Eden, and they no longer had access to the tree of life, which was their source of *zoe*. When man was created in the image of God, he was created with the capacity to gain fellowship with God on spiritual, life-giving level, essentially becoming part of the family of God. When Adam and Eve were expelled from the Garden of Eden, they retained the "image of God," but they lost that intimate and live-giving fellowship with God.

This level of fellowship and the live-giving *zoe* are restored to a person when they believe in Jesus as the Son of God and the Messiah and count on his death and resurrection. In John 17, Jesus gives an enlightening definition of eternal *zoe*.

> *John 17:3 And this is **eternal life (zoe)**, that they know you, the only true God, and Jesus Christ whom you have sent. (ESV)*

Jesus defines an intrinsic aspect of eternal *zoe*, as the intimate level of knowledge and communication that exists for the believer. No longer is the believer dependent on a priest or other means of making supplication to God, Jesus, or the Holy Spirit. They have direct access, because God now lives within the believer, making them a new creation, a child of God capable of crying out, "Abba" (father), just like a little child would call out to its own father.

This level of intimacy is a restoration of the intimacy that Adam and Eve had the privilege of enjoying but ultimately despised.

It is interesting that the tree of life that is mentioned (in Genesis) in the Garden of Eden does not appear again in the Bible until the end of the book of Revelation. We see it again here as John describes the new heaven and new earth. There is a river of life that flows through and straddling it is the large tree of life with leaves for the healing of the nations.

Thus, *zoe* has come full circle. Man believed Satan instead of God, thereby Satan stole the "sheep" from the pen of the Garden of Eden, and they were killed. And it has remained so; this has been the state of all mankind since then. Man lost access to *zoe* and immortality. They had no hope but death and destruction.

But, God had a plan of redemption, which he has carried out through the life, death, and resurrection of Jesus Christ, his only begotten son. Through believing in Jesus, a person can be restored back to that level of fellowship and again have access to the tree of *zoe*. (The tree of *zoe* represents the *zoe* that flows from the indwelling Holy Spirit in the *psuche* of the believer due to the grace that comes from believing in Jesus.)

Destroy

Ultimately, Satan's end game is the destruction of man. Without *zoe*, man has no hope of immortality. Without *zoe*, unbelievers will ultimately be destroyed in the lake of fire, which is the second death.

It is no coincidence that Satan is called the "Destroyer" in Revelation 9:11.

Rev. 9:11 *They have as king over them the angel of the bottomless pit. His name in Hebrew is* Abaddon, *and in Greek he is called* **Apollyon** *[root is* **apollumi***].* *(ESV)*

Though Satan is the thief that has come to steal, kill, and destroy, we have the assurance that Jesus has come to overcome Satan's work and bring eternal life to believers. We have the assurance that we will in no way be destroyed into the eon. We will be resurrected to eternal life.

Believers receive *zoe* (eternal life) when they believe. They cross over from a status of death to a status of life (*zoe*) at that very moment. Their psuche has been deposited with the indwelling *zoe*, preserving their *psuche* for eternal life. The believer **will** die an earthly death but that is not their end. They will be resurrected to eternal life on the resurrection day.

Some believers who are still living on the day of Jesus' return will not suffer an earthly death but will join those believers who have already died (Paul calls them "those who have fallen asleep" and the "dead in Christ"). For more on this, see 1 Thessalonians 4:13-18.

The believers' Psuche has been deposited
with the indwelling Zoe, preserving
their Psuche for Eternal Life (Zoe).
Believers that die an earthly death
can rest assured that will not be their end.
They will be resurrected to Eternal Zoe
on the resurrection day.

If the Dead Are Not Raised, Then We Will Perish

*1 Cor. 15:16-18 For if the dead are not raised, not even Christ has been raised. And if Christ has not been raised, your faith is futile and you are still in your sins. Then, those also who have fallen asleep in Christ have **perished** (apollumi). (ESV)*

Paul's emphasis here is that if Jesus has not been raised, then our faith is basically useless, since no one will be raised from the dead. Believers would just remain in their sins (in a status of death). Thus, those believers who have already died an earthly death (fallen asleep) would have perished (*apollumi*).

Does it make sense that Paul would be saying that these believers would be in Hell? If you hold to the traditional view that *apollumi* means "ruin" and infers **eternal torment** in Hell, then that is your only logical conclusion from this verse.

No, of course not. Paul is implying that "perishing" means never recovering from death (i.e., no hope of being raised from the dead). To perish would mean that their death is permanent or utter destruction. They would have perished (died) with no hope of resurrection.

Thanks be to God that is not the case!

Jesus did rise from the dead, is eternally alive at this very moment, and is our certain hope of eternal *zoe*!

Matthew 7:13 *Enter by the narrow gate. For the gate is wide and the way is easy that leads to* **destruction**, *and those who enter by it are many. For the gate is narrow and the way is hard that leads to* **life (zoe)**, *and those who find it are few (ESV)*

The above statement by Jesus, is very straightforward. It is clearly speaking of destruction. Jesus provides a stark contrast. There are two gates, one leads to destruction, the other leads to zoe.

Romans 9:21-23 *Or does the potter not have authority over the clay, to make from the same lump a vessel that is for honorable use and one that is for ordinary use? And what if God, wanting to demonstrate his wrath and to make known his power, endured with much patience vessels of wrath prepared for* **destruction**? *And he did so in order that he could make known the riches of his glory upon vessels of mercy that he prepared beforehand for glory (LEB)*

In the verse above, Paul is clearly refering to the destruction of those who are under God's wrath, and have refused to accept the death of Jesus on their behalf.

Phillipians 1:27-28 Only let your manner of life be worthy of the gospel of Christ, so that whether I come and see you or am absent, I may hear of you that you are standing firm in one spirit, with one mind striving side by side for the faith of the gospel, and not frightened in anything by your opponents. This is a clear sign to them of their **destruction***, but of your salvation, and that from God. (ESV)*

Phillipians 3 :18-20 For many, of whom I have often told you and now tell you even with tears, walk as enemies of the cross of Christ. Their end is **destruction***, their god is their belly, and they glory in their shame, with minds set on earthly things. But our citizenship is in heaven, and from it we await a Savior, the Lord Jesus Christ (ESV)*

In both sections of verses above, Paul is clearly stating to the Phillipians that those who oppose the gospel of Christ will be destroyed.

The following verses are from Peter's letter in the book of 2 Peter. Peter is also clearly speaking of the destruction of those who deny Jesus.

2 Peter 2:1-3 But false prophets also arose among the people, just as there will be false teachers among you, who will secretly bring in destructive heresies, even denying the Master who bought them, bringing upon themselves swift **destruction***. And many will follow their sensuality, and because of them the way of truth will be blasphemed. And in their greed they will exploit you with false words. Their condemnation from long ago is not idle, and their* **destruction** *is not asleep (ESV)*

2 Peter 2:12 But these, like irrational animals, creatures of instinct, born to be caught and **destroyed***, blaspheming about matters of which they are ignorant, will also be* **destroyed** *in their* **destruction** *(ESV)*

2 Peter 3:3-16 Above all knowing this, that in the last days scoffers will come with scoffing, following according to their own desires and saying, "Where is the promise of his coming? For ever since the fathers fell asleep, all things have continued just as they have been from the beginning of creation." 5 For whe] they maintain this, it escapes their notice that the heavens existed long ago and the earth held together out of water and through water by the word of God, by means of which things the world that existed at that time was **destroyed** *by being inundated with water. But by the same word the present heavens and earth are reserved for fire, being kept for the day of judgment and* **destruction** *of ungodly people.*

Now, dear friends, do not let this one thing escape your notice, that one day with the Lord is like a thousand years, and a thousand years is like one day. The Lord is not delaying the promise, as some consider slowness, but is being patient toward you, because he does not want any to **perish***, but all to come to repentance. But the day of the Lord will come like a thief, in which the heavens will disappear with a rushing noise, and the celestial bodies will be destroyed by being burned up, and the earth and the deeds done on it will be disclosed.*

273

*Because all these things are being destroyed in this way, what sort of people must you be in holy behavior and godliness, while waiting for and hastening the coming of the day of God, because of which the heavens will be destroyed by being burned up and the celestial bodies will melt as they are consumed by heat! But according to his promise, we are waiting for new heavens and a new earth in which righteousness resides. Therefore, dear friends, because you[j] are waiting for these things, make every effort to be found at peace, spotless and unblemished in him. And regard the patience of our Lord as salvation, just as also our dear brother Paul wrote to you, according to the wisdom that was given to him, 16 as he does also in all his letters, speaking in them about these things, in which there are some things hard to understand, which the ignorant and unstable distort to their own **destruction**, as they also do the rest of the scriptures. (LEB)*

In the following verses from the Book of Acts, Peter is preaching to a crowd that contained members from the mob that had influenced the decision to crucify Jesus.

> *Acts 3:15-23* *and you killed the Author of **life (zoe),** whom God raised from the dead. To this we are witnesses...*
>
> *..."And now, brothers, I know that you acted in ignorance, as did also your rulers. But what God foretold by the mouth of all the prophets, that his Christ would suffer, he thus fulfilled. Repent therefore, and turn back, that your sins may be blotted out, that times of refreshing may come from the presence of the Lord, and that he may send the Christ appointed for you, Jesus, whom heaven must receive until the time for restoring all the things about which God spoke by the mouth of his holy prophets long ago. Moses said, 'The Lord God will raise up for you a prophet like me from your brothers. You shall listen to him in whatever he tells you. And it shall be that every **soul (psuche)** who does not listen to that prophet shall be destroyed from the people.' (ESV)*

Notice how Peter tells them:

- They killed the "author of zoe"
- God raised Jesus from the dead. The resurrection of Jesus forms the very core of the message of salvation, specifically because as the source of zoe, Jesus brings resurrection to eternal zoe, on the resurrection day. Resurrection is also fundamental to the message of salvation because it is eternal death (destruction) that Jesus saves us from.
- Any psuche that does not listen to that prophet (Jesus) shall be destroyed

Peter does not say anything about eternal torment. He is clearly and simply stating that the obstinate unbeliever will be destroyed.

Life
Defined

37

Where Did Things Go Wrong?

If what we have concluded about *psuche* and *zoe* are, in fact, what Jesus taught, then we should expect to see some indication that Christians in the early church held to this teaching.

That is **exactly** what we find.

Early church leaders frequently wrote about gaining eternal *zoe* and being saved from the penalty of death.

What do we not find? We don't see any reference to the "immortality of the soul" or "everlasting torment" until late in the second century AD.

Paul's Warning

> **Col. 2:8** *See to it that no one takes you captive by philosophy and empty deceit, according to **human tradition**, according to the elemental spirits of the world [this can also read as the "fundamental beliefs of the world system"], and not according to Christ. (ESV)*

The apostle Paul warned against allowing existing philosophies, traditions, and belief systems to infiltrate and take captive the sound doctrine according to Christ.

Shouldn't We Respect Tradition?

Traditions are typically very good things and have a great deal of value as people pass on values and beliefs from one generation to another. However, when a tradition is based on a false assumption, it should be respectfully challenged.

Tradition can also be a bad thing. Greek tradition held to the belief in the immortality of the soul for many centuries before the birth of Christianity. This belief became an invasive, insidious virus that spread into Christianity by the beginning of the third century AD. As many Greeks became Christians, some of their Greek traditions infiltrated the church. Some of these beliefs heavily influenced incorrect Christian doctrines that remain to this day.

As we saw in the verse above, Paul made a stern warning about this possibility in his letter to the Colossians church.

What if Martin Luther (out of a sense of respect) had deferred to the traditions of his day? Would he have still proceeded with posting his *Ninety-Five Theses*? Would he still have taken a defiant stand against what was one of the strongest traditions and forces in the history of the world?

Our goal should be to respect tradition in as far as it complies with the truth that we see in God's word. If it does not, then we are bound to respectfully disagree.

See what Jesus had to say about traditions in Mark 7:1-13.

*Mark 7:1-13 And the Pharisees and some of the scribes who had come from Jerusalem gathered to him. And they saw that some of his disciples were eating their bread with unclean—that is, unwashed—hands. (For the Pharisees and all the Jews do not eat unless they wash their hands ritually, thus **holding fast to the traditions of the elders**. And when they come from the marketplace, they do not eat unless they wash. And there are many other traditions which they have received and hold fast to—for example, the washing of cups and pitchers and bronze kettles and dining couches.) And the Pharisees and the scribes asked him, "Why do your disciples not live according **to the tradition of the elders**, but eat their bread with unclean hands?" So he said to them, "Isaiah prophesied correctly about you hypocrites, as it is written, 'This people honors me with their lips, but their heart is far, far away from me. And they worship me in vain, teaching as doctrines the commandments of men.' **Abandoning the commandment of God, you hold fast to the tradition of men.**" And he said to them, "**You splendidly ignore the commandment of God so that you can keep your tradition**. For Moses said, 'Honor your father and your mother,' and, 'The one who speaks evil of father or mother must certainly die.' But you say, 'If a man says to his father or to his mother, "Whatever benefit you would have received from me is corban" (that is, a gift to God), you no longer permit him to do anything for his father or his mother, **thus making void the word of God by your tradition that you have handed down**, and you do many similar things such as this." (LEB)*

What if Peter and John had listened to the high priest, priests, and Jewish council and kept their mouths shut when commanded to do so by this very council? If they had indeed kept quiet and observed the tradition of the elders, we would have no gospel at all today.

> *Acts 4:19-20 But, Peter and John answered them, "Whether it is right in the sight of God to listen to you rather than to God, you must judge, for we cannot but speak of what we have seen and heard." (ESV)*

Infiltration of the Belief of the "Immortal Soul"

One of the most damaging world views that infiltrated and captivated the church is the error of believing that man has an immortal soul. Man does not have a soul; he **is** a soul. Also, man is mortal, not immortal.

The concept of the "immortal soul" was not taught by Jesus, the New Testament authors, the apostles, nor the Apostolic Fathers.

Let's define "Apostolic Fathers." The term "Apostolic Fathers" is not a biblical term but has been historically used to describe those early church leaders who taught the teachings of Christ as they learned them from the apostles. In other words, they had not personally heard the teachings of Jesus but had sat at the feet of the apostles who had and were now passing on these teachings. This was the first generation removed, so to speak, from the apostles.

We have many writings of the Apostles, which have been accepted as part of the New Testament. Writings of the Apostolic Fathers were not accepted into the canon of the New Testament and rightfully so, as these men were not personal witnesses of Jesus' life, death, resurrection, and teaching. However, their writing does give us an accurate understanding as to what they believed.

The concept of the "immortal soul" does not appear in early church writings until 150 years after the birth of the church. By this time, the Greek culture (the widely predominant culture of Christianity during the first several centuries) began to influence and infiltrate Christian thought. Plato introduced the idea of the "immortal soul" many centuries earlier. This belief was widely and firmly held by the typical citizen of the Roman Empire. This belief deeply influenced Greek culture and permeated Christian beliefs during the first few centuries of the early church. Many of the Christian converts from the Roman Empire integrated parts of this belief into their Christian faith.

By the third century AD, the concept of the "immortal soul" had become widely accepted in Christian circles and powerfully influenced how scripture was interpreted. By the time Christianity was legalized by the Roman Empire in AD 311, the notion of "immortal life" being a gift of God was held by the minority. The idea of the "immortal soul" became the official doctrine of the Roman Empire, which declared Christianity as its national religion by AD 380. About a century later, Augustine cemented the belief of the immortal soul as a bulwark of Christian doctrine. From this point forward, any effort to curb the idea of the "immortal soul" was heavily censored and even punishable as heresy.

I do not feel there is enough room in this book to present this evidence, especially when others have done an excellent job bringing this truth to light. There are many who have undertaken an astute study on the writings of the Apostolic Fathers and other prominent leaders in the first few centuries of the church.

See the links at the end of this book to get a better understanding of what the earliest leaders of the Christian world (after the apostles) firmly believed. These studies also reveal the slow emergence and infiltration of the fallacy of the "immortal soul" over the course of a couple centuries, displacing the clear teachings of Jesus and the New Testament writers.

> One of the most damaging world views that infiltrated the church was the erroneous belief that man has an immortal soul. The truth is, that man does not have a soul, he is a soul. Also man is mortal, not immortal.

Life
Defined

38

What is Hades?

The word *Hades* is often translated as "Hell" in English translations. Using the actual Greek word *Hades* would be a much better choice, so as to not confuse this word with *Gehenna*.

Gehenna is almost always translated as "Hell." Unfortunately, many English translations use the word "Hell" for translating both *Hades* and *Gehenna*. This is much like the issue of translating both *zoe* and *psuche* as "life." This oversimplification of the scriptures has masked the important differences intended in the original words. The consequences of this has resulted in several disastrous misunderstandings.

This truly confuses the issue of the after-life, as the words *Hades* and *Gehenna* are not equivalent. Neither Jesus nor any New Testament author would have ever thought of equating these two words. On the contrary, they used different words because they represented different things!

Hades is the Greek word that is equivalent to the Hebrew word *Sheol*, which is used throughout the Hebrew Old Testament. In the Old Testament, Sheol is portayed as the place of the dead and nothing more. In fact, Sheol is sometimes thought of as the "grave." It was never portrayed as a place of torment, nor a place of paradise, or depicted as some sort of dichotomous realm.

The Greek word *Hades* means the "unseen" and is a general term for the abode of the dead. *Hades* is associated with torment in the New Testament because of Jesus' story of Lazarus and the rich man, in which the text mentions that the rich man looked up within *Hades* and saw Lazarus (see Luke 16:19-31 below).

Luke 16:19-31 *Now a certain man was rich, and dressed in purple cloth and fine linen, feasting sumptuously every day. And a certain poor man named Lazarus, covered with sores, lay at his gate, and was longing to be filled with what fell from the table of the rich man. But even the dogs came and licked his sores. Now it happened that the poor man died, and he was carried away by the angels to Abraham's side. And the rich man also died and was buried. And in* **Hades** *he lifted up his eyes as he was in torment and saw Abraham from a distance, and Lazarus at his side. And he called out and said, 'Father Abraham, have mercy on me, and send Lazarus so that he could dip the tip of his finger in water and cool my tongue, because I am suffering pain in this flame!' But Abraham said, 'Child, remember that you received your good things during your life, and Lazarus likewise bad things. But now he is comforted here, but you are suffering pain. And in addition to all these things, a great chasm has been established between us and you, so that those who want to cross over from here to you are not able to do so, nor can they cross over from there to us.' So he said, 'Then I ask you, father, that you send him to my father's house, for I have five brothers, so that he could warn them, in order that they also should not come to this place of torment!' But Abraham said, 'They have Moses and the prophets; they must listen to them.' And he said, 'No, father Abraham, but if someone from the dead goes to them, they will repent!' But he said to him, 'If they do not listen to Moses and the prophets, neither will they be convinced if someone rises from the dead.'"* (LEB)

In this text, Jesus specifically refers to *Hades*, not *Gehenna*. Lazarus is depicted as being in Abraham's bosom while the rich man is in torment. There is a chasm separating them, but the scripture does not infer that the rich man is in *Hades* and Lazarus is in heaven. Rather, they are both in *Hades* with a chasm separating them. *Hades* is the interim place of the dead, before the resurrection and judgment day take place.

> Neither Jesus nor any New Testament author would have ever thought of equating Hades with Gehenna. On the contrary, they used different words because they represented different things!

In Luke's account, the rich man is in tormented in *Hades*. While this torment of the rich man within Hades may last for millennia, it will eventually come to an end. *Hades* will be destroyed on the day of judgment. See the following verse from the end of Revelation where on the day of judgement, the first two things to be thrown in the lake of fire, are death and *Hades*.

> *Revelation 20:4 Then Death and Hades were thrown into the lake of fire. This is the second death, the lake of fire. (ESV)*

Upon being cast into the "lake of fire" *death* and *Hades* will destroyed forever. Thus, this interim venue (*Hades*) will come to an end.

The Connection Between Death and Hades

Each time *Hades* is mentioned in the book of Revelation, *Hades* and death are always associated with each other. This makes total sense. After a person dies, they enter *Hades*, which is a venue or phase of waiting until the resurrection.

> *Rev. 6:7-8 When he opened the fourth seal, I heard the voice of the fourth living creature say, "Come!" And I looked, and behold, a pale horse! And its rider's name was **Death, and Hades** followed him. (ESV)*

Notice the interesting statement that Jesus makes in the verse below. **Jesus holds the keys to death and *Hades*.** This is hugely significant. Jesus will set believers free from death and *Hades* and give them Eternal Life. Neither death nor *Hades* can prevail against the salvation that comes via believing the truth about Jesus' identity.

There is no way out of Hades without Jesus freeing that person from death. On resurrection day, Jesus will free all who have trusted and believed in him from the grip of Hades. These people will be raised from death to eternal zoe.

> *Rev. 1:17-18 When I saw him, I fell at his feet as though dead. But, he laid his right hand on me, saying, "Fear not, I am the first and the last, and the living one. I died, and behold I am alive forevermore, and **I have the keys of death and** Hades." (ESV)*

Note: *The traditional view understates the significant role of the destruction of death and Hades because it is blinded to it's importance. This event goes hand-in-hand with the resurrection as the ultimate resolution of the state of death that mankind has existed in since the Garden of Eden. Yet this pinnacle achievement of God's rescue of man is robbed of it's importance in the traditional view. The traditional view is so focused on "eternal torment in Hell" that it misses the true focus that the Bible places on resurrection and the destruction of death and Hades.*

*Rev. 20:11-15 Then, I saw a great white throne and him who was seated on it. From his presence earth and sky fled away, and no place was found for them. And I saw the dead, great and small, standing before the throne, and books were opened. Then, another book was opened, which is the book of life. And the dead were judged by what was written in the books, according to what they had done. And the sea gave up the dead who were in it, **death and** Hades gave up the dead who were in them, and they were judged, each one of them, according to what they had done. Then, **death and** Hades were thrown into the lake of fire. This is the **second death, the lake of fire**. And if anyone's name was not found written in the **book of life (zoe)**, he was thrown into the **lake of fire**. (ESV)*

On the day of judgment, both death and *Hades* will be destroyed. Therefore, the reference in Luke 16 to the torment that the rich man is going through in *Hades* is not permanent. *Hades* will cease to exist after the judgment that is described in the book of Revelation.

Remember, both death and *Hades* are thrown into the "lake of fire", which is the **second death**. The lake of fire is *Gehenna*. Each time Jesus used the word *Gehenna* in the synoptic gospels, he used it as a metaphor referring to the future lake of fire.

The first and second resurrection will both have occurred by the day of judgment. No one will be left in *Hades*, since both those rising to eternal *zoe* and those resurrecting for the second death will no longer be in *Hades*. (They will no longer be dead, as all will be resurrected at this point.)

Jesus *permanently* ends death for all who have believed in him, and they are resurrected to eternal *zoe*. Those whose names are not written in the book of *zoe* are thrown into the lake of fire, which is aptly called the "second death."

They will ultimately be destroyed, killed, dead forever. This would be known as "everlasting punishment," not "everlasting punishing." There is a difference.

Two Paradigms Regarding *Hades*

There are some who argue that the story of the rich man and Lazarus is actually more like a parable, with Jesus using a popular existing belief from the cultural folklore of that time to incriminate the Pharisees for their long-held view that wealth was sign of God's blessing, and that poverty or ill health was a sign of God's disfavor. After all, the entirety of Luke 16 deals with Jesus speaking to the greed and presumptuous pride of the Pharisees.

A similar story was commonly used by the Pharisees to indicate their assurance of going to Abraham's bosom, while almost everyone else would go to torment. This folklore was not based on scripture but was a popular belief during the Maccabean period. For instance, the terms "Abraham's bosom" and the idea of a chasm in the after-life is not described anywhere else in the Bible, yet was a popular notion among the Jews at that time.

For more detail on this, I would refer you to an interesting article at the following link:

http://www.christadelphia.org/pamphlet/p_lazarus.htm

If this is so, then Jesus turned this folktale on it's head, rebuking the Pharisees. It is thought that Jesus intentionally used the "rich man" to allude to Caiphus (the high priest) as all of the components in the story of the rich man as Jesus tells the story, would be interpreted by the Pharisees as directly implicating Caiphus.

However, others believe this story of *Hades* is an actual account of this "intermediate holding place" of the dead and that the story of the rich man and Lazarus should be taken literally as Jesus recalling an actual historical event.

I do not wish to delve into this debate over Hades because this is not the focus of this book. An exact understanding of what happens during this interim period of *Hades* is not essential to understanding Jesus' teachings on *eternal zoe, death, and immortality.*

My focus is on Jesus' ultimate purpose, which is to save man from eternal death and give him eternal life. I do not want to get distracted by a debate over the exact nature of this interim period of the after-life (Hades), and miss the main focus of Jesus' teachings throughout the gospels.

Hades Is Not Gehenna

But, one thing is for certain: *Hades* is not *Gehenna*. *Hades* is clearly going to be destroyed on the day of judgment. *Hades* is therefore an interim state and is not indicative (in any way) of what takes place in *Gehenna* on the day of judgment.

Many who hold to the traditional view use this story of the rich man and Lazarus as the foundation of their teaching that when a person dies, they immediately go to heaven or hell after death. By doing so, they are forced to interpret *Gehenna* and *Hades* as meaning essentially the same thing. This is a perfect example of how influential a paradigm can be in blinding a person to reality.

I include several links at the end of the book that deal with *Hades*, *Sheol*, and the story of the rich man and Lazarus.

There is also a link to an insightful article on the history of *Sheol*'s use in the Old Testament. *Sheol* is the Hebrew equivalent of the Greek word *Hades*. The author shows how *Sheol* is a term used for the state of the dead. In fact, it is the state of man's condition when they die . . . they are dead.

One thing is for certain: Hades is not Gehenna. Hades is clearly going to be destroyed on the day of judgment. Hades is therefore an interim state and is not indicative (in any way) of what takes place in Gehenna on the day of judgment.

Soul Sleep

"Soul sleep" is the idea that the dead are asleep and are later awakened on the resurrection day. Those who hold to the idea of "soul sleep" believe that the dead are asleep. Therefore they would not have any sensation of suffering, well-being, etc.. There is a great deal of support in the Old and New Testament for this belief. If you take the story of the rich man and Lazarus literally then it is likely that you would reject this idea of soul sleep.

I have listed a few scriptures below, from the New Testament that support the idea of "soul sleep". Notice that the gospel writers consistently show Jesus as depicting someone who had passed away as being asleep. Indeed, the apostle Paul also refers to believers who are already dead as being asleep.

Matthew 9:24 he said, "Go away, for the **girl is not dead but sleeping**." And they laughed at him. *(ESV)*

Mark 5:39 And when he had entered, he said to them, "Why are you making a commotion and weeping? The child **is not dead but sleeping**." *(ESV)*

Luke 8:52 And all were weeping and mourning for her, but he said, "Do not weep, for **she is not dead but sleeping**." *(ESV)*

John 11:11-15 He said these things, and after this he said to them, "**Our friend Lazarus has fallen asleep**, but I am going so that I can **awaken** him." So the disciples said to him, "Lord, if he has fallen **asleep**, he will get well." **Now Jesus had been speaking about his death**, but they thought that he was speaking about **real sleep**. So Jesus then said to them plainly, "Lazarus has **died**, and I am glad for your sake that I was not there, so that you may believe. But let us go to him. *(LEB)*

1 Corinthians 15:6 Then he appeared to more than five hundred brothers at one time, most of whom are still alive, though some have fallen **asleep**. *(ESV)*

*1 Corinthians 15:17-18 And if Christ has not been raised, your faith is futile and you are still in your sins. Then those also who have fallen **asleep** in Christ have perished. (ESV)*

*1 Corinthians 15:20 But in fact Christ has been raised from the dead, the firstfruits of those who have fallen **asleep** (ESV)*

*1 Corinthians 15:50-52 I tell you this, brothers: flesh and blood cannot inherit the kingdom of God, nor does the perishable inherit the imperishable. Behold! I tell you a mystery. We shall not all **sleep**, but we shall all be changed, in a moment, in the twinkling of an eye, at the last trumpet. For the trumpet will sound, and the dead will be raised imperishable, and we shall be changed. (ESV)*

*1 Thessalonians 4:13 But we do not want you to be uninformed, brothers, about those who are **asleep**, that you may not grieve as others do who have no hope (ESV)*

*1 Thessalonians 4:14 For since we believe that Jesus died and rose again, even so, through Jesus, God will bring with him those who have fallen **asleep** (ESV)*

*1 Thessalonians 4:15 For this we declare to you by a word from the Lord, that we who are alive, who are left until the coming of the Lord, will not precede those who have fallen **asleep** (ESV)*

*1 Thessalonians 5:9-10 For God has not destined us for wrath, but to obtain salvation through our Lord Jesus Christ, who died for us so that whether we are awake or **asleep** we might live with him. (ESV)*

Again, I do not want to wade into this argument about Hades, (this interim period or place of the dead), as that is not the focus of this book. I just want to make you aware of "Soul Sleep" in case you have never heard of it.

The purpose of "Life Defined" is to show that the Bible very clearly teaches Conditionalism, not Traditionalism. I hope you can see the significance of Jesus' teaching on life, death and eternity and how important it is to accurately convey this truth.

Notable Conditionalists

Four of the great reformers of Christianity who were Conditionalists (who also held to the belief of "soul sleep") are listed below:

- **John Wycliffe**: translated the Bible into Middle English from Latin in 1382.
- **John Huss**: A famous priest and reformer who preferred trusting in the scriptures rather than the pope, was burned at the stake by the Catholic church in 1415.
- **William Tyndale**: the first person to translate the New Testament from the original Greek into English. This happened about the same time as the invention of the printing press. His printed Bibles spread all over Europe. Tyndale was executed (strangled and then burned at the stake) by Henry VIII for producing this translation.
- **Martin Luther**: the most notable reformer, usually credited with starting the reformation, although the works of others like Wycliffe, Huss and Tyndale definitely contributed to the environment in which this occurred.

Martin Luther boldly stood against the Pope's declaration that the soul was immortal. For more information on Luther's position on this topic as well as his belief in"soul sleep", I would recommend reading the article on the following web page:

https://www.truthaccordingtoscripture.com/documents/death/fr oom/luther-conditionalism.php#.XBaW03BjNPY

It is noteworthy that John Calvin (another reformer who came onto the scene while Luther was still alive) *severely* attacked the position of "soul sleep" that these other prominent reformers had held to. Calvin wrote a viscious pamphlet attacking those who held to "soul sleep" entitled "Psychopannychia". At the end of the day, due to Calvin's aggressive and tenacious writing (and the fact he was the last in this long line of Reformers) his doctrine won out for the long term.

Most Protestants hold Calvin and Luther in the same high esteem yet are unaware of their strong difference on this topic.

Calvin can be credited (infamously in my opinion) with overtaking the great work of these men who had correctly clarified the message (Conditionalism) of the gospel. Calvin was one of the strongest proponents of the idea of "eternal torment in Hell." Had Calvin not visciously discounted the beliefs of these other men, then Conditionalism would likely would have become the predominant belief throughout Christianity today.

> Martin Luther boldly stood against the Pope's declaration that the soul was immortal

Jesus Went to *Hades* When He Was Crucified

On the day of Pentecost the apostle Peter preached to a large crowd, many of whom would become believers in Christ that day upon being convicted by his sermon. Peter begins by explaining who Jesus was and that they (the crowd) had killed him. Yet God rasied him from the dead, because it was impossible for Jesus to be held by death.

> ***Acts 2:22-24*** *"Men of Israel, hear these words: Jesus of Nazareth, a man attested to you by God with mighty works and wonders and signs that God did through him in your midst, as you yourselves know—this Jesus, delivered up according to the definite plan and foreknowledge of God, you crucified and killed by the hands of lawless men. God raised him up, loosing the pangs of death, because it was not possible for him to be held by it." (ESV)*

Peter continues his sermon by quoting from King David (from Psalm 16:9-11).

> ***Acts 2:25-32*** *"For David says concerning him, 'I saw the Lord always before me, for he is at my right hand that I may not be shaken; therefore my heart was glad, and my tongue rejoiced; my flesh also will dwell in hope. For you will not abandon my* **soul** *(***psuche***) to* **Hades***, or let your Holy One see corruption. You have made known to me the paths of* **life** *(***zoe***); you will make me full of gladness with your presence.'"*
>
> *"Brothers, I may say to you with confidence about the patriarch David that he both died and was buried, and his tomb is with us to this day. Being therefore a prophet, and knowing that God had sworn with an oath to him that he would set one of his descendants on his throne, he foresaw and spoke about the* **resurrection** *of the Christ, that he was not abandoned to* **Hades***, nor did his* **flesh see corruption***. This Jesus God raised up, and of that we all are witnesses."* *(ESV)*

Peter points out that King David is dead and buried. (In other words, David has not been resurrected). He explains that God had

295

promised David that he would someday set one of David's descendants upon David's throne. This man would be known as the "Holy One," better known as the Messiah (Hebrew) or the Christ (Greek).

Peter also explains that David prophecied that God would not leave (abandon) Jesus' *psuche* in *Hades*. In other words, God would raise Jesus from the dead.

In addition, Jesus' flesh did not see corruption (Jesus' body did not decay). This certainly would not be true about David as Peter explains that David's tomb was still with them.

In summary, Peter's sermon about Jesus contained these main points:

> ➤ The crowd participated in killing Jesus, according to the plan and foreknowledge of God the Father.
> ➤ God did not leave Jesus' *psuche* in *Hades*. (Jesus was resurrected)
> ➤ God did not allow Jesus' body to decay. (Jesus was resurrected)

We can see that Peter understood *Hades* as a place of the dead. He doesn't explain anything else about *Hades*, just that God was not going to leave or abandon Jesus' *psuche* there. It is in fact Jesus' resurrection from death (being raised from *Hades*), that is the focal point of Peter's sermon, that everything else in his sermon hinges upon.

> Peter explains David's prophecy that God would not leave Jesus' **psuche** in Hades. In other words, God would raise Jesus from the dead.

What Paul Says about *Hades* and Mortality

Now that you know a bit more about *Hades* and man's mortality, let us take a closer look at what Paul says in 1 Corinthians 15. There is an important word here that we have missed.

> ***1 Cor. 15:50-57*** *But I say this, brothers, that flesh and blood is not able to inherit the kingdom of God, nor can corruption inherit incorruptibility. Behold, I tell you a mystery: we will not all fall asleep, but we will all be changed, in a moment, in the blink of an eye, at the last trumpet. For the trumpet will sound, and the dead will be raised imperishable, and we will be changed. For it is necessary for this perishable body to put on incorruptibility, and this mortal body to put on immortality. But whenever this perishable body puts on incorruptibility and this mortal body puts on immortality, then the saying that is written will take place:*
>
> *"Death is swallowed up in victory.*
>
> *55 Where, O **death** is your victory?* (**the actual Greek word is Hades, not death!**)
>
> *Where, O death, is your sting?*
>
> *Now the sting of death is sin, and the power of sin is the law. But thanks be to God, who gives us the victory through our Lord Jesus Christ!* (LEB)

See the actual Greek-English Interlinear text on the following page.

1 Corinthians 15:55 The Greek word in 15:55 is not "death" but *Hades*. This verse reads more accurately as, "Oh *Hades*, where is your victory?"

Greek	Translit.	Strong's	Parsing	Gloss	Gloss 2
ΠΟΥ	pou	G4226	Part Int	?-where	where ?
ΣΟΥ	sou	G4675	pp 2 Gen Sg	OF-YOU	
ΘΑΝΑΤΕ	thanate	G2288	n_ Voc Sg m	DEATH !	
ΤΟ	to	G3588	L_Nom Sg n	THE	
ΚΕΝΤΡΟΝ	kentron	G2759	n_ Nom Sg n	PIERCer	sting
ΠΟΥ	pou	G4226	Part Int	?-where	where ?
ΣΟΥ	sou	G4675	pp 2 Gen Sg	OF-YOU	
ΑΔΗ	hadE	G86	n_ Voc Sg m	UN-PERCEIVED !	unseen !
ΤΟ	to	G3588	L_Nom Sg n	THE	
ΝΙΚΟC	nikos	G3534	n_ Nom Sg n	CONQUEST	victory

55 O death, where [is] thy sting? O grave, where [is] thy victory?

The point Paul is making here, is that *Hades* will not have victory over the believer. The believer will be resurrected from *Hades*. (This is obvious from reading the entirety of 1 Corinthians 15:50-57 shown on the previous page.)

This is a major deviation from the Traditionalist view. The traditional view is that *Hades* is a place of torment for the unbeliever. Therefore, it is no surprise that *Hades* was not translated literally in this verse, as this would not fit the Traditionalist paradigm.

Hades Cannot Prevent Believers from Escaping Death

Toward the end of Jesus' ministry, he asks his closest disciples a very important question. He asks them, "Who do people say that I am?"

They give him an answer, and then Jesus turns the question directly to them . . . "Who do **you** say that I am? "

Jesus' ministry up to this point had been a living testimony to his closest disciples, revealing who he really was. They had not only listened to his teaching for nearly three years but had personally witnessed his miracles and observed his day-to-day living.

Now, Jesus presents the question directly to them: "Do you believe in me?" See the following conversation from the gospel according to Matthew.

> *Matt. 16:13-18 Now, when Jesus came into the district of Caesarea Philippi, he asked his disciples, "Who do people say that the Son of Man is?" And they said, "Some say John the Baptist, others say Elijah, and others Jeremiah or one of the prophets." He said to them, "But, who do you say that I am?"*
>
> *Simon Peter replied, "You are the Christ, the Son of the living God." And Jesus answered him, "Blessed are you, Simon Bar-Jonah! For flesh and blood has not revealed this to you, but my Father who is in heaven. And I tell you, you are Peter, and on this rock I will build my church, and the gates of **Hell** (Hades) shall not prevail against it." (ESV)*

Notice that the last verse translates *Hades* into English as "Hell." This is a huge mistake! *Hades* is not *Gehenna* in any way imaginable. This laxity in translation is a big part of the problem we are dealing with. However, there are some English translations that correctly insert the word *Hades* here instead of Hell, which is commendable.

Back to the context of the verses above. Peter answers Jesus' question by making a firm statement of faith that he believes Jesus is the Messiah, the Son of the living God. Based upon this confession, Jesus says that his church will be built upon this truth (the truth that Jesus is the Messiah, the Son of the living God).

Don't miss this next part . . .

Jesus then states that the gates of *Hades* will not overcome the church!

I have often heard this verse being incorrectly used to refer to the realm of Satan and his demonic forces and that this so-called realm of Satan (*Hades*) would not have enough power to overcome Christ's church. In other words, some people use this verse to portray Hell as Satan's headquarters.

This is not at all what this verse is saying. Satan has nothing to do with *Hades* other than the fact that it is his deception of Adam and Eve that has put us all into the certainty of death that we are born into.

Let me repeat this: Satan has nothing to do with *Hades*, other than the fact that he has been successful in getting all of us to enter Hades when our temporal life on earth is over. Remember, in John chapter 8 Jesus referred to Satan as a murderer from the beginning. Satan has in essence murdered all mankind. We are born into a state of death that has existed since mankind was expelled from the Garden of Eden, and lost access to the tree of zoe.

Satan stands as both the deceiver and the accuser of all mankind. Satan's ultimate goal at this point is to continue to deceive mortals in order to prevent them from believing in Jesus.

Satan does not have a headquarters located in *Hades*, or *Gehenna* for that matter. Satan's headquarters is actually the world you live in. His reign of darkness covers the whole earth. It is only through the "light of life" (zoe) that Jesus provides to the believer that one can escape this darkness.

Back to the verse. Jesus says that *Hades* will not overcome the church (those that are believers). This is because the gates of *Hades* will not be able to prevent believers from escaping the sentence of death. Jesus will free believers from *Hades* to receive eternal *zoe*.

There will be no more dying from that point on, hence the destruction of death. There will no longer be a state of the "unseen" dead (*Hades*), as there will not be anyone to inhabit such a state. Everyone will have been resurrected to receive Eternal Life or to be cast into the lake of fire, which is the second death.

Think back to the verse just quoted from King David, in Acts 2. As with many prophecies from the Old Testament, there are two fulfillments. However, there is something very unique about this prophecy (Psalm 16:9-11). The second fulfillment (Jesus resurrection) took place *before* the first fulfillment. Normally double fulfillments indicate that the first fulfillment occurred during the time and in the context of the Old Testament. This would be considered a type or shadow of the ultimate fulfillment which would come later through Jesus.

The first fulfillment (David's resurrection) has yet to occur. Though David has not yet been resurrected, he expressed his complete confidence that this will happen at some point in the future. He speaks of his assurance that God will not abandon him to *Hades*. He was confident, based on the fact that God had shown him the path to *zoe*. We do not know exactly what God revealed to David, but it was enough for David to rest in confidence.

Remember that in John 10:10, Jesus said he had come so that his sheep might have *zoe*. Jesus has come to end the sentence of death once and for all for those who believe in him.

> Jesus says that Hades will not overcome the church. This is because the gates of Hades will not be able to keep believers from escaping the sentence of death. Jesus will free believers from death and Hades to receive eternal **zoe**.

One Final Comment Regarding *Hades*: What It Is *Not*

Hades is not "purgatory" in any sense whatsoever.

Purgatory was a concept fabricated by men, that evolved over a period of several centuries. By the eleventh century AD, purgatory was a belief firmly held by the Roman Catholic Church. According to this belief man must undergo a purging of sin after death (or purification) in a place called "purgatory" before being allowed into heaven.

There are so many things wrong with this belief, it would take me a long time to go into them all—but primarily, the main fact would be that such a place is never mentioned in the Bible.

The belief in purgatory has generated subsequent errors that are even more disturbing. The notion of being able to purchase "indulgences" for those that have died became prevalent in the Roman Catholic Church by the fifteenth century. The purchased "indulgence" would supposedly enable the dead person in question to pass through purgatory much more quickly.

The notion of those still alive being able to purchase "indulgences" in order to expedite forgiveness or purification of someone in purgatory was one of the primary reasons that drove Martin Luther, a Catholic priest at the time, to produce his Ninety-Five Theses against the Roman Catholic Church. There is no biblical support for "purgatory" or "indulgences."

39

What is Tartaroo?

There is one other word that is translated as "Hell" one time in the New Testament. This occurs in 2 Peter 2:4, when Peter speaks of the angels that sinned long ago.

> *2 Pet. 2:4 For if God did not spare angels when they sinned, but cast them into **Hell** (tartaroo) and committed them to chains of gloomy darkness to be kept until the judgment. (ESV)*

Peter is referring to a temporary place of confinement for some fallen angels (demons). They are to be kept there until the day of judgment that takes place after the second resurrection.

Tartaroo is obviously a place where these demons are confined with chains of gloomy darkness. What these chains consist of is unknown and irrelevant. The point here is that these particular demons have been taken out of action, and are being held there until the day of judgment.

Luke 8:26-33 And they sailed to the region of the Gerasenes, which is opposite Galilee. And as he got out on the land, a certain man from the town met him who had demons and for a considerable time had not worn clothes and did not live in a house, but among the tombs. And when he saw Jesus, he cried out, fell down before him, and said with a loud voice, "What do I have to do with you, Jesus, Son of the Most High God? I beg you, do not torment me!" For he had commanded the unclean spirit to come out of the man. (For it had seized him many times, and he was bound with chains and shackles and was guarded, and breaking the bonds he would be driven by the demon into the deserted places. So Jesus asked him, "What is your name?" And he said, "Legion," because many demons had entered into him. And they began imploring him that he would not order them to depart into the abyss. Now there was a large herd of pigs feeding there on the hill, and they implored him that he would permit them to enter into those pigs. And he permitted them. So the demons came out of the man and entered into the pigs, and the herd rushed headlong down the steep slope into the lake and were drowned. (LEB)

These verses record when Jesus encountered a man possessed by a legion of demons. When confronted by Jesus, the demons pleaded with him not to send them into the abyss. This is likely a reference to *tartaroo*. It is a temporary place of darkness and torment where the demons would be held until the day of judgment.

This is obviously a place the demons greatly feared. Why Jesus spared these particular demons from this fate at that time is not clear.

40

What is *Gehenna*?

The word *Gehenna* occurs twelve times in the New Testament. Eleven of these are used by Jesus himself in his teachings.

Jesus' Use of Apocalyptic Terminology

Jesus heavily quotes from the Old Testament throughout the gospels. His reference to Old Testament scripture and prophecies would always reflect the *true intended thrust of those scriptures*, even if the contemporary view of those same scriptures was incorrect.

In fact, when Jesus alludes to Gehenna, he often combines two separate apocalyptic prophecies from the Old Testament. He actually mixes these two prophecies of total and massive destruction of wicked men, in several instances where he uses the word Gehenna. Gehenna itself is a direct reference to one of these dreadful prophecies of death and destruction. The other reference which is mixed in with several of the Gehenna verses incorporates terminology directly from the last chapter of the prophetic book, Isaiah.

Even if we are clueless about what Jesus is talking about in our contemporary times, Jesus was very intentional when he pulled two very graphic prophecies about death, judgement and slaughter from the Old Testament. He knew exactly what he was doing. He was not creating and interjecting some new concept on the fly. When Jesus used these two prophecies together, he intended to point to the ultimate day of judgement, which will involve massive slaughter, death and destruction. Neither of these prophecies from the old testament depict long term suffering or eternal torment. Rather, they clearly depict massive slaughter, with countless dead corpses.

For example, when Jesus spoke of *Gehenna*, he occasionally added phrases to emphasize this totally destructive nature of *Gehenna*. The traditional view argues that this terminology indicates "never ending torment", such as being continuously eaten by worms, where the person is always eaten, but never devoured, and always burning, but never consumed by the fire.

Jesus never made these insinuations. In fact, the Jews that heard him mention *Gehenna* would have associated the infamous valley of Hinnom with earlier prophecies of slaughter from the old testament. Jews with an accurate knowledge of Old Testament scripture would have associated *Gehenna* with a dreadful reputation as a place of horror, shame, disgust, and God's judgment against Judah, with the certainty of slaughter and *utter destruction*.

These Jews would not have associated Jesus' statements about *Gehenna* with "never ending torment" or "eternal suffering".

When Jesus quoted from Old Testament prophecies, he always reflected the true intended thrust of those scriptures, even if the contemporary view of those same scriptures was incorrect.

When Jesus alludes to Gehenna, he often combines two separate apocalyptic prophecies from the Old Testament. He mixes these two prophecies of the massive slaughter of wicked men, to emphasize this totally destructive nature of Gehenna.

Lake of Fire – The Second Death

Jesus used the word *Gehenna* as a metaphor to refer to the "lake of fire." The idea of the "lake of fire" is used several times by John in the book of Revelation. Twice he clearly defines the **lake of fire** as the **second death**. The second death will occur on the day of judgment after the second resurrection.

> ***Rev. 2:11*** *He who has an ear, let him hear what the Spirit says to the churches. The one who conquers will not be hurt by the **second death**. (ESV)*

> ***Rev. 20:16*** *Blessed and holy is the one who shares in the first resurrection! Over such the **second death** has no power, but they will be priests of God and of Christ, and they will reign with him for a thousand years. (ESV)*

> ***Rev. 20:14-15*** *Then, death and Hades were thrown into the lake of fire. **This is the second death, the lake of fire**. And if anyone's name was not found written in the book of life (zoe), he was thrown into the **lake of fire**. (ESV)*

> ***Rev. 21:8*** *But as for the cowardly, the faithless, the detestable, as for murderers, the sexually immoral, sorcerers, idolaters, and all liars, **their portion will be in the lake that burns with fire and sulfur, which is the second death** (ESV)*

The gospel according to Matthew records seven instances of *Gehenna*, while three occur in the gospel according to Mark, and one occurs in the gospel according to Luke.

The other instance occurs in the book of James, when *Gehenna* is used by James, the brother of Jesus. The apostle John never used the word *Gehenna* in his gospel or in any of his writings. Nor did Paul use it in any of his writings.

In Matthew, Jesus uses the word *Gehenna on four separate occasions.* In two of these instances, Jesus uses *Gehenna* multiple times in the same conversation.

I've listed each occurrence below:

*Matt. 5:22 But, I say to you that everyone who is angry with his brother will be liable to judgment; whoever insults his brother will be liable to the council; and whoever says, 'You fool!' will be liable to the **Hell (Gehenna)** of fire." (ESV)*

*Matt. 5:27-30 "You have heard that it was said, 'You shall not commit adultery.' But, I say to you that everyone who looks at a woman with lustful intent has already committed adultery with her in his heart. If your right eye causes you to sin, tear it out and throw it away. For it is better that you lose one of your members than that your whole body be thrown into **Hell (Gehenna)**. And if your right hand causes you to sin, cut it off and throw it away. For it is better that you lose one of your members than that your whole body go into **Hell (Gehenna)**." (ESV)*

*Matt. 10:28 "And do not fear those who kill the body but cannot kill the **soul (psuche)**. Rather fear him who can destroy both **soul (psuche)** and body in **Hell (Gehenna)**." (ESV)*

*Matt. 18:7-9 "Woe to the world for temptations to sin! For it is necessary that temptations come, but woe to the one by whom the temptation comes! And if your hand or your foot causes you to sin, cut it off and throw it away. It is better for you to enter **life (zoe)** crippled or lame than with two hands or two feet to be thrown into the eternal fire. And if your eye causes you to sin, tear it out and throw it away. It is better for you to enter **life (zoe)** with one eye than with two eyes to be thrown into the **Hell (Gehenna)** of fire." (ESV)*

Matt. 23:15 *"Woe to you, scribes and Pharisees, hypocrites! For you travel across sea and land to make a single proselyte, and when he becomes a proselyte, you make him twice as much a child of **Hell (Gehenna)** as yourselves." (ESV)*

Matt. 23:33 *"You serpents, you brood of vipers, how are you to escape being sentenced to **Hell (Gehenna)**?" (ESV)*

In Mark's gospel, Jesus uses the word Gehenna 3 times in a single conversation.

Mark 9:42-48 *"Whoever causes one of these little ones who believe in me to sin, it would be better for him if a great millstone were hung around his neck and he were thrown into the sea. And if your hand causes you to sin, cut it off. It is better for you to enter **life (zoe)** crippled than with two hands to go to **Hell (Gehenna)** to the unquenchable fire. And if your foot causes you to sin, cut it off. It is better for you to enter **life (zoe)** lame than with two feet to be thrown into **Hell (Gehenna)**. And if your eye causes you to sin, tear it out. It is better for you to enter the kingdom of God with one eye than with two eyes to be thrown into **Hell (Gehenna)**, where 'their worm does not die and the fire is not quenched.'" (ESV)*

Luke's gospel records Jesus using Gehenna once, very similar to the verse in Matthew 10:28

Luke 12:4-5 *"I tell you, my friends, do not fear those who kill the body, and after that have nothing more that they can do. But, I will warn you whom to fear: fear him who, after he has killed, has authority to cast into **Hell (Gehenna)**." (ESV)*

Finally, James uses the word Gehenna once in his letter.

*James 3:5-6 So also the tongue is a small member, yet it boasts of great things. How great a forest is set ablaze by such a small fire! And the tongue is a fire, a world of unrighteousness. The tongue is set among our members, staining the whole body, setting on fire the entire course of life, and set on fire by **Hell (Gehenna)**. (ESV)*

Gehenna Was Used as a Metaphor, But It Is a Real Place

Gehenna is the actual name of a valley located just outside of Jerusalem. In the mind of the Jew in Jesus' day, the *Gehenna* valley was historically associated with a prophetic curse of judgment. In fact, *Gehenna* was dreadfully infamous; its history was abhorrent to them. Most Jews that heard Jesus use the word *Gehenna* would have immediately associated it with a judgment of massive deadly slaughter, utter destruction, and annihilation. They would not have associated it with eternal suffering or torment.

> Jews that heard Jesus use the word **Gehenna** would have associated it with a judgment of massive deadly slaughter and utter destruction. They would not have associated it with eternal suffering or torment.

Etymology of the Word *Gehenna*

The history of *Gehenna* goes back to the days of the kingdom of Judah about seven to eight centuries earlier. The nation of Judah during that time had assimilated pagan rituals from the nations surrounding them of worshipping Baal. One of these rituals associated with Baal worship was the sacrifice of children upon the red-hot altar of Baal (and Moloch) as these living babies were sacrificed (killed) in the fire.

This practice took place in an area that became known as Topheth, within the Valley of Hinnom. By the time of Jesus, this Valley of Hinnom became known as *Gehenna* in the Greek language.

God responded to this horrific practice of child sacrifice with a most severe prophecy of judgment. See the following verses from the Old Testament, which depicts this idolatry of Judah and God's response.

> **2 Chron. 28:1-3** *Ahaz was twenty years old when he began to reign, and he reigned sixteen years in Jerusalem. And he did not do what was right in the eyes of the Lord, as his father David had done, but he walked in the ways of the kings of Israel. He even made metal images for the Baals, and he made offerings in the **Valley of the Son of Hinnom** and burned his sons as an offering, according to the abominations of the nations whom the Lord drove out before the people of Israel. (ESV)*

Ahaz was the king of Judah for sixteen years, in about 730 BC. Ahaz succumbed to pressure from Assyria to adopt the worship of Baal, which included making idols. One of the practices of worship to Baal included the ritual of burning their children alive on one of these idols. This took place in the Valley of Ben Hinnom (later known in Greek as *Gehenna*).

> **2 Chron. 33:1-6** *Manasseh was twelve years old when he began to reign, and he reigned fifty-five years in Jerusalem. And he did what was evil in the sight of the Lord . . . And he burned his sons as an offering in the **Valley of the Son of Hinnom**, and used fortune-telling and omens and sorcery, and dealt with mediums and with necromancers. He did much evil in the sight of the Lord, provoking him to anger. (ESV)*

King Manasseh continued with this detestable practice of sacrificing children in the fire in the Valley of Ben Hinnom. He was the grandson of Ahaz.

Josiah was the grandson of Manasseh. Josiah actually made an earnest effort to turn the kingdom of Judah back to worshipping the true God and to do away with the idolatrous practices of his father Amon and his grandfather Manasseh.

This section is a bit long but is a very interesting and powerful story about King Josiah, who was dedicated to repenting and restoring Judah to faithfully following the true God.

> *2 Kings 23:1-16 Then, the king sent, and all the elders of Judah and Jerusalem were gathered to him . . . And he read in their hearing all the words of the Book of the Covenant that had been found in the house of the Lord. And the king stood by the pillar and made a covenant before the Lord, to walk after the Lord and to keep his commandments and his testimonies and his statutes with all his heart and all his soul, to perform the words of this covenant that were written in this book. . . .*
>
> *. . . And he deposed the priests whom the kings of Judah had ordained to make offerings in the high places at the cities of Judah and around Jerusalem; those also who burned incense to Baal, to the sun and the moon and the constellations and all the host of the heavens. . . . And he defiled **Topheth**, which is in the **Valley of the Son of Hinnom**, that no one might burn his son or his daughter as an offering to Molech. (ESV)*

We see where Josiah desecrated Topheth. This desecration likely involved the breaking of idols and altars into pieces and then burning them into ashes or grinding them into dust. The desecration would also involve filling the area with dead men's bones or burning the bones first and then spreading the ashes over the area. In any case, the place became abhorrent to the Jews from then on, even unto the days of Jesus.

Josiah was the last "righteous" king that Judah had. After Josiah's death, the nation of Judah basically fell away and abandoned seeking God and his word.

The Prophecy of the Destruction of Judah

Jeremiah was a prophet in Judah from about 630-580 BC. During this time, he makes a prophecy regarding the destruction of Judah. Listen to the harsh words of judgment that God places upon Judah.

> ***Jer. 7:30-34*** *"For the sons of Judah have done evil in my sight, declares the Lord. They have set their detestable things in the house that is called by my name, to defile it. And they have built the high places of **Topheth, which is in the Valley of the Son of Hinnom,** to burn their sons and their daughters in the fire, which I did not command, nor did it come into my mind. Therefore, behold, the days are coming, declares the Lord, when it will no more be called **Topheth, or the Valley of the Son of Hinnom, but the Valley of Slaughter; for they will bury in Topheth, because there is no room elsewhere.** And the dead bodies of this people will be food for the birds of the air, and for the beasts of the earth, and none will frighten them away. And I will silence in the cities of Judah and in the streets of Jerusalem the voice of mirth and the voice of gladness, the voice of the bridegroom and the voice of the bride, for the land shall become a waste." (ESV)*

Jer. 19:1-15 Thus said Yahweh, "Go and buy a potter's earthenware jar, and take some of the elders of the people, and some of the leaders of the priests, and go out to the **Valley of Ben Hinnom**, which is at the entrance of the Gate of the Potsherd, and proclaim there the words that I speak to you. And you shall say, 'Hear the word of Yahweh, O kings of Judah and inhabitants of Jerusalem. Thus says Yahweh of hosts, the God of Israel: "Look, I am about to bring **disaster** upon this place so that everyone who hears it his ears will ring. Because they have forsaken me, and they have defaced this place, and they have made smoke offerings in it to other gods whom they have not known, they, nor their ancestors, nor the kings of Judah, and they have filled up this place with the blood of the innocent, and they have built the high places of Baal, to burn their children in the fire, burnt offerings to Baal, which I commanded not, and I ordered not, and it did not come to my mind.

"Therefore look, days are about to come," declares Yahweh, "when this place will no longer be called **Topheth or the Valley of Ben Hinnom, but the Valley of the Slaughter.** And I will lay waste the plans of Judah and Jerusalem in this place, and I will bring them to ruin by the sword before their enemies, and by the hand of those who seek their life, and I will give their dead bodies as food to the birds of heaven and to the animals of the earth. And I will make this city a horror, and an object of hissing, everyone who passes by it will be appalled, and will hiss because of all its wounds. And I will cause them to eat the flesh of their sons, and the flesh of their daughters, and each one will eat the flesh of his neighbor in the siege and in the distress which their enemies and those who seek their life inflict on them."'

*"Then you shall break the jar before the eyes of the men who go with you. And you shall say to them, 'Thus says Yahweh of hosts: "So I will break this people and this city as one breaks the vessel of the potter, so that it is not able to be repaired again. **And in Topheth they will bury until there is no room to bury**. Thus will I do to this place," declares Yahweh, "and to its inhabitants, to make this city like Topheth. And the houses of Jerusalem and the houses of the kings of Judah will be unclean like the place of Topheth, all the houses where they made smoke offerings upon their roofs to all the host of heaven, and where they poured out libations to other gods."'"*

Then Jeremiah came from Topheth, where Yahweh had sent him to prophesy, and he stood in the courtyard of the house of Yahweh and said to all the people, "Thus says Yahweh of hosts, the God of Israel, 'Look, I am about to bring to this city and upon all its towns all the disaster that I have pronounced against it, because they have hardened their neck to not hear my words.'" (LEB)

Jeremiah again pronounces judgment upon Judah. Notice what he says about the "Valley of Ben Hinnom" (*Gehenna*). Remember, *Gehenna* is the word that Jesus uses as a metaphor for the lake of fire.

The context of all these verses from the prophets is one of judgment, a massive slaughter with complete and utter destruction. There is no connotation of a lingering or everlasting torment, only numberless dead corpses.

> The context of these prophecies is one of judgment, a massive slaughter with complete and utter destruction. There is no connotation of a lingering or everlasting torment, only countless dead corpses.

Where the Worm Never Dies and Fire Never Goes Out

The following verse from Mark show Jesus use of the phrases: "where the worm never dies and where the fire is not quenched."

> *Mark 9:42-48 "Whoever causes one of these little ones who believe in me to sin, it would be better for him if a great millstone were hung around his neck and he were thrown into the sea. And if your hand causes you to sin, cut it off. It is better for you to enter life (zoe) crippled than with two hands to go to* **Hell (Gehenna) to the unquenchable fire.** *And if your foot causes you to sin, cut it off. It is better for you to enter life (zoe) lame than with two feet to be thrown into* **Hell (Gehenna).** *And if your eye causes you to sin, tear it out. It is better for you to enter the kingdom of God with one eye than with two eyes to be thrown into* **Hell (Gehenna),** *'where their worm does not die and the fire is not quenched.'"* (ESV)

Reminder: Jesus inserts quotes from Old Testament scriptures frequently during in his teachings. These quotes from the Old Testament are prophecies of doom, slaughter, and utter destruction—not eternal torment.

*Isa. 66:24 And they shall go out and look on the dead bodies of the men who have rebelled against me. **For their worm shall not die, their fire shall not be quenched,** and they shall be an abhorrence to all flesh. (ESV)*

Jesus quotes this idea of "their worm shall not die, and their fire is not quenched" from this very last verse of the book of Isaiah.

Notice that Isaiah is not talking about people who are eternally suffering in torment. He is clearly speaking of dead corpses after a great and terrible slaughter.

The idea of "their worm shall not die" is referring to the maggots that will consume the dead corpses that are laying everywhere after a great slaughter. In other words, the idea is that their destruction will be complete; there will be no end to the worms, until there is no more decaying flesh for them to eat. There is no portrayal of worms eating a conscious person. There is no idea conveyed of suffering but rather of complete destruction.

> The idea of "their worm shall not die" is referring to the maggots that will consume the dead corpses that are laying everywhere after a great slaughter

Similarly, the idea of "their fire shall not be quenched" is also referring to the final destruction of those dead corpses upon the battlefield. Corpses will be burned until they are utterly and totally gone. The fire that burns them will not be quenched. This is not referring to some sort of eternal fire but rather an unquenchable fire that will not be extinguished until all the dead bodies have been completely consumed (utterly destroyed) by the fire. Again, there is no idea conveyed of suffering or of eternal torment. Dead corpses do not feel pain.

317

The scripture above speaks of those who will go out and look upon dead bodies. There is nothing implied about tormenting conscious people. Rather, they are looking upon dead and decaying bodies that are being eaten by maggots, or burned in pyres or heaps to get rid of them.

Jesus' use of this phrase is not alluding to eternal torment but to the great day of judgment and slaughter, which is prophesied in the very last verse of Isaiah.

Note: *Jesus is tying this prophecy by Isaiah (Isaiah 66:24) to the prophecies made by Jeremiah (Jeremiah 7:30-34 and 19:1-15) when Jeremiah spoke of the judgment that will take place in the Valley of Hinnom (Gehenna). Neither of these prophecies involved eternal torment. There is certain to be a period of suffering in such slaughters, but those who are being slaughtered will be completely destroyed.*

Weeping and Gnashing of Teeth

Luke 13:24-30 "Strive to enter through the narrow door. For many, I tell you, will seek to enter and will not be able. When once the master of the house has risen and shut the door, and you begin to stand outside and to knock at the door, saying, 'Lord, open to us,' then he will answer you, 'I do not know where you come from.' Then, you will begin to say, 'We ate and drank in your presence, and you taught in our streets.' But, he will say, 'I tell you, I do not know where you come from. Depart from me, all you workers of evil!' **In that place there will be weeping and gnashing of teeth, when you see Abraham and Isaac and Jacob and all the prophets in the kingdom of God but you yourselves cast out.** *And people will come from east and west, and from north and south, and recline at table in the kingdom of God. And behold, some are last who will be first, and some are first who will be last." (ESV)*

Another phrase that is traditionally attributed to eternal torment in *Gehenna* is the phrase "weeping and gnashing of teeth." Jesus uses this phrase several times in his teachings to refer to the intense anger, regret, and sorrow of those who have been left out (or cast out) of the kingdom of God.

> These quotes from the Old Testament are prophecies of doom, slaughter, and utter destruction - not eternal torment

Notice the other phrase: "when you see." This is the actual trigger for weeping and gnashing of teeth, not the torment.

When those unbelievers realize that they have been left behind and are doomed, they will experience fear, sorrow, utter despair, and intense rage. Such is the description of weeping and gnashing of teeth.

While this phrase indicates intense anger and regret from being left behind and thrown into eternal fire, the weeping and gnashing of teeth **is *not* indicative of eternal suffering**.

It has been presumed to mean that by those who hold to the traditional view who want to see it that way. But, there is no imperative by Jesus' use of the phrase that supports this.

As you can see, the weeping and gnashing of teeth are due to anger, rage, and regret from being cast outside and not able to enter. This phrase doesn't allude to physical pain or eternal torment. Gnashing of teeth indicates extreme rage, while weeping would indicate sorrow and regret.

*Matt. 13:40-42 Just as the weeds are gathered and burned with fire, so will it be at the end of the age. The Son of Man will send his angels, and they will gather out of his kingdom all causes of sin and all law-breakers, and throw them into the fiery furnace. In that place there will be **weeping and gnashing of teeth**. (ESV)*

Some will argue that the verse above indicates that weeping and gnashing of teeth are due to pain and suffering in the fiery furnace. I can see where that might seem to make sense if you were determined to take that path.

However, this verse is actually describing the destruction that is going to take place on the day of judgment. There will indeed be weeping and gnashing of teeth, as rage and despair overtake those who are about to be destroyed. How long those who are thrown into the fiery furnace will suffer before they are destroyed is not mentioned. But, the complete destruction of these people is certain. They will ultimately be annihilated. They will not be tormented forever.

Ps. 112:10 The wicked man sees it and is angry; he gnashes his teeth and melts away; the desire of the wicked will perish! (ESV)

As you can see in this Psalm, the phrase "he gnashes his teeth" is used as an expression of intense anger, not as a reference to pain. This is a direct reference to the anger of the wicked man, who sees the blessing of the man who fears the Lord.

Notice that the wicked man melts away, and his desires will perish.

Acts 7:54 Now, when they heard these things they were enraged, and they ground their teeth at him. (ESV)

Here in the book of Acts, we see the Jews becoming so angry at Stephen that they ground their teeth at him. In their intense anger they stoned Stephen to death.

Learning the Vocabulary of Judgement (by Edward Fudge)

I highly recommend the following video of a lecture done by Edward Fudge. Fudge does a thorough job of reviewing multiple scriptures regarding the topics discussed in the preceeding pages. The video quality is not great, but the audio is fine and the content is excellent.

https://www.youtube.com/watch?v=VXVugW3TEsY

You can also find this lecture by searching for the following at youtube.com:

"Debunking Proof Texts for Eternal Torment - Edward Fudge Lecture, 2"

Note: Fudge passed away in 2017. He did not know me nor was aware of this book. In other words, he may or may not not have endorsed or agreed with all of my views.

The Ultimate Question about Hell

In Revelation 20, the apostle John (also the author of the gospel according to John) states that on the final day of judgment those whose names are found in the book of *zoe* will be given Eternal *zoe*. Those whose names are not found in the book of *zoe* will be thrown into the lake of fire which is the second death.

> *Rev. 20:13-15 And the sea gave up the dead who were in it, death and Hades gave up the dead who were in them, and they were judged, each one of them, according to what they had done. Then, death and Hades were thrown into the **lake of fire**. **This is the second death, the lake of fire**. And if anyone's name was not found written in the **book of life (zoe)**, he was thrown into the **lake of fire**. (ESV)*

So the question about Hell comes down to this. Based on what you now know about *psuche* and *zoe*, how do you interpret the second death?

Would you agree with the traditional view, which defines the "second death" as eternal separation from God and being cast into

Hell as a place of eternal torment, continuous burning, continuously being eaten by worms, and everlasting darkness?

Would you agree with the traditional view, which defines Jesus' repeated use of the word "perishing" (utter destruction) as meaning eternal separation from God and being cast into Hell as a place of eternal excruciating torment?

Note: It is important to remember that we are all already initially separated from God (we are all initially in a status of death). It is only when we are born again, via the imputation of zoe, that we are reunited with God on a spiritual level.

Maybe it would just be better to take Jesus and John at their word. Let us assume the "second death" means the second death. Likewise, utter destruction means utter destruction.

Clarifying Satan's Connection to *Gehenna*

Satan is not directly connected to *Gehenna*, as many believe. However, it **will** be Satan's ultimate destination. But it is not his place at this time.

I mentioned earlier that *Gehenna* is not a headquarters for Satan. It is not his dwelling place, as it has been depicted for centuries. In fact, it will become his final place of punishment, where he and his angels will be tormented forever.

Keep in mind that this is not their place today; they currently have free range throughout the world of men, seeking to deceive and enslave men to darkness. They seek to keep mankind enslaved on the path to death.

> *Rev. 20:10 . . . and the devil who had deceived them was thrown into the lake of fire and sulfur, where the beast and the false prophet were, and they will be tormented day and night forever and ever. (ESV)*

But, the devil's (Satan's) time is coming, when he will be thrown into the lake of fire. It appears that Satan and his angels will be tormented forever.

But, that is not the case for humans.

Difference between Humans and Angels

Let's take a look at a statement that Jesus makes about angels. In Luke 20:34-36, Jesus makes a comment about those who are worthy to participate in the age to come, and the resurrection (to eternal zoe).

> *Luke 20:34-36 And Jesus said to them, "The sons of this age marry and are given in marriage, but those who are considered worthy to attain to that age and to the resurrection from the dead neither marry nor are given in marriage, **for they cannot die anymore, because they are equal to angels and are sons of God, being sons of the resurrection.** (ESV)*

Jesus says those believers will be like the angels, for they cannot die anymore. They are equal to the angels (in that sense). They have become children of God, children of the resurrection.

Remember, it is the spirit of God, that gives zoe. When a person believes in Jesus as the messiah, counts on his death and resurrection as their source or salvation, and live their life henceforth in trust and continual dependence upon this salvation, they are born again. This new birth is not of the flesh, but of the spirit of God, they become children of God, assured of eternal zoe, and being children of the resurrection to zoe.

This gift of immortality, upon the resurrection, will make the child of God like the angels, in the sense that they can no longer die!

Zoe will culminate it's final effect in the believer as they are raised to immortal zoe, with an imperishable body. It is specifically "**zoe**" **(life as God has it)** which is deposited into the psuche of the believer, via the indwelling Spirit of God, that imparts immortality.

As we take one last look at John chapter 5, think about the following:

God has zoe in himself, and he has granted Jesus to have zoe in himself. Thus, Jesus can give zoe to whomever he is pleased to give it. Zoe comes from the Holy Spirit, which is inherently part of God and the Jesus.

> *John 5:21-29 For as the Father raises the dead and gives them life, so also the Son gives life to whom he will. For the Father judges no one, but has given all judgment to the Son, that all may honor the Son, just as they honor the Father. Whoever does not honor the Son does not honor the Father who sent him. Truly, truly, I say to you, whoever hears my word and believes him who sent me has eternal life. He does not come into judgment, but has passed from death to life.*
>
> *"Truly, truly, I say to you, an hour is coming, and is now here, when the dead will hear the voice of the Son of God, and those who hear will live. For as the Father has life in himself, so he has granted the Son also to have life in himself. And he has given him authority to execute judgment, because he is the Son of Man.*
>
> *Do not marvel at this, for an hour is coming when all who are in the tombs will hear his voice and come out, those who have done good to the resurrection of life, and those who have done evil to the resurrection of judgment. (ESV)*

Humans have been in an initial state of death, since Adam and Eve were banished form the Garden of Eden and the Tree of Life (zoe).

Only God, Jesus, and the Holy Spirit are the "source" of zoe, that can be "given" to another creature.

It seems plausible that the angels were given immortality when they were created, although no angel has "zoe" inherent from within them, in other words, they cannot bestow "zoe" upon any other creature.

However, this verse from Luke seems to indicate that angles are not capable of dying. Thus Jesus statement that those believers who are considered worthy to attain to the resurrection will be like the angels in the sense that they can no longer die, makes complete sense, when you understand the purpose of the resurrection.

The salvific effect of the resurrection is that it resurrects us from death! The effect of that is that we can no longer die, or remain dead. We will be given immortality via the gift of zoe into the ages.

Having said all of this, could it be that the reason that Satan and his angels will be tormented forever is because as angels they were created with (given) immortality?

This seems to be a plausible explanation, although the Bible is not emphatically clear about this. There are some who believe that Satan and his angels will be destroyed. I am not going to lose any sleep over this either way. God will see that Satan and his demons (fallen angels) will get what they deserve.

Life
Defined

41

Zoe For All Men

Romans 5:17-18 For if, because of one man's trespass, death *reigned through that one man, much more will those who receive the abundance of grace and the free gift of righteousness reign in* life (zoe*) through the one man Jesus Christ. Therefore, as one trespass led to* condemnation *for all men, so one act of righteousness leads to justification and* life (zoe) *for all men. (ESV)*

Question: If one trespass of Adam lead to condemnation for all men, then what did the actual "condemnation" consist of?

Was the condemnation supposed to be "Hell"? Did God pronounce an "eternity of torment" for Adam and Eve, that then progressed on down to all men?

What was the punishment for Adam? It was this... **death**.

Adam's access to the "Tree of Life" was taken away. He and Eve were banished from the garden. God told them their destiny was that they would die and return to dust and ashes. From they came and to dust they would return.

This has been the state of man ever since. It is only through Jesus' death, substituted for our death, that this sentence was taken away, for those whose believe in Jesus as Messiah, Lord and Savior.

As a result of believing in the one man's (Jesus') act of righteousness, people are justified by this act of faith and receive the **gift of zoe**. This *zoe* preserves that person's *psuche* for eternal *zoe*, they are now immortal, they have exchanged the status of death for *zoe*.

The idea of "Hell" as it is perceived by people today, did not exist in Genesis, or anywhere in the Old Testament. In fact, the notion of "eternal torment" was nowhere in Jesus mind when he spoke of Gehenna. It was only later (about 150 years after Jesus' resurrection), that this false notion began to infiltrate into Christian circles as more and more of the Greek cultural beliefs began to mix with Christian teaching.

If you read all of Romans chapter 5, you will see why the "resurrection" plays such an important part in this whole section by Paul. It is the resurrection of Jesus, that displayed Jesus' power and victory over death. It is Jesus' resurrection, that gives the believer assurance of their own resurrection. You see, it is not "eternal torment" that is the issue here, nor anywhere else in Paul's writings. Remember, Paul never mentions Gehenna (Hell) in any of this writing. ***That's because "eternal torment" is a non-issue.*** "Eternal torment" is a straw man injected by Satan to detract from the real argument of Jesus. Satan has always been and always will be a deceiver, twisting any truth coming from God.

If Satan cannot just outright deceive a person from believing in Jesus, then he will do the next best thing. He will twist and distort the real message of Christ, so that people will be confused about the original message. This distortion alone, contributes to reducing fruit in the life of the believer and is a major deterence to unbelievers accepting the message of salvation that is available through Jesus.

To answer my first question, "Hell" really is the actual condemnation that Genesis is talking about. You see, when Jesus refers to "Gehenna" in the 3 synoptic gospels, as well as the fire that is never quenched and the worm that never dies, he is mixing two metaphors that reference back to 2 apocalyptic scriptures in the Old Testament. This is discussed in detail in the previous chapters.

When Jesus spoke of Gehenna, he was referring to the day of judgement, when those who have rejected Jesus will be killed (destroyed), in the lake of fire, which is the second death.

42

Revelation 14 & 20

Earlier we discussed that many of Jesus statements were direct references to scripture from the Old Testament. Indeed, without understanding these connections it is impossible to have an accurate understanding of what of Jesus meant.

This also holds true for many statements made by New Testament authors and certainly holds true for the apostle John who as we have seen, has written the gospel of John and the book of Revelation. Nowhere is this more evident than in the book of Revelation, where John uses vivid imagery to depict future events including the day of judgement.

In order to accurately understand this prophetic imagery, we have to understand the imagery that John is directly connecting to from the Old Testament.

Two of the most controversial sections of verses are found in the book of Revelation, in chapters 14 and 20. If you try to explain these sections without understanding their connection to their correlated imagery found in the Old Testament, you will indeed interpret these verses incorrectly.

At this point, I would like to direct you to a video of Chris Date where he is speaking in a debate. Chris is one of the main contributors to the website RethinkingHell.com. Chris does an excellent job of explaining these verses and their connection to Old Testament scripture.

Chris is a solid Christian young man, with a firm faith in Jesus. I highly respect him, and have no hesitation recommending what he has to say regarding these issues.

The debate is fairly long, however if you pick up at 18:33 into the debate and listen until about 28:00, you will hear the main points regarding Revelation 14, 20 and a correlated section from Matthew 13. This section of video lasts about 10 minutes.

To find the link to Chris' debate do a search on YouTube for: "Chris Date - Conditional Immortality: A Comprehensive Case". (As of November, 2018)

Note: *Neither Chris Date nor RethinkingHell.com has read or reviewed my book at the time of this publishing. Therefore they might not endorse or agree with all my views in this book.*

I have listed the scriptures below as a reference for you as you listen to Chris's comments.

Matthew 13:24-30 *He put another parable before them, saying, "The kingdom of heaven may be compared to a man who sowed good seed in his field, but while his men were sleeping, his enemy came and sowed weeds[c]among the wheat and went away. So when the plants came up and bore grain, then the weeds appeared also. And the servants[d] of the master of the house came and said to him, 'Master, did you not sow good seed in your field? How then does it have weeds?' He said to them, 'An enemy has done this.' So the servants said to him, 'Then do you want us to go and gather them?' But he said, 'No, lest in gathering the weeds you root up the wheat along with them. Let both grow together until the harvest, and at harvest time I will tell the reapers, "**Gather the weeds first and bind them in bundles to be burned, but gather the wheat into my barn.**"""* (ESV)

Matthew 13:36-43 *Then he left the crowds and went into the house. And his disciples came to him, saying, "Explain to us the parable of the weeds of the field." He answered, "The one who sows the good seed is the Son of Man. The field is the world, and the good seed is the sons of the kingdom. The weeds are the sons of the evil one, and the enemy who sowed them is the devil. The harvest is the end of the age, and the reapers are angels. **Just as the weeds are gathered and burned with fire, so will it be at the end of the age.**

The Son of Man will send his angels, and they will gather out of his kingdom all causes of sin and all law-breakers, and throw them into the fiery furnace. In that place there will be weeping and gnashing of teeth. Then the righteous will shine like the sun in the kingdom of their Father. He who has ears, let him hear. (ESV)

Malachi 4:1-3 For behold, the day is coming, burning like an oven, when all the arrogant and all evildoers will be stubble. The day that is coming shall set them ablaze, says the Lord of hosts, so that it will leave them neither root nor branch. 2 But for you who fear my name, the sun of righteousness shall rise with healing in its wings. You shall go out leaping like calves from the stall. 3 And you shall tread down the wicked, for they will be ashes under the soles of your feet, on the day when I act, says the Lord of hosts. (ESV)

Revelation 14:9-11 And another angel, a third, followed them, saying with a loud voice, "If anyone worships the beast and its image and receives a mark on his forehead or on his hand, 10 he also will **drink the wine of God's wrath, poured full strength into the cup of his anger**, and **he will be tormented with fire and sulfur in the presence of the holy angels and in the presence of the Lamb**. 11 And **the smoke of their torment goes up forever and ever, and they have no rest, day or night**, these worshipers of the beast and its image, and whoever receives the mark of its name." (ESV)

Revelation 20:10-15 And the devil who deceived them was thrown into the lake of fire and sulphur, where the beast and the false prophet also are, and they will be tormented day and night forever and ever. And I saw a great white throne and the one who was seated on it, from whose presence earth and heaven fled, and a place was not found for them. And I saw the dead—the great and the small—standing before the throne, and books were opened. And another book was opened, which is the book of life (zoe), and the dead were judged by what was written in the books, according to their deeds. And the sea gave up the dead who were in it, and Death and Hades gave up the dead who were in them, and each one was judged according to their deeds. And Death and Hades were thrown into the lake of fire. This is the second death—the lake of fire. And if anyone was not found written in the book of life (zoe), he was thrown into the lake of fire. (LEB)

*Jude 7 just as Sodom and Gomorrah and the surrounding cities, which likewise indulged in sexual immorality and pursued unnatural desire, **serve as an example by undergoing a punishment of eternal fire**. (ESV)*

*2 Peter 2:4-6 For if God did not spare angels when they sinned, but cast them into Hell (tartaroo) and committed them to chains of gloomy darkness to be kept until the judgment; if he did not spare the ancient world, but preserved Noah, a herald of righteousness, with seven others, when he brought a flood upon the world of the ungodly; **if by turning the cities of Sodom and Gomorrah to ashes he condemned them to extinction, making them an example of what is going to happen to the ungodly** (ESV)*

2 Peter 3:5-7 *For they deliberately overlook this fact, that the heavens existed long ago, and the earth was formed out of water and through water by the word of God,* **and that by means of these the world that then existed was deluged with water and perished. But by the same word the heavens and earth that now exist are stored up for fire, being kept until the day of judgment and destruction of the ungodly.** *(ESV)*

Ezekial 20: 47-48 *Say to the forest of the Negeb, Hear the word of the Lord: Thus says the Lord God, Behold, I will kindle a fire in you, and it shall devour every green tree in you and every dry tree.* **The blazing flame shall not be quenched, and all faces from south to north shall be scorched by it. All flesh shall see that I the Lord have kindled it; it shall not be quenched."** *(ESV)*

Amos 5:5-6 *Seek me and live; or cross over to Beersheba; for Gilgal shall surely go into exile, and Bethel shall come to nothing." Seek the Lord and live,* **lest he break out like fire in the house of Joseph, and it devour, with none to quench it for Bethel** *(ESV)*

Jeremiah 7:32-33 *Therefore, behold, the days are coming, declares the Lord, when it will no more be called Topheth, or the Valley of the Son of Hinnom,* **but the Valley of Slaughter; for they will bury in Topheth, because there is no room elsewhere.** *And the* **dead bodies of this people** *will be food for the birds of the air, and for the beasts of the earth, and none will frighten them away. (ESV)*

Obadiah 16 *For as you have drunk on my holy mountain, so all the nations shall drink continually;* **they shall drink and swallow, and shall be as though they had never been.** *(ESV)*

Genesis 19:23-29 The sun had risen on the earth when Lot came to Zoar. Then the Lord rained on Sodom and Gomorrah **sulfur and fire from the Lord out of heaven**. And he overthrew those cities, and all the valley, and all the inhabitants of the cities, and what grew on the ground. But Lot's wife, behind him, looked back, and she became a pillar of salt.

And Abraham went early in the morning to the place where he had stood before the Lord. And he looked down toward Sodom and Gomorrah and toward all the land of the valley, and he looked and, behold, the **smoke of the land went up like the smoke of a furnace.** (ESV)

Isaiah 34:8-10 For the Lord has a day of vengeance, a year of recompense for the cause of Zion. And the streams of Edom shall be turned into pitch, and her soil into **sulfur; her land shall become burning pitch. Night and day it shall not be quenched**; its smoke shall go up forever. (ESV)

Matthew 25:45-46 Then he will answer them, saying, 'Truly, I say to you, as you did not do it to one of the least of these, you did not do it to me.' And these will go away into **eternal punishment**, but the righteous into **eternal life (zoe)**." (ESV)

Life
Defined

43

Resurrection... the Defining Factor

The traditional viewpoint believes that a person goes to heaven or Hell as soon as they die. If that is true, then how do you explain the need for resurrection?

How do you explain the important role that the Bible gives to the resurrection? Why does the Bible say it was important that Jesus was resurrected from the dead?

Was Jesus resurrected to save believers from Hell? Or death?

Traditionalists often claim Jesus went to Hell when he died (i.e., *Hell as they define it*), but the Bible does not say that anywhere!

Instead, in the verses that the traditional view claims supports this idea (Acts2:22-36), Peter is quoting from Psalm 16 where Peter indicates that David was prophesying about Jesus. In Psalm 16, David prophesies that God would not leave Jesus' body to decay, nor leave him in *Sheol*. *Sheol* in the Old Testament was loosely interpreted as a place of the dead or the grave. *Hades* is the Greek equivalent to the Hebrew word *Sheol*. Peter does not use the word "Gehenna" here, but uses the Greek word Hades. Gehenna and Hades are not equivalent in any way. Yet, many bibles translate them both into the English word "Hell". Those who hold to the traditional view will use the word Hell and Hades interchangeably (and inconsistently) in order to support their confusing views.

Look closely at David's statement. Peter's main point in quoting from David in this passage from Psalm 16, is to point out that David *died*, and that his *tomb still remains*. In other words, David is still dead, and still in his tomb. Thus David's body did indeed decay, and he is still in Hades. Peter's emphasis is that David's prophesy is not refering to David himself, but rather to the resurrection of Jesus from the dead.

When Jesus died, God indeed did not abandon his pusche to Hades, nor did Jesus' body decay (see corruption). God raised Jesus from the dead on the third day.

Peter's emphasis on the resurrection of Jesus is to show Jesus' victory over death. Hell (Gehenna) has nothing to do with this section of scripture.

> *Acts 2:24-31* *God raised him (Jesus) up, loosing the pangs of death, because it was not possible for him to be held by it. For David says concerning him,*
>
> *"'I saw the Lord always before me, for he is at my right hand that I may not be shaken; therefore my heart was glad, and my tongue rejoiced; my flesh also will dwell in hope.*
>
> *For you will not abandon my soul to Hades, or let your Holy One see corruption.*
>
> *You have made known to me the paths of life (zoe); you will make me full of gladness with your presence.'*
>
> *"Brothers, I may say to you with confidence about the patriarch David that he both died and was buried, and his tomb is with us to this day. Being therefore a prophet, and knowing that God had sworn with an oath to him that he would set one of his descendants on his throne, he foresaw and spoke about the resurrection of the Christ, that he was not abandoned to Hades, nor did his flesh see corruption. (ESV)*

Resurrection is Victory Over Death

Resurrection is the primary objective that Jesus accomplished. Jesus did not come to save people from eternal torment in Hell, but rather to save people from eternal death (destruction).

If a person is already in heaven or Hell after they die, then explain the purpose of the resurection! A common traditional explanation for the resurrection, is that a person is given a new imperishable body during the resurrection, so that they can then go thru a formal judgment, and then return back to Hell to resume their excruciating torment, or return to a heavenly environment as their reward.

Seriously?

Is this the significance of the resurrection? Is the resurrection merely a blip in the road of the after-life?

Or on the other hand, could the resurrection be the culmination of all that the Bible speaks of in the old and new testaments, as well as the fulfillment of all promise of scripture?

Jesus resurrection is the pinnacle of the Bible. This is because Jesus has overcome and defeated death.

The resurrection was the exclamation point of Jesus' purpose, which he completed via his death on the cross, and subsequent resurrection from the dead.

There will indeed be a resurrection on the day of judgement. All mankind will be resurrected from the dead. Those whose names are written in the "Book of Life (zoe)" will be raised to eternal life (zoe). Those whose names are not in the book of life, will be destroyed in the lake of fire, which John aptly calls the "second death" several times in the Book of Revelation.

Collosians 1:18 *And he is the head of the body, the church. He is the beginning, the **firstborn from the dead**, that in everything he might be preeminent. (ESV)*

Revelation 1:4-5 *Grace to you and peace from him who is and who was and who is to come, and from the seven spirits who are before his throne, and from Jesus Christ the faithful witness**, the firstborn of the dead**, and the ruler of kings on earth (ESV)*

I Corinthians 15:12-26 *Now if Christ is proclaimed as **raised from the dead**, how can some of you say that there is no resurrection of the dead? But if there is no resurrection of the dead, then not even Christ has been raised. And if Christ has not been raised, then our preaching is in vain and your faith is in vain. We are even found to be misrepresenting God, because we testified about God that he raised Christ, whom he did not raise if it is true that the dead are not raised. For if the dead are not raised, not even Christ has been raised. **And if Christ has not been raised, your faith is futile and you are still in your sins**. **Then those also who have fallen asleep in Christ have perished**. If in Christ we have hope in this life only, we are of all people most to be pitied. **But in fact Christ has been raised from the dead, the firstfruits of those who have fallen asleep**. For as by a man came death, by a man has come also the resurrection of the dead. For as in Adam all die, **so also in Christ shall all be made alive**. But each in his own order: Christ the firstfruits, then at his coming those who belong to Christ. Then comes the end, when he delivers the kingdom to God the Father **after destroying every rule and every authority and power**. For he must reign until he has put all his enemies under his feet. **The last enemy to be destroyed is death**. (ESV)*

44

Hell No – The Book of Acts

Let me ask you a question. If Hell was the main problem that Jesus came to save us from, don't you think that this message would have been preached in the early church? Wouldn't we see a dire warning to those who had never heard the gospel, that they must escape the fires of Hell?

Do you realize, that the word Hell (Gehenna) is never mentioned in the book of Acts? Neither Peter, nor Paul, nor Stephen, nor anyone else ever mentions Hell, or eternal torment anywhere in the book of Acts. On the other hand, they frequently mention Jesus being raised from the dead, and the real hope of resurrection for those who believe.

However, the Greek word Hades, is mentioned in Acts 2:27, with reference to a quote from the Old Testament, where King David prophecies that "God will not abandon Jesus' *psuche* in Hades". As you should know by now, Hades is the place of the dead. In the old testament, the Hebrew word "Sheol" (equivalent to the Greek word Hades) is often simply portrayed as the grave. I covered Hades in a previous chapter, but suffice to say, that Hades is the place of the dead. Some simply consider it to be no more than the grave where all mankind is in a state of sleep until the resurrection day. Others believe it is a place of conscious torment and paradise. The condition of torment or paradise would depend on which side of the chasm a person would be located within Hades, as depicted in Jesus story of the rich man and Lazarus in Luke 16. I am not taking on stand on either side of this Hades argument. This is an insignificant issue compared to the matter of death, *zoe* and the huge consequences due to the false understanding about Gehenna.

It is very important to take note of this fact: the Greek word Hades that is used in Acts 2, is **NOT** the Greek word Gehenna! There is a huge difference! I hear preachers occasionally saying that Jesus went to Hell when he died, and then he was later resurrected. This is so wrong! Jesus did not go to Hell. When Jesus died, he just died, his *psuche* was killed.

Trying to make Jesus' death into something else, diminishes from the powerful message that is portrayed in the book of Acts. Jesus was resurrected **from death**. It is only because of his resurrection from death, that any of us has hope being raised from the dead. Death is the problem, the only problem. Resurrection via the gift of eternal zoe, is the only solution to this problem.

> **Death is "the" problem.**
>
> Resurrection via the gift of Eternal Zoe,
>
> is the only solution to this problem
>
>
> Resurrection to "Life" is directly tied to Zoe
>
>
> There is no resurrection without Zoe

Death is the problem that Paul emphasizes over, and over again in the book of Acts. When God raised Jesus from Hades, it was simply his *psuche* that was resurrected.

> *Acts 2:22-32* "*Men of Israel, hear these words: Jesus of Nazareth, a man attested to you by God with mighty works and wonders and signs that God did through him in your midst, as you yourselves know— this Jesus,[c] delivered up according to the definite plan and foreknowledge of God, you crucified and killed by the hands of lawless men. God raised him up, loosing the pangs of death, because it was not possible for him to be held by it.*
>
> *For David says concerning him,* "*'I saw the Lord always before me, for he is at my right hand that I may not be shaken; therefore my heart was glad, and my tongue rejoiced; my flesh also will dwell in hope.* ***For you will not abandon my soul (psuche) to Hades,*** *or let your Holy One see corruption.* ***You have made known to me the paths of life (zoe)****; you will make me full of gladness with your presence.'*
>
> *"Brothers, I may say to you with confidence about the patriarch David that he both died and was buried, and his tomb is with us to this day. Being therefore a prophet, and knowing that God had sworn with an oath to him that he would set one of his descendants on his throne, he foresaw and spoke about the resurrection of the Christ, that he was not* ***abandoned to Hades,*** *nor did his flesh see corruption. This Jesus God raised up, and of that we all are witnesses. (ESV)*

Here, in Acts chapter 2, we see the very first sermon (by Peter) that occurs after Jesus resurrection, on the day of Pentecost. Peter points out that Jesus was killed, but that God would not abandon Jesus' *psuche* to Hades.

Peter is quoting from Psalm 16, where King David states his own confidence that God will not abandon his *psuche* to Hades. David was speaking of the grave, or unseen place of the dead. David was confident that God would not leave him there. His confidence was based upon the fact that God had shown him the path to life (zoe).

> **Acts 3:14-15** *But you denied the Holy and Righteous One, and asked for a murderer to be granted to you, and you killed the Author of life (zoe), whom God raised from the dead. To this we are witnesses. (ESV)*

In another sermon by Peter, he is preaching to an audience containing may people who had been responsible for condemning Jesus to death. He indeed accuses them of killing the "author of zoe". What a powerful statement! He then then states that God raised Jesus from the dead, and that he (Peter) was a personal witness of this resurrection.

This is the approach we should all consider. It is indeed our sin... yours and mine, that condemned Jesus to death. For it was in God's plan to atone for our death sentence, by killing Jesus, and then resurrecting him. It is only because Jesus was resurrected, declaring victory over death, that you and I have hope of eternal life. His resurrection and zoe provide you and I with hope beyond the grave.

> **Acts 3:22-24** *Moses said, 'The Lord God will raise up for you a prophet like me from your brothers. You shall listen to him in whatever he tells you. And it shall be that every soul who does not listen to that prophet shall be **destroyed** from the people.' And all the prophets who have spoken, from Samuel and those who came after him, also proclaimed these days. (ESV)*

The above verse contains a quote from Moses. Moses is prophecying that anyone who does not listen to the future prophet (referring to Jesus) shall be destroyed. Does that sound like eternal torment? Or does that sound like *destruction*?

In the following verses, we see the resurrection of Jesus, the salvation that is tied directly to resurrection, and the connection of resurrection to zoe.

Neither Hell nor eternal torment are ever mentioned

> **Acts 4:1-2** *And as they were speaking to the people, the priests and the captain of the temple and the Sadducees came upon them, 2 greatly annoyed because they were teaching the people and proclaiming in Jesus* **the resurrection from the dead.** *(ESV)*

> **Acts 4:8-12** *Then Peter, filled with the Holy Spirit, said to them, "Rulers of the people and elders, if we are being examined today concerning a good deed done to a crippled man, by what means this man has been healed, let it be known to all of you and to all the people of Israel that by the name of Jesus Christ of Nazareth, whom you crucified,* **whom God raised from the dead**—*by him this man is standing before you well. This Jesus is the stone that was rejected by you, the builders, which has become the cornerstone.* **And there is salvation in no one else,** *for there is no other name under heaven given among men by which we must be saved." (ESV)*

> **Acts 11:15-18** *As I began to speak, the Holy Spirit fell on them just as on us at the beginning. And I remembered the word of the Lord, how he said, 'John baptized with water, but you will be baptized with the Holy Spirit.' If then God gave the same gift to them as he gave to us when we believed in the Lord Jesus Christ, who was I that I could stand in God's way?" When they heard these things they fell silent. And they glorified God, saying, "Then to the Gentiles also God has granted repentance that leads to* **life (zoe).***" (ESV)*

*Acts 13:36-41 For David, after he had served the purpose of God in his own generation, fell asleep and was laid with his fathers and saw corruption (corruption means decay of his body), **but he whom God raised up (resurrected) did not see corruption**. Let it be known to you therefore, brothers, that through this man forgiveness of sins is proclaimed to you, and by him everyone who believes is freed from everything from which you could not be freed by the law of Moses.*

*Beware, therefore, lest what is said in the Prophets should come about: "'Look, you scoffers, be astounded and **perish (utterly destroyed)**; for I am doing a work in your days, a work that you will not believe, even if one tells it to you.'" (ESV)*

*Acts 13:46-48 And Paul and Barnabas spoke out boldly, saying, "It was necessary that the word of God be spoken first to you. **Since you thrust it aside and judge yourselves unworthy of eternal life (zoe)**, behold, we are turning to the Gentiles. For so the Lord has commanded us, saying,*

*"'I have made you a light for the Gentiles, that you may bring salvation to the ends of the earth.'" And when the Gentiles heard this, they began rejoicing and glorifying the word of the Lord, and as many as were appointed to **eternal life (zoe)** believed. (ESV)*

In the verses above, Paul is telling the audience that Jesus was resurrected, that indeed God raised him and that his body did not decay. He warns the scoffers that they will perish (be destroyed). He then speaks of *eternal zoe*.

Notice that Paul did not speak of going to *Hell*, but rather that the scoffers would be destroyed.

The verses on this page, speak of the hope of the resurrection, which is only available because of Jesus resurrection and victory over death. There is no mention of Hell or eternal torment. This is because death is the issue. Eternal torment was not mentioned, because it was not even on the radar at that time. This false belief was injected into Christian doctrine a few hundred years later.

Acts 17:30-32 The times of ignorance God overlooked, but now he commands all people everywhere to repent, because he has fixed a day on which he will judge the world in righteousness by a man whom he has appointed; and of this he has given assurance to all by raising him from the dead." Now when they heard of the resurrection of the dead, some mocked. But others said, "We will hear you again about this." (ESV)

Acts 23:6 Now when Paul perceived that one part were Sadducees and the other Pharisees, he cried out in the council, "Brothers, I am a Pharisee, a son of Pharisees. It is with respect to the hope and the resurrection of the dead that I am on trial." (ESV)

Acts 24:20-21 Or else let these men themselves say what wrongdoing they found when I stood before the council, other than this one thing that I cried out while standing among them: 'It is with respect to the resurrection of the dead that I am on trial before you this day.'" (ESV)

Acts 25:18-19 When the accusers stood up, they brought no charge in his case of such evils as I supposed. Rather they had certain points of dispute with him about their own religion and about a certain Jesus, who was dead, but whom Paul asserted to be alive. (ESV)

Remember, death is the problem that Paul emphasizes in the book of Acts. Then he always presents Jesus substitutionary death and resurrection as the solution to the problem. In the verses below, Paul is preaching to Festus and King Agrippa.

> **Acts 26:22-29** *Therefore I have experienced help from God until this day, and I stand here testifying to both small and great, saying nothing except what both the prophets and Moses have said were going to happen,* **that the Christ was to suffer and that as the first of the resurrection from the dead, he was going to proclaim light both to the people and to the Gentiles.***"*

> *And as he was saying these things in his defense, Festus said with a loud voice, "You are out of your mind, Paul! Your great learning is driving you insane!" But Paul said, "I am not out of my mind, most excellent Festus, but am speaking words of truth and rationality. For the king knows about these things, to whom also I am speaking freely, for I am not convinced that these things in any way have escaped his notice, because this was not done in a corner. Do you believe the prophets, King Agrippa? I know that you believe."*

> *But Agrippa said to Paul, "In a short time are you persuading me to become a Christian?" And Paul replied, "I pray to God, whether in a short time or in a long time, not only you but also all those who are listening to me today may become such people as I also am, except for these bonds!" (LEB)*

It is Paul's preaching of the resurrection of the dead, that prompts Festus to accuse Paul of being insane. The idea of the resurrection of the dead seems impossible to Festus, and Paul risks his life by preaching such an implausible idea. Yet, Paul is not afraid of dying. He is determined to preach the good news of Jesus' salvation for all who will listen and hopefully believe.

45

Take It at Face Value – Don't Twist It

Most scripture is meant to be taken at face value. We must be careful not to attempt to explain what something means, by twisting it to mean something else, just to fit a particular doctrine.

A Few Examples that State the Obvious

2 Timothy 2:10 which now has been manifested through the appearing of our Savior Christ Jesus, **who abolished death and brought life (zoe) and immortality** to light through the gospel. *(ESV)*

➤ Jesus abolished the sentence of death for the believer

➤ Jesus brought zoe and immortality to light through the good news (gospel) of his teaching. Zoe and immortality are tied together. It is zoe that imparts immortality to the believer. The Holy Spirit conveys zoe into a person when they become a believer.

John 3:16 For God so loved the world, that he gave his only Son, that whoever believes in him **should not perish (apollumi) but have eternal life (zoe)** *(ESV)*

➤ This verse is very straight forward, when you understand what Jesus said throughout the gospel of John.

*Romans 6:23 For the **wages of sin is death**, but the free gift of God is **eternal life (zoe)** in Christ Jesus our Lord. (ESV)*

➢ This is as simple to understand as it can possibly be. Paul would have never imagined that believers would eventually twist this verse into the horrible mindset that is so prevalent today.

Let me ask you a question about this verse. When Paul wrote this verse, did he in the most complete manner he was capable of, express what he understood the gospel to be? Did he accidentally or intentionally leave out extremely important details?

Do you realize Paul never mentions Hell (Gehenna) in any of his writing? If eternal torment in Hell, was part of what believers were being saved from, don't you think he would have thought to mention that in the book of Romans, or 1st or 2nd Corinthians? Or any of his other books? Do you know Paul is credited with writing practically half of the books in the new testament? Isn't it odd that he would not even mention Hell or everlasting torment in any of these?

On the other hand, Paul frequently emphasizes death as the problem faced by mankind. He teaches about zoe that brings immortality to the believer, which is only available through Jesus, as the only solution to this problem of death. He talks definitively about the resurrection to eternal zoe!

John (the apostle) wrote the Gospel of John, which is the foundation of the study of this book, as well as writing 1st, 2nd, 3rd John and the Book of Revelation. John never mentions Hell (Gehenna) in any of these books. Yet he frequently and consistently speaks of death being the main issue.

Luke wrote the book of Acts (see the previous chapter), which details the history of the newly born church, which started shortly after Jesus resurrection and into the years to come. Throughout all of the book Acts, which includes Peter's sermons, Stephen's sermon, and Paul's pleas and teachings throughout his missionary journeys, there is no mention of Hell or eternal torment. If Hell were the main issue that mankind was to be saved from, shouldn't Paul or Peter have mentioned that somewhere?

> **Matthew 10:28** *And do not fear those who kill the body but cannot kill the soul (psuche), Rather fear him who can destroy (apollumi) both soul (psuche) and body in Hell (Gehenna). (ESV)*

The traditional view takes the word *destroy* (apollumi) in the above verse and tries to twist it to mean "ruin", and use that context to say that those who are not saved will be "ruined" by their eternal, excruciating torment in Hell for eternity. If you try to interpret this verse in that way, then what do you do with the next verse (below) from Luke 13:1-5?

> **Luke 13:1-5** *Now at the same time some had come to tell him about the Galileans whose blood Pilate had mixed with their sacrifices. And he answered and said to them, "Do you think that these Galileans were sinners worse than all the Galileans, because they suffered these things? No, I tell you, but unless you repent you will all **perish (apollumi)** as well! Or those eighteen on whom the tower in Siloam fell and killed them—do you think that they were sinners worse than all the people who live in Jerusalem? No, I tell you, but unless you repent, you will all **perish (apollumi)** as well!" (LEB)*

If you interpret Luke 13:1-5 to mean *ruin*, you have to deal with the "likewise" statement that Jesus uses. Jesus uses these two recent newsworthy items of his day, to break the notion that his listeners held to, that bad things like this happened to people who were sinners, or that they deserved these untimely deaths.

Jesus is refuting this notion, by telling them that these people who were killed were not any worse than anyone else. He then goes on to tell his listeners that unless they repent, they will **all likewise** perish (be destroyed). As we know from Jesus' teachings that we have seen in this book, all men exist in state of death, and unless they believe, they will die in their sin. They will not have hope of this death sentence being removed.

351

But, if perish (apollumi) should be interpreted as "ruin", as the traditional view would have us believe, then what does **likewise** mean? Did the Galileans that were killed suffer ruin? Did the eighteen that died when the tower fell on them suffer ruin? Of course not. They were all killed. They died. This is what Jesus is referring to. He does not imply in any way that these people were killed and then went on to eternal torment (ruin).

> *Matthew 7:13 Enter by the narrow gate. For the gate is wide and the way is easy that leads to* **destruction**, *and those who enter by it are many. For the gate is narrow and the way is hard that leads to* **life (zoe)**, *and those who find it are few. (ESV)*

If you didn't know that Jesus was speaking of *zoe*, when the English word life is used here, then the meaning of this verse becomes enigmatic. Not only will you miss the fact that Jesus is speaking of zoe, he is also directly contrasting zoe to destruction, which Jesus does frequently during his ministry. We have seen this theme throughout the gospel of John, as well as in the synoptic gospels.

Jesus is again being straightforward here. Enter by the narrow gate that leads to *zoe*, or stay on the wide easy path that leads to *destruction*.

Or you can make this twisted and complicated, and say that *destruction* means everlasting excruciating torment and suffering for those that take the easy and wide path. If you choose to say that, then you are changing Jesus words.

> Jesus is making a clear statement. Enter by the narrow gate that leads to Zoe, or stay on the wide easy path that leads to destruction.

46

Finally, Thank You

I would like to express my gratitude to you for reading all the way through this book. I hope this has been helpful in clarifying Jesus' message and in your accepting the eternal life (*zoe*), which is only available through faith in Jesus the Christ.

Perhaps the day will come, in the age of the new heaven and earth, when you and I will meet and have the opportunity to reflect on God's sufficient saving grace through Jesus, as well as his good and sovereign daily grace to each of us through our unique journeys.

Remember John's final words in his gospel regarding *Zoe* . . .

> *John 20:31* . . . *these are written so that you may believe that Jesus is the Christ, the Son of God, and that by believing you may have* **zoe** *in his name.* *(ESV)*

Su Z Kane

47

About the Author

Su Z Kane is not the real name of the author, but a pen name.

Su Z Kane is an aptronym. It is my heart's desire and prayer that every one who reads this book, will remember that within the *psuche* of all believers, abides the zoe of Jesus, via the indwelling Holy Spirit.

It is this *zoe* of God, that gives all believers immortality, as well as restoring the deep, rich, continous abiding fellowship with the Father, Son, and Spirit that we can enjoy while we are still living in this life (*psuche*) on earth.

If you are a believer and remember nothing else from this book, please hold on to the fact that your *psuche* is indwelt by the life giving *zoe* of God, and this gift of *zoe*, makes you a child of God.

One of the most prevalent forms of *psuche* that occurs in the new testament is "psuchane", pronounced Su-Kane. The middle initial of the pen name, "Z" represents the indwelling *Zoe* of God.

Su Z Kane is merely an aptronym to remind you of who you are in Christ. Nothing more.

Your *psuche*, has been saved, through the indwelling gift of *zoe*. This will ultimately result in eternal life (*zoe* unto the ages) for the believer, upon the day of resurrection.

Welcome to immortality my friend.

MC Elmore

> *Psalm 23:4-6 Even though I walk through the valley of the* **shadow of death**, *I will fear no evil, for you are with me; your rod and your staff, they comfort me. Surely goodness and mercy shall follow me all the days of my life,* **and I shall dwell in the house of the Lord** *forever. (ESV)*

48

A Tribute to Edward Fudge

I would like to give tribute to a man who I have come to regard as the vanguard of the Conditionalist movement in this century. (There were others before him, though none in recent decades who are as noteworthy that I am aware of.)

Edward Fudge spent about forty years of his life devoted to bringing the truth of the Bible's teaching to this subject. He knew that correctly understanding the truth about Gehenna, Hades, immortality, and eternal life was not a matter of salvation. He showed grace for those who disagreed with him. He was truly a sweet spirited and tender-hearted man.

However, he knew the importance of having a correct understanding of Jesus' and the Bible's teaching on this topic. His exhaustive biblical research has revealed truth which will hopefully become the new paradigm of Christians in the decades and centuries to come.

Many have said that the Old Testament does not teach much about Hell, and they are correct in the sense of "Hell" as it is typically understood in the traditional sense.

However, Fudge brings out the overwhelming truth about the numerous instances of the judgment of God toward the wicked, which are foretold throughout the Old Testament. This judgment is the destruction of the ungodly, which is in total agreement with Jesus' teachings on *Gehenna* and John's teachings in Revelation on the second death.

I strongly recommend Fudge's latest book, *The Consuming Fire (Third Edition)*, which he completed shortly before his death, in November of 2017.

I never met him personally and he did not know me.

Fudge was truly the authority on this subject. I regret not getting to know him. After reading much of his work and watching many of his videos, I can only say that he was a child of God, a man fully devoted to rightfully dividing the word of truth, a gentleman, a loving family man, and quite obviously, a man who garnered the love and respect of all who truly knew him.

Fudge inspired and mentored several younger individuals who have picked up the torch. One group he was closely associated with is the group of Christians who regularly contribute to the website **RethinkingHell.com**.

As of this date I strongly recommend their articles, videos, conferences, and other resources they provide.

There is also the website of **EdwardFudge.com**, which is still maintained by his family at this time. There are many great articles there as well.

You can also do a search on YouTube.com to see several videos of him speaking or debating.

Several of his videos can be seen here:

https://www.truthaccordingtoscripture.com/documents/death/wicked.php#.W-N8aJNKhPZ

Note: No one associated with Edward Fudge or these websites necessarily endorses me or my views.   Mr. Fudge never knew me and my direct interaction with these other groups has been little or none as of the time of this publication.

49

My Primary Resources

I have heavily used certain resources for my own word studies as a basis for this book. I would like to share a few of these, in case you would like to utilize these while conducting your own study.

Interlinear New Testament

One of the most valuable tools online is the Greek-English Interlinear New Testament, which can be found at:

> ➤ http://www.scripture4all.org/OnlineInterlinear/Greek_Index.htm

Greek-English Interlinear New Testaments have been used as reference material for generations by serious Bible scholars. The online access to this resource is a wonderful study tool.

Greek Dictionary

Strong's Analytical Concordance (book form) is an excellent tool for identifying the use and locations of Greek words in the New Testament.

Some aspects of *Strong's Concordance* are also available online. One of the best online resources for *Strong's Dictionary* that I have found is at this link:

> ➤ http://Biblehub.com/strongs.htm

Online Bible

Another great online resource is the entire Bible, which can quickly be searched by book and chapter. This is an excellent tool for quickly finding verses of interest and being able to read them in various translations.

> ➤ https://www.Biblegateway.com/

50

Recommended Resources

Recommended Reading

The Fire that Consumes (Third Edition)

by Edward Fudge

Rethinking Hell: Readings in Evangelical Conditionalism

by Christopher M. Date, Gregory G. Stump and Joshua W. Anderson

The Doctrine of Immortality in the Early Church

by John H. Roller

Recommended Websites

www.lifeddefined.life

http://rethinkinghell.com

https://edwardfudge.com

https://www.truthaccordingtoscripture.com/Hell.php

Further Word Study

If you are interested in doing more of your own study on *psuche* or *zoe*, please see the webpages below.

The following links will take you to the Strong's definitions, as well as listings of all the Greek renderings of the word *psuche* and *zoe*.

Psuche

http://Biblehub.com/greek/5590.htm

Zoe

http://Biblehub.com/str/greek/2222.htm

51

Links Related to Topics

The links listed below can be easily reached by clicking on their links on our website at:

www.lifedefined.life/links

Note: All links are listed without permission. The owners and associates of these websites may not endorse or agree my views in this book.

Links to More Discussion about the Word "Perish"

https://www.truthaccordingtoscripture.com/documents/death/perish.php#.W-OCILtjNPY

http://www.rethinkingHell.com/2017/02/fixing-john-316-500-years-after-the-reformation/

http://Biblehub.com/greek/622.htm

Links to More Discussion on "Conditionalism"

http://rethinkingHell.com/statement/

http://rethinkingHell.com/2016/08/conditional-immortality-an-acceptable-view/

http://rightreason.org/2011/an-open-letter-to-my-traditionalist-friends/

https://www.truthaccordingtoscripture.com/documents/death/immortality-gift.php#.WrzsfC74-UI

https://www.truthaccordingtoscripture.com/documents/death/defense-conditional-immortality/introduction.php#_

Link to Reformationists' views on "Conditionalism"

https://www.afterlife.co.nz/2010/05/immortality-of-the-soul-in-the-Bible/

Links to Early Church Beliefs on the Mortality of *Psuche*

https://truthmattersradio.wordpress.com/2009/02/22/the-history-of-Hell-with-dr-john-roller/

http://www.truthaccordingtoscripture.com/documents/death/apostolic-fathers-immortality.php#.Wh1d9VV5WUl

http://www.truthaccordingtoscripture.com/documents/death/immortality-early-church/apostolic-fathers.php#.Wg2MH1V5WUk

https://www.afterLife.co.nz/history-of-Hell/

https://www.jba.gr/The-origins-of-the-doctrine-of-the-immortality-of-the-Soul.htm

Links Regarding Immortality and the Story of the "Rich Man and Lazarus"

https://edwardfudge.com/2012/03/the-rich-man-lazarus-2/

https://www.truthaccordingtoscripture.com/documents/death/the-rich-man-and-lazarus-dawson.php#

http://www.christianmonotheism.com/truthmatters/podcast%2029%20--%20David%20Burge%20--%20Objections%20to%20Conditional%20Immortality.mp3

http://www.christadelphia.org/pamphlet/p_lazarus.htm

Link to Old Testament History and Meaning of *Sheol*, the Hebrew Equivalent of the Greek Word *Hades*

https://www.truthaccordingtoscripture.com/documents/death/sheol.php#.Wr1eny74-Uk

Link Regarding "Fire Is Not Quenched"

http://rethinkingHell.com/2012/11/the-fire-is-not-quenched-annihilation-and-mark-948-part-2/

Links Regarding "Weeping and Gnashing of Teeth"

https://edwardfudge.com/2014/01/gnashing-of-teeth/

https://www.truthaccordingtoscripture.com/documents/death/defense-conditional-immortality/chapter-8.php#_

http://www.patheos.com/blogs/christiancrier/2015/08/15/what-does-gnashing-of-teeth-mean-in-the-Bible/

Informative Links on the Subject of Hell (*Gehenna*)

http://www.truthaccordingtoscripture.com/documents/death/wicked.php#.Wg2GxlV5WUk

https://jesuswithoutbaggage.wordpress.com/2015/07/07/outer-darkness-weeping-and-gnashing-of-teeth-in-matthew/

https://www.truthaccordingtoscripture.com/Hell.php